101
THOUGHTS
FROM THE
WORD

Volume Four

101
THOUGHTS
FROM THE
WORD

Volume Four

BOOK OF SERIES

DAVID T. PECKHAM

authorHOUSE®

AuthorHouse™
1663 Liberty Drive
Bloomington, IN 47403
www.authorhouse.com
Phone: 1-800-839-8640

First published by AuthorHouse   10/15/2011

ISBN: 978-1-4670-6072-1 (sc)
ISBN: 978-1-4670-6071-4 (ebk)

Library of Congress Control Number: 2011918186

Printed in the United States of America

Scripture quotations are taken from the New King James Version unless otherwise noted.
AMP–Amplified Version; KJV–King James Version; NLT–New Living Translation; NIV–New International Version; RSV–Revised Standard.

Poems ascribed to DTP are by the author.

CONTENTS

GOD/MAN SERIES

THE LORD'S PRAYER SERIES

THE WORD OF GOD

"THE Word of God is as a garden of fruit and flowers—luscious with the sweetness, penciled with the beauty, and fragrant with the perfume of CHRIST. All its shadows, types, and prophecies, all its doctrines, precepts, and promises testify of HIM. Search the Scriptures in whatever part, or view them from whatever standpoint you may, of CHRIST they speak, and to CHRIST they lead. The star of the east pendent over the lowly manger of Bethlehem pointed not more truly, conducted not more surely the wise men to the spot where the infant Savior lay, than does this "more sure word of prophecy, which is as a lamp shining in a dark place," lead the mind inquiring for truth, the sinner in search of the Savior, the disciple in quest of his Lord, to Christ, the way, the truth, the life. Let us, dear reader, often walk within this Divine enclosure, this sacred garden, where the north wind and the south wind blows—the *law* humbling and condemning, the *gospel* comforting and saving—and eat the pleasant fruits, and inhale the perfume of Sharon's Rose." *Octavius Winslow, Go to Jesus.*

"The Bible is the opening of the heart of God. It is God's heart unveiled, each throb inviting the mourner, the poor in spirit, the widow, the fatherless, the bereaved, the persecuted, the sufferer, yes, every child of affliction and grief to the asylum and sympathy, the protection and soothing of His heart. Oh, thank God for the comfort and consolation of the Scripture! Open it with what sorrow and burden and perplexity you may, be it the guilt of sin, the pressure of trial, or the corrodings of sorrow, it speaks to the heart such words of comfort as God only could speak.

"Have you ever borne your grief to God's Word, especially to the experimental Psalms of David, and not felt that it was written for that particular sorrow? You have found your grief more accurately portrayed, your state of mind more truly described, and your case more exactly and fully met, probably in a single history, chapter, or verse, than in all the human treatises that the pen of man ever wrote.

"Fly to the Word of God, then, in every sorrow! You will know more of the mind and heart of God than you, perhaps, ever learned in all the schools before. Draw, then, O child of sorrow, your consolation from God's Word. Oh, clasp this precious Word of comfort to your sorrowful heart, and exclaim, 'It is mine! The Jesus of whom it speaks is mine, the salvation it reveals is mine, the promises it contains are mine, the heaven it unveils is mine, and all the consolation, comfort, and sympathy which wells up from these hidden springs, is MINE." *Octavius Winslow, The Preciousness of God's Word.*

INTRODUCTION

Reading: Ephesians 1:1-6
"Having predestined us to adoption as sons by Jesus Christ to Himself,
according to the good pleasure of His will" Ephesians 1:5

What is a Christian? In these days of so many brands of Christianity, with its hundreds of denominations (and hundreds of divisions within the denominations), sects and cults, the world has a genuine right to ask this question. A Christian is not defined by what he believes, but by who he is. A Christian, as defined by one of today's leading theologians, is *"One who has God as his Father" J.I. Packer, Knowing God, Ch 19.*

The concept of knowing God as a Father was new when Jesus preached His Sermon on the Mount (Matthew 5:3-7:27). During this sermon Jesus referred to God as *"Your Father"* 12 times, *"My Father"* once, and *"Our Father"* once. The Fatherhood of God was implied in the Old Testament (Hosea 11:1; Malachi 1:6), but the intimacy of the Father/son relationship was limited to His own people, the "seed of Abraham" (Exodus 4:22-23). The nation of Israel was God's son, and He dealt with them as such, but for an individual to enjoy such a relationship was not expressed.

There are 250 references in the New Testament that speak of Christians having a Heavenly Father, and that they have a unique Older Brother. The New Testament concept of the Fatherhood of God broadens it to those who "are Christ's," not to the entire world population, or limited to the children of Israel. The common conception that all mankind are children of God is never taught in scripture; all are His creation, but not all His children. We become children of God, not by the process of human birth, but by spiritual birth: "Most assuredly, I say to you, unless one is born again, he cannot see the kingdom of God" (John 3:3).

Another analogy by which we are made sons of God is *adoption:*

"For as many as are led by the Spirit of God, these are sons of God.
For you did not receive the spirit of bondage again to fear, but you

received the Spirit of adoption by whom we cry out, 'Abba, Father'"
Romans 8:14-15.

For a childless man to insure himself an heir to his estate and carry on his family name, he would often adopt an adult male as his son. This was a common practice during the time of Jesus and the establishment of the church. As is the custom of adoption today, a legally adopted child assumes every right and privilege of a naturally born son, the primary difference being the blood of his adoptive father does not flow through his veins.

"When the fullness of the time had come, God sent forth His Son, born of a woman, born under the law, to redeem those who were under the law, that we might receive the adoption as sons. And because you are sons, God has sent forth the Spirit of His Son into your hearts, crying out, 'Abba, Father!' Therefore you are no longer a slave but a son, and if a son, then an heir of God through Christ"
Galatians 4:4-7.

As sons of God we have unique privileges with family responsibilities, and are subject to family discipline. Until the reformation in the 17th century, a Christian's relationship to God was, for the most part, based on fear and bondage, with a slave like association with Him, rather than that of a Father/son. This concept still pervades in some branches of the church today.

The obvious consideration is—before we can be sons, we must have a Father, and this is exactly how the New Testament introduces this most wonderful concept of the intimacy between God and His children. Intimacy is what the Christian faith is all about, and is made possible by the miraculous birth, life, death, resurrection, and ascension of the "Only begotten Son of God," Jesus Christ.

"If you want to judge how well a person understands Christianity, find out how much he makes [understands] of the thought of being God's child, and having God as his Father. If this is not the thought that prompts and controls his worship and prayers and his whole outlook on life, it means he does not understand Christianity very well at all." J.I. Packer, Knowing God, chapter 19.

The relationship between God and His elect are described in several ways throughout scripture, but we will defer these thought to a future series of thoughts. Suffice it to say that the relationship of Father and son exposes not only the intimacy between the two, but also the rights and privileges of the Father's children.

"The Spirit Himself bears witness with our spirit that we are children of God, and if children, then heirs—heirs of God and joint heirs with Christ" Romans 8:14-17.

Another aspect we will be considering of our adoption into the family of God is the permanence of it. We all know families in which the parent/child relationship has been severed, or is severely strained beyond recognition, and sometimes reconciliation seems impossible. This is not so in the relationship between our Heavenly Father and His redeemed children. Our conduct as Christians must be strongly influenced by the recognition and acceptance of our spiritual adoption. One who truly loves his human father does everything in his power to please him, and make him proud of him. If our behavior brings the father we love sorrow and disappointment, we will do all we can to restore the pride he once had in us.

As we consider this magnificent theme. my prayer is that together we will be granted a greater and fresher appreciation of what it means to be adopted into the family of God.

Puritan Quote:

"Christian contentment is that sweet, inward, quiet, gracious frame of spirit, which freely submits to and delights in God's wise and fatherly disposal in every condition" Jeremiah Burroughs, 1599-1646.

THE FATHERHOOD OF GOD

Reading: Matthew 6:1-15
"Our Father in heaven, hallowed be Your name" Matthew 6:9

Before we can have sons we must have a father, and fathers come in all shapes and sizes—good fathers and bad fathers, some are loved and some hated, some consulted and some ignored, some we love to go home and visit, while others are left behind as their children mature into adulthood, and leave home at the earliest possible moment with no intention of ever returning. I thank God constantly that my father and mother were of the good kind, and remember with joy the words of my father when he said to me, "I am very proud of you." I, therefore, have an advantage over those who have never enjoyed a close relationship with their father, for I can readily apply some of the qualities of a good father to my Heavenly Father. When God says, 'I love you with an everlasting love,' I have some basis upon which to understand what He means.

On the other hand, those whose relationship with their earthly father is strained or almost non-existent, take great comfort in the fact that their Heavenly Father provides with abundance those elements of a good father that is/was missing from their earthly relationship. So, the Fatherhood of God to His children is, or should be, a matter of great significance to them. Unfortunately, this filial relationship between God and His children is often relegated to the meaningless repetition of the so called Lord's Prayer on Sunday mornings—meaningless, that is, to many who repeat it in parrot-like fashion.

The concept of God as Father is not new with the teachings of Christ, but His relationship with individual believers is. The Old Testament presents God as the Father of Israel:

> *"When Israel was a child, I loved him, and out of Egypt I called My son" Hosea 11:1; see also Jeremiah 31:19.*

Of the many prayers recorded in the Old Testament, never is Jehovah addressed as "Father" yet, when His disciples asked Jesus how to pray, He commenced with "Our Father." When David or the prophets spoke of God as their Father, it was always within the context of His people as a nation, or in prophesy concerning Jesus (cp. Psalm 89:26-29; Isaiah 63:16; 64:8-9; Jeremiah 3:19-20). What a surprise this must have been to them, especially when He included Himself in the address.

The Fatherhood of God is the axle upon which all New Testament doctrine turns. Everything that makes the New Testament better than the Old, and which makes a difference between Christianity and Judaism, is summed up in the Fatherhood of God. Father is like the Christian name for God. If it were not for God the Father, Jesus would not be known to mankind as the Sent One:

> *"Therefore, holy brethren, partakers of the Heavenly calling, consider the Apostle (apostolos, one who is sent) and High Priest of our confession, Christ Jesus, who was faithful to Him who appointed Him" Hebrews 3:1-2 (parenthesis added).*

The hub of the entire gospel message is John 3:16-17, "For God (the Father) so loved the world that He gave His only begotten Son, that whoever believes in Him should not perish but have everlasting life. For God did not send (apostello) His Son into the world to condemn the world, but that the world through Him might be saved" (parenthesis added).

Some churches emphasize God the Son in their teaching to the almost exclusion of God the Father. The same can be said of many that lay emphasis on God the Holy Spirit. To concentrate on Jesus Christ or the Holy Spirit is not wrong, unless it is to the exclusion of God the Father. "There are three that bear witness in heaven: the Father, the Word, and the Holy Spirit; and these three are one" 1 John 5:7. Denominations, sects and cults, are started because one person or a group of persons decide one particular doctrine should be emphasized over all others. Some are named after the doctrine, i.e. Baptist, Methodist, Congregational, Presbyterian, Pentecostal, Seventh Day Adventist, etc.

One of the first things the Holy Spirit has taught me in my quest to know the Father, is the reality that this is exactly who He is—my Father.

The relationship I have with Him is a personal one; He is "my" Father. Somehow, it is different to say He is "our Father" when, for instance, I repeat the Lord's Prayer, which I did every Sunday morning in church. I can get lost in the "our," but not in the "my." It is like attending a church with a large congregation where one is scarcely known—I can get lost in the crowd and never be held accountable for my walk with the Lord, or lack of it. That is how I feel with the words "Our Father." I can remain distant in the numbers while still acknowledging God as "our" Father who is in heaven, but how different when I see Him and acknowledge Him as "my" Father.

God has established a personal relationship with me—with me as an individual. If God is indeed my Father, I must understand that, in His love for me, He will discipline me when I need it, both for my good and for the upholding of His faithfulness. He is a Just God, an attribute He does not discard because He is my Father. This is the same relationship all born again believers have with the Father, yet they are all individuals and personal. I have met several people who deny God because "God would never want to have a personal relationship with me." They believe in a god who created the heavens and earth, but then released it to see what would happen. Such a god would not be interested in a personal relationship with something He created. How sad; this is exactly the purpose of God.

Puritan Quote:

"Give me a father that is angry with my sins, and that seeks to bring me back, even though it be by chastisement. Thank God you have got a father that can be angry, but that loves you as much when he is angry as when he smiles upon you" C.H. Spurgeon—1834-1892.

THE LOVE OF GOD

Reading: 1 John 3:1-2
"Behold what manner of love the Father has bestowed on us, that we should be called children of God!" 1 John 3:1.

What an introductory word when considering the love of God, especially within the context of the adoption of believers into the family of God. The Greek word 'eido' implies not only to look but to 'know, be aware, consider, perceive' what you are looking at. Stop what you are doing and stand back, gaze in awe and amazement at the love of God! Absorb into your very psyche, your heart of hearts, what it is you see. This is a different word than when John the Baptist said, "Behold! The Lamb of God who takes away the sin of the world!" John 1:29. Here it carries more of the element of surprise—"Look, see, This is the Lamb of God . . ."

I am reminded of the event when God told Ezekiel: "'Son of man, feed your belly, and fill your stomach with this scroll that I give you.' So I ate, and it was in my mouth like honey in sweetness" (Ezekiel 3:3). He was not to simply nibble on the scroll, but to consume it entirely so his body would digest it, therefore becoming a part of him. Is it not the case here, fellow believer? "Behold!" take it and digest the love of God that has made you one of His adopted children. Do not read these words with a glancing eye, but stop right here and make this truth a reality in your heart. Digest it and make it a necessary part of your understanding of who God is, and what He has done for you, and what you mean to Him. This, I believe, is one of those marvelous credentials the depths of which we will never fully understand until we are in His presence "for (then) we shall see Him as He is" (1 John 3:2):

"For now we see in a mirror, dimly, but then face to face. Now I know in part, but then I shall know just as I also am known" 1 Corinthians 13:12.

Our adoption into the family of God is not a benefit for which we applied, for it is has been "lavished" (NIV) on us by our Heavenly Father. It is a gift from Him who loves us with an everlasting love (Jeremiah 31:3):

"In this is love, not that we loved God, but that He loved us and sent His Son to be the propitiation for our sins" 1 John 4:10.

In Roman culture, adoption was more the practice of the rich and influential who had failed to produced a son. In order that such a family had an heir, a young man would be adopted solely for that purpose. Such a candidate would be one who himself was born and raised into a family of wealth and influence (usually a second son, seldom the eldest), one who had proven himself to be intellectual and qualified in the eyes of the adoptive parents to be heir of their estate. That which makes our adoption by Almighty God truly rich and influential and so amazing, is that He chooses those who are dead in their "trespasses and sins" (Ephesians 2:1,5) and who rightfully must say with David, "I am a worm, and no man" (Psalm 22:6). Listen to the words of God to Israel: "Remember, if you are Christ's then you are Abraham's seed and heirs according to the promise" (Galatians 4:26):

"Fear not, you worm Jacob, you men of Israel! I will help you," says the LORD and your Redeemer, the Holy one of Israel" Isaiah 41:14.

Is this not amazing love? We are not fit for a place in God's family. We have nothing that qualifies us to become a member of His family—we fail in every aspect, yet, writes the Apostle John, "Beloved, now we are children of God."

"Behold, what exotic [foreign to the human heart] love the Father has permanently bestowed upon us, to the end that we may be named [born ones, bairns] of God. And we are" 1 John 3:1-2, Kenneth S. Wuest, An Expanded Translation.

That is the amazing thing, is it not? "And we are!" There might be times when we feel differently, but then we must always remember that our adoption depends upon His faithfulness, and He never fails, always remaining true to His promise and purpose.

"Stop! Stand in awe at the magnitude of exotic love our Father has permanently lavished on us, that we are called sons of God. And we are" A paraphrase from several translations.

"Knowing who we are in Christ, and understanding what we possess in Christ, is foundational to living a life that is well pleasing to Christ" Albert N. Martin.

It is one thing to believe we have been adopted into the family of God and that He is our Father, but do we understand what it means. What benefits and privileges do we have as God's children? What responsibilities and obligations do we have? These are some of the matters we will discuss as our thoughts regarding our spiritual adoption continue.

Amazing Father, let me never forget for one moment that I am your adopted child, an heir of your promises and blessed with every spiritual blessing in Christ Jesus. Help me to fully absorb this wonderful reality into the depths of my soul. Whenever I have a spare moment, turn my thoughts to your glorious love when you made me your son, your heir and brother to Jesus. When I wake in the morning, and lay my head on the pillow at night, remind me that I am your son. Fill my heart with thanks and praise, and may the tears of joy frequent my cheeks as the reality of my sonship to you is digested by my soul. Abba, Father, I stand in awe as I gaze upon your magnificent, unfathomable and unchanging love that raised me out of my trespasses and sins, and placed my feet firmly on Jesus, the Rock of my salvation. From your ever grateful prodigal son.

Puritan Quote:
"O how shall I the goodness tell,
Father, which Thou to me hast showed?
That I, a child of wrath and hell,
I should be called a child of God"
Charles Wesley 1707-1788.

9

THE LOVE OF GOD — CONT'D

Reading: 1 John 3:1-2
"Behold what manner of love the Father has bestowed on us, that we should be called children of God!" 1 John 3:1.

Many who love the Lord Jesus Christ and believe in Him as their Savior, turn to one particular passage of scripture when they require reassurance in the face of an enemy confrontation. For me that particular scripture is the first chapter of Ephesians. Once we begin reading this chapter it is difficult to know where to stop—so don't, keep reading, and absorb the many blessings that are yours because God has made you one with His Son. At the outset Paul establishes our inclusion into the family of God: "Just as He chose us in Him before the foundation of the world, that we should be holy and without blame before Him in love, having predestined us to adoption as sons by Jesus Christ to Himself" (Ephesians 1:4-5).

"In the beginning God created the heavens and the earth." So declares the first verse of the bible, but before that event took place God did something else—He chose us to be His children. This is not something that John Calvin wrote, nor the reformers or puritans, but the Holy Spirit, God Himself. He chose us to be "holy and without blame before Him in love" so He could adopt us into His family. Jesus calls those who deny Him sons "of your father, the devil" (John 8:44). Paul writes that "all have sinned and fall short of the glory of God" (Romans 3:23), and the All-Righteous and Holy God cannot take into His family any who are even slightly tainted with sin. His first act, therefore, is to make us "holy and without blame" so we can be acceptable to Him. Once He has done that (it is called justification) every obstacle has been removed, and He can proceed with the adoption process.

J.I. Packer writes in his treatise Concise Theology, "*Justification is the basic blessing on which adoption is founded; adoption is the crowning blessing [of salvation] to which justification clears the way.*" God must try us in criminal (judicial) court before taking us to Family Court, where He will take out papers adopting us into His family. We must be declared innocent of all charges in order to qualify for adoption. Words such as pure, clean, white as snow, without blemish, without fault, are all biblical terms describing those who have been justified in the court of God's justice. God accomplishes this by what is called "transference." This is a twofold process: 1) our sins are transferred to Jesus Christ (Isaiah 53:6), and 2) His righteousness is transferred to us (Romans 4 :5-6).

> *"And you, who once were alienated and enemies in your mind by wicked works, yet now He has reconciled in the body of His flesh through death, to present you holy, and blameless, and above reproach in His sight" Colossians 1:21-22.*
> *"But God demonstrates His own love toward us, in that while we were still sinners, Christ died for us" Romans 5:8.*

This is the only way by which a holy God can establish a relationship with unholy man—man must be like Him, in His image. God communed with Adam before he sinned, but once he sinned he was dismissed from His presence, and this filial communication was blocked for ever (Gen 3:8, 23-24). But then:

> *"When the fullness of the time had come, God sent forth His Son, born of a woman, born under the law, to redeem those who were under the law, that we might receive the adoption as sons" Galatians 4:4-5.*

Paul again addresses the activity of God—before time the adoption plan was framed, and, in the fullness of time, it was fulfilled. The very reason for Christ becoming Man was to make it possible for God to adopt children into His family. The sin problem had to be dealt with before any child of wrath (Ephesians 2:3) could be made a child of God. Redemption is the means and adoption is the purpose, therefore, all who are redeemed are automatically adopted into God's family:

> *"In this the love of God was manifested toward us, that God has sent His only begotten Son into the world, that we might live through*

Him. In this is love, not that we loved God, but that He loved us and sent His Son to be the propitiation for our sins" 1 John 4:9-10.

The intense and overwhelming suffering and death Jesus endured was so the purpose of the Father might be fulfilled, and that purpose is the adoption of sons (Eph 1:3-6). The experience of the three "Gs" was so we might call God "Abba, Father." Gabbatha—the place of shameful trial (John 19:13); Gethsemane—the place of intense agony (Matthew 26:36-39); Golgotha—the place of forsaking and death (John 19:17-18)—all this so we might be called children of God.

"For it was fitting for Him, for whom are all and by whom are all things, in bringing many sons to glory, to make the captain of their salvation perfect through sufferings" (Hebrews 2:10). Jesus' work and ministry was made complete by His sufferings. "It is finished" he shouted with a final cry of victory: God can now fulfill His plan by adopting many sons and daughters into His family.

When John saw the New Jerusalem (not a thing but persons) descending from heaven, the One who sat on the throne said,

"'Behold, I make all things new.' And He said to me, 'Write, for these words are true and faithful.' And He said to me, 'It is done! I am the Alpha and the Omega, the Beginning and the End. I will give of the fountain of the water of life freely to him who thirsts. He who overcomes shall inherit all things, and I will be his God and he shall be My son'" Revelation 21:5-7.

The crowning glory of a completed purpose and plan—"I will be his God and he shall be My son." Such glory! Such grace! Such love!

Puritan Quote:
"There are three things that earthly riches can never do; they can never satisfy divine justice, they can never pacify divine wrath, nor can they ever quiet a guilty conscience. And till these things are done, man is undone" Thomas Brooks (1608-1680).

THE GRACE OF GOD

Reading: Ephesians 1:4-6
". . . just as He chose us in Him before the foundation of the
world . . . having predestined us to adoption as sons by Jesus Christ to
Himself, according . . . to the praise of the glory of His grace . . ."
Ephesians 1:6.

Imagine receiving a birthday gift from God (which is not too much of an exaggeration), and the time has come for you to open it. Written on the box in large letters are the words—MY BLESSINGS TO YOU. You open the box with great anticipation and out pours many smaller boxes, the contents of which are identified by a single word written on them. One of the first boxes you see is identified by the word—ADOPTION.

In his letter to the believers at Ephesus, Paul begins by listing the most wonderful blessings (gifts) given to "the faithful in Christ Jesus." At the top of the list is the sovereign act of election, "He chose us in Him before the foundation of the world" (vs 4). He continues to explain this wonderful gift by adding, "Having predestined us to adoption as sons by Jesus Christ to Himself" (vs 5). The source and purpose of this gift is identified as "the good pleasure of His will, to the praise of the glory of His grace" (vss 5-6).

Previously, we saw from 1 John 3:1 that our adoption into God's family is an expression of His love, "Behold what manner of love the Father has bestowed on us, that we should be called children of God!" Both the love and grace of God are clear expressions of our adoption into His family, neither randomly on His part nor by luck on ours, but "according to the good pleasure of His will" (vs5).

"Where sin abounded, grace abounded much more" Romans 5:20.

Even though the depths and power and consequences of sin are extremely great, yet the grace of God is greater still. The word translated "abounded much more" literally means to "super-abound" or "over abound."

Satan's negatives are always "over-abounded" by God's positives. We were by nature children of the devil (1 John 3:10) but now, by God's grace, we are children of God. The grace of God is super-abundant in its ability to overcome the ravages of sin.

"And of His fullness we have all received, and grace for grace. For the law was given through Moses, but grace and truth came through Jesus Christ" John 1:16-17.

The grace of God is personified in His Only-begotten Son Jesus Christ. The grace of God is an outworking of "His fullness" of which we participate, because at our new birth and adoption we are made one with Jesus Christ. The word for adoption means 'the placing as a son'—showing us that our becoming sons of God is an active work of God, not just the signing of a paper. When my wife and I adopted our eldest son, I remember clearly when, for the first time, the worker placed him into our arms. His adoption was more than signatures on a piece of paper, but the literal placing of this child into our arms. He immediately became our son, was given our name, and was now as much a member of our family as his brother and sister who were born to us later. What a joyful day that was, a day we shall never forget, and one for which we will always be thankful. Our son was the perfect gift from God.

Our text today states that this marvelous transaction called spiritual adoption is "to the praise of the glory of His grace." This tells us that our adoption into God's family is the result of His grace; we are His sons due to it. He has made us objects of His grace—by His choice, not because He could find anything in us to warrant it. He has taken one who was at enmity with Himself, one who constantly violated His holiness and whose rightful state stood him in line to endure the wrath and judgment of the Almighty, this one God has showered with His grace by giving him the gift of adoption, and by so doing has forgiven him of all his sin. He has declared him faultless in His eyes, never to stand before the Judge of heaven and earth and hear the conclusive words, "Depart from Me, you cursed, into the everlasting fire prepared for the devil and his angels" (Matthew 25:41-42). I know this is not a popular doctrine in many churches today, but even when considered as a slightest possibility it makes the grace of God in adoption a most glorious and incomprehensible act.

> *"Behold [stand back, consider with awe and amazement] what manner of love the Father has bestowed on us, that we should be called children of God! Beloved, now we are children of God; and it has not yet been revealed what we shall be, but we know that when He is revealed, we shall be like Him, for we shall see Him as He is" 1 John 3:1-2.*

The Westminster Shorter Catechism summarizes spiritual adoption in the following manner: "Adoption is the act of God's free grace by which we become His sons with all the rights and privileges of being His." This is straightforward yet profound; simple yet overwhelming. The definition of grace is "to freely receive that which we do not deserve." The definition of mercy is "to not receive that which we do deserve." As children of God we are recipients of God's mercy and grace, both of which are illustrations or extensions of His love.

Adoption is like Justification—it is a once-and-for-all act, not a process like sanctification. At the very moment we are born again the act of adoption takes place. Adoption is not something God bestows on us later. It is one of the three great manifestations of God's love with which we are endowed the very moment we are saved—the Holy Spirit, Justification, and Adoption—all three are free gifts from God, all three acts of free grace.

Grace! It is a foreign sound
To one who is dead in sin;
To one who in sin's grasp is bound,
No life or light within.

But, to him who in Christ is found,
'Tis life and joy and peace;
Grace, oh, what an amazing sound,
From sin it gives release.

'Twas love that brought my Savior down,
And grace that set me free.
With thanks and praise, Him I'll crown,
Until His face I see.

Adopted into God's family,
A child of God I am;
My Father, God most holy,
My Brother, His perfect Lamb.

As eternity rolls on,
His grace I'll never forget,
My robes of white I'll don,
For love and grace have met.

Oh, praise my soul, the King,
From death to life I've come.
For ever, then, I'll sing,
For grace, its work has done.
DTP

THE SPIRIT OF GOD

Reading: Galatians 4:1-7
"And because you are sons, God has sent forth the Spirit of His Son into your hearts, crying out, 'Abba, Father!'" Galatians 4:6

Until recently, whenever I saw or read the words "Abba, Father," I immediately thought of the wonderfully intimate relationship our Savior had with His Father. While I still believe this is very true, it is not limited to that. If I was asked "Where in the bible do we find the words "Abba, Father," I would accurately reply they were the words of Jesus in the Garden of Gethsemane. Again, this is true, but it is much more than that—much, much more. These words represent the apex of all the blessings that are ours because we have been placed in Jesus Christ by our Heavenly Father. To be sons of God, to be adopted into His family, is the zenith of all the privileges we have because we are recipients of God's grace.

Along with Jesus we are sons of God; not in essence, yet nevertheless sons in every other sense of the word. "And because we are sons, God has sent forth the Spirit of His Son into your hearts, crying out, 'Abba, Father.'" Just as the Father sent Jesus (Galatians 4:4-5), so He sent His Spirit to complete the transaction of actually making us His sons (vss 4-5). Jesus made our adoption possible, and the Spirit of God oversees the transaction—He signed the adoption papers.

God the Father designed the plan (along with the Son and Holy Spirit), God the Son made it possible by taking care of the sin problem that stood as an obstacle to the plan being fulfilled, and God the Holy Spirit performs the transaction. Once again, as in the physical creation (let us make man) the three Persons of the Triune God performed the adoptive transaction. Every act of God is a joint operation whereby the Father, Son and Holy Spirit faithfully and perfectly perform their work according to His divine purpose and for His glory.

The greatest of all privileges given to His children is that we approach our Heavenly Father on a very intimate basis, calling Him "Abba, Father."

What a privilege, what an honor, what a relationship. While all other relationships are wonderful in their own right, I personally yearn for a deepening of understanding and experience of what it truly means to call my God "Abba, Father." Actually these privileges are more than that—they are rights. Because we are members of our natural family, certain elements are not just privileges, they are rights. We have the right to live in our parent's home, eat their food, and participate in family gatherings and events—all because we are children of our parents. It is no different in our Heavenly family:

> *"But as many as received Him, to them He gave the right to become children of God, to those who believe in His name: who were born, not of blood, nor of the will of the flesh, nor of the will of man, but of God" John 1:12-13.*

The word translated "right" or as in the KJV "power" is *'exousia,'* which means authority. As children of God we have the right to claim His promises, and to fully expect Him to be faithful to those promises. We have the authority and the right to call the Creator of the universe "Abba, Father." Yes, it is a privilege, a great and wonderful privilege, yet it is so much more, it is our right, a right given to us by the Spirit of God.

These words are used only three times in the New Testament, and one of the things common to all three occasions is the concept of crying out. The first usage is by Jesus, our elder Brother, when He was under extreme stress in the Garden of Gethsemane. He told His disciples, "My soul is exceedingly sorrowful, even to death" (Mark 14:34), so much so that "an angel appeared to Him from heaven, strengthening Him. And being in agony, He prayed more earnestly" (Luke 22:43-44). Mark records He was "troubled and deeply distressed" (Mark 14:33). This describes an event that was much more than a child sitting on his father's lap looking adoringly into his face. This was a cry of agony, a cry of deepest anguish. Yes, Jesus is God, nevertheless He was petrified at what the very next day held for Him. He would be separated from His Father, the first and only time in eternity.

So these words are presented in Paul's letter to the Roman believers:

"For you did not receive the spirit of bondage again to fear, but you received the Spirit of adoption by whom we cry out, 'Abba, Father'"
Romans 8:15.

"Cry out" is the word 'krazo,' meaning to call aloud, scream (shriek, exclaim, implore). Again, "krazo' is used implying that our cry "Abba, Father" is one made out of desperation and anxiety. This is the impression given in the well known verse, "Let us therefore come boldly to the throne of grace that we may obtain mercy and find grace to help in time of need" (Hebrews 4:16). I need help, I am beside myself, I can see no way out—"Abba, Father, help me!" Because I am His child I have the right to cry out to my Heavenly Father.

This in no way implies I cannot enjoy this right of intimacy when I simply wish to "Be still, and know that [He is] God" (Psalm 46:10). The Holy Spirit is giving us the right and ability to address God with the same language as does Jesus. We have many examples of Jesus calling God "Father," but only one as "Abba, Father." Truly, this is one more sign that Jesus is our Brother, as we both have the same Father.

This right Jesus Himself described when He said, "All things have been delivered to Me by My Father, and no one knows the Son except the Father. Nor does anyone know the Father except the Son, and the one to whom the Son wills to reveal Him" (Matthew 11:27). Adoption is a legal status, and means little unless the Father reveals Himself to us as "Our Father." He then sends His Spirit into our hearts enabling us to internally feel the reality of our new relationship of Father and Son, and to address the one true and living God as "Abba, Father." Our Heavenly Father sends His Spirit into our hearts with a wonderful message—"I am El Shaddai, Almighty God, and now, because you are My sons and daughters, you may call Me 'Abba, Father.'"

Puritan Quote:

"And what is "the spirit of adoption, whereby we cry Abba, Father?" It is a sweet compound of faith that knows God to be my Father, love that loves him as my Father, joy that rejoices in him as my Father, fear that trembles to disobey him because he is my Father and a confident affection and trustfulness that relies upon him, and casts itself wholly upon him, because it knows by the infallible witness of the Holy Spirit, that Jehovah, the God of earth and heaven, is the Father of my heart" C.H. Spurgeon—1834-1892.

INTIMACY

Reading: Galatians 4:1-7
"And because you are sons, God has sent forth the Spirit of His Son into your hearts, crying out, 'Abba, Father!'" Galatians 4:6

What is spiritual intimacy with our Heavenly Father? Just about every author has a different opinion, but it all boils down to one thing—knowing God. This is true, but there are different degrees of knowing God. The argument can be made that every person who is born again knows God—a relationship has been established—He is our Father and we are His children. But, how deep is our knowledge and understanding of who He is? How free are we when we approach Him? What is our attitude? In order to enjoy an intimate relationship with God, we need to grasp hold of this Father/son concept. If we approach Him every time as our King and ourselves as citizens of His kingdom, we will probably never enjoy this intimacy.

Apart from the Father/son understanding, the other relationship that speaks to me of intimacy is that of the Shepherd/sheep. To be sought by the Shepherd, and be laid across His shoulders and hear Him rejoicing, induces a certain quality of intimacy, yet even that does not compare to the relationship I have with God as my Father.

To know God does not in itself establish intimacy. Untold numbers of children have strained relationships with their earthly father—they know them, yet do have an intimate relationship with them. They may know them too well, and that is the reason for their poor relationship.

In his wonderful book "Knowing God," J.I. Packer writes:

"The conviction behind this book is that ignorance of God—ignorance both of His ways and of the practice of communion with Him—lies at the root of much of the church's weakness today. Two unhappy trends seem to have produced this state of affairs.

Trend one is that Christian minds have been conformed to the modern spirit: the spirit, that is, that spawns great thoughts of man and leaves room for only small thoughts of God. Trend two is that Christian minds have been confused by the modern skepticism."

Ignorance of God is, I believe, the primary reason why so many Christians lack an intimate relationship with their Heavenly Father. How can Christians learn to know Him better when the only time they pick up their bible is to take it to church on Sunday mornings? Sadly, a practice that is becoming more and more popular is when the scripture reading is projected on to a large screen at the front of the church. I remember, during my last visit to the Faroe Islands, I was given the opportunity to speak at a conference meeting where 150 older folk had gathered for a week of bible study and fellowship. I asked them to raise their bible in the air if they had it with them—not one person failed to raise their bible. It was a rich sight.

"Oh, the fullness, pleasure, and sheer excitement of knowing God on earth" Jim Elliot.

We learn to know God in two primary ways—reading His Word every day and praying every day. In both scenarios the Holy Spirit will reveal God to our hearts. Without practicing these two functions of the Christian life, a believer will remain young in the faith and ignorant of who God is.

Paul wrote in his letter to the Philippian believers, "That I may know Him and the power of His resurrection" (Philippians 3:10), and to the Ephesians:

"For this reason I bow my knees to the Father of our Lord Jesus Christ, from whom the whole family in heaven and earth is named, that He would grant you, according to the riches of His glory, to be strengthened with might through His Spirit in the inner man, that Christ may dwell in your hearts through faith; that you, being rooted and grounded in love, may be able to comprehend with all the saints what is the width and length and depth and height—to know the love of Christ which passes knowledge; that you may be filled with all the fullness of God" Ephesians 3:14-19.

This is the definition of an intimate relationship with God. This should be the desire of every believer's heart, that for which he or she should crave and earnestly strive, counting all things as loss for the excellence of the knowledge of Christ Jesus my Lord (Philippians 3:8.). Nothing else matters but that I gain a closer understanding of who my Heavenly Father is. Knowledge is not understanding. I have read books filled with biblical knowledge that left me dry because it was obvious the author knew about God (doctrine) yet did not understand Him. My spiritual life was almost destroyed because I plunged myself into doctrine and neglected my spiritual growth. If I had spent just a small portion of the time in prayer and devotions as I did in doctrinal study, things would have been different. Christians require a balance between these two areas—nothing but doctrine will smother that abundant life Christ promised His followers, yet ignore doctrine altogether and you will never grow in Christ.

Mephibosheth was invited by King David to become a member of his royal household because he was the son of his good friend Jonathan. At their first meeting, Mephibosheth "fell on his face and prostrated himself." But David took him and sat him at the royal table, and said, "As for Mephibosheth . . . he shall eat at my table like one of the king's sons." (2 Samuel 9:11). Read the entire account in 2 Samuel 9, and apply it to the relationship to which God, our King, has brought us. Mephibosheth was "lame on both his feet" yet, when he sat at the king's table, his legs were covered by the table cloth. So it is with us, our lameness is covered by the table cloth of God's saving grace and Christ's righteousness.

Intimacy with the Almighty God is the high privilege of every child of God, and is one of the blessings made available because we are "in Him," and accepted with Jesus as His sons and daughters.

Puritan Quote:

"Our prayers and God's mercy are like two buckets in a well. One ascends and one descends. Our prayers ascend to God in Heaven, and His mercies and blessings descend upon us" (Ezekiel Hopkins, 1634-1690).

DISCIPLINE

Reading: Hebrews 12: 5-13
"My son, do not despise the chastening of the LORD" Hebrews 12:5

The time has arrived when we need to consider that which is probably the least favorite of all the privileges and benefits given to us as adopted children of God. "For whom the LORD loves He chastens, and scourges every son whom He receives" Hebrews 12:6.

How well some of us remember the words of our human father as he was about to "apply the board of education to the seat of learning;" yes, that which is now sadly spoken of as "child abuse"—a spanking. His words, "I am doing this because I love you" were received by us with silent contempt:

"In this the children of God and the children of the devil are manifest: Whoever does not practice righteousness is not of God"
1 John 3:10.

We are either children of God or children of the devil—there is no middle ground, no shared parentage. Our Heavenly Father's purpose is to conform us to the image of His Only Begotten Son, Jesus Christ, and, to achieve this, He frequently has to discipline us. The chastising hand of God does not take us outside the realm of His love, but rather is proof of it: "For whom the LORD loves He chastens."

Our scripture reading today opens the door of understanding regarding this sometimes avoided and frequently misunderstood subject. Five dimensions of God's paternal discipline are addressed:

1) The origin of God's paternal discipline.

The two words 'loves' and 'receives' are in the present continual tense. In other words, what is the origin of God's continuing discipline? The answer is simple; it is His infinite, eternal, and unchangeable love. If He did not love His sons and daughters He would not undertake the task of disciplining them:

"Just as He chose us in Him before the foundation of the world, that we should be holy and without blame before Him in love" Ephesians 1:4.

His purpose is that we might be "holy and without blame" and, from the beginning to the end, the source of it is His "love."

a)   In love He predestined us to adoption—Ephesians 1:4
b)   In love He drew us to Himself—Jeremiah 3:3
c)   In love He preserves us and sees to it that we shall never be separated from Him—Romans 8:33-39.

The Father's love is the source of every act of discipline. All discipline is applied from the righteous indignation of God as our Father, not as our Judge. In the light of this read Psalm 38—can these possibly be the words of a believer? Yes, they can and are; the discipline of our Father can be very severe; He will do whatever it takes to achieve His goal—our conformity to Jesus Christ. Some require a slap on their spiritual backside while others need a 2x4. Sometimes the effects are temporary, while for others it is lifelong. Wounds leave scars, and scars are a constant reminder of the reason for the discipline. Jesus carried the scars from His wounds even in His resurrected body.

2) The subject of God's paternal discipline:

His adopted children, each of them without exception, are the subjects of His discipline. God has no undisciplined, unchastened children.

The following are quotes from various persons:

"Corrections are pledges of our adoption and badges of our sonship."

"God punishes His enemies but chastens His children. The one is the judicial application of His wrath, the other is proof of His parental love."

"The scourge of the judge is widely different than the rod of the Father."

"God had one natural Son without corruption, but no adopted sons without correction."

"A gracious soul may look through the darkest cloud and see God smiling at Him."

"The subjects of God's paternal discipline are all of His children."

"Affliction, in some form or another, is leveled by God to every individual whom He regards with peculiar favor as the necessary means of promoting his spiritual profit."

3) *The nature of God's paternal discipline.*

Three words are used to describe the nature of our Father's discipline: chastened, rebuked (reproved), and scourged.

Chastened—a chastening can be either in the form of admonition or discipline. Other words used to describe this function are nurture, tutoring, and instruction—training with discipline.

Reproved—a verbal rebuke—2 Timothy 4:2, Revelation 3:19—a call to desist. The Holy Spirit will often issue the rebuke to "Stop what you are doing." As Paul writes to Timothy:

"Preach the word; be instant in season, out of season; reprove, rebuke, exhort with all longsuffering and doctrine" 2 Timothy 4:2.

He uses the spoken word and the written word to speak to us. Conviction is the work of the Holy Spirit, and its purpose is always to bring us closer to conformity with the Lord Jesus Christ.

Scourged—this word is used only seven times—six when applying to Jesus, and once in our reading in Hebrews. God sometimes takes severe measures to get our attention on things that are important in our spiritual lives. There are times when we do not respond to our Father's chastening and reproof, so He applies a more severe form of discipline. God will achieve His purpose and is willing to do whatever it takes to do it. It may seem harsh, but the child of God who is the recipient of such severe discipline, will one day thank Him in all sincerity for not leaving him to his own devices.

Puritan Quote:

"Chastening is an effect of God's love. It is not only consequential unto it, but springs from it" John Owen—1616-1683.

DISCIPLINE (CONT'D)

Reading: Hebrews 12: 5-13
"My son, do not despise the chastening of the LORD" Hebrews 12:5

Previously, we commenced some thoughts regarding God's paternal discipline under the three headings of:

1) *The origin of God's paternal discipline—His love.*
2) *The subject of God's paternal discipline—every person adopted into His family.*
3) *The nature of God's paternal discipline—chastening, reproof and scourging.*

Now I would like to continue these thoughts under two more headings:

4) *The goal of God's paternal discipline:*

We touched on this previously when we observed that our Heavenly Father's goal is to conform us to the image of His Only Begotten Son, Jesus Christ:

"For our profit, that we may be partakers of His holiness . . . [and the} peaceable fruit of righteousness" Hebrews 12:10-11.

It is our Father's desire and eternal goal that we should be holy—just like Jesus. "You shall be holy, for I the LORD your God am holy" (Leviticus 19:2; also Lev 11:44; 20:7; 1 Peter 1:16). Holiness is who God is, and His every attribute springs from it. If we are to be like Him, we must be holy, something we are incapable of achieving without God's intervention—discipline.

The benefit of discipline is that it yields fruit. It does not say it might bring forth fruit, but that it does. There is no doubt about it. When God does a work in the heart of His children, it does achieve its intended purpose. When God purges His vine, it is that it may bear more fruit—(John 15:2). When God cultivates His ground (the hearts of His adopted children), it will bring forth herbs satisfying to Him (Hebrews 6:7).

The fruit desired by the Father is the "peaceable fruit of righteousness." Remember, there is no righteousness acceptable to God other than His own. Therefore, when we are born again, the righteousness of Jesus Christ is imputed to us. God's discipline does not make our unrighteousness righteous, but promotes Christ's righteousness in us, and increases its fruit. Paul prays for the Philippian believers that they might be

"filled with the fruits of righteousness which are by Jesus Christ, to the glory and praise of God" Philippians 1:11. See also 2 Corinthians 9:10.

Also, this fruit of righteousness, which discipline brings about, is peaceable:

"The work of righteousness will be peace, and the effect of righteousness, quietness and assurance forever" Isaiah 32:17, see also James 3:18.

Those children of the Living God who have been taken through, or are going through, great trials, testify to the peace they experience; a peace that passes all understanding. When they recognize and accept that God is in control, and His desire is for their spiritual profit, there is an indescribable peace that overrides all worry and panic. What an experience it is to rest in the knowledge that our Heavenly Father's hand is on you for your spiritual and eternal welfare: *"By these fruits of righteousness our hearts are quieted, our minds composed, all tumults allayed, and we are able to "possess our souls in patience" John Owen.*

5) The proper response to God's paternal discipline:
Our response can be categorized under three headings:
a) Expect it
b) Understand it
c) Submit to God in it.

If you are God's adopted child you must expect His discipline. You are a member of His family, and you will be brought into conformity with Jesus, you will increase in holiness, and you will bear the fruit of righteousness. Not only is this the desire of our Heavenly Father, it is the desire of each one who has been born again by the Spirit of God. The severity of our discipline depends on what we need to be brought into line with God's purpose. If we rebel, our discipline will be greater than if we readily submit to His will

When "fiery trials" come your way, recognize them for what they are—a means by which you can grow spiritually. If you truly belong to Him you will recognize His hand of discipline, and, as James writes:

"My brethren, count it all joy when you fall into various trials, knowing that the testing of your faith produces patience. But let patience have its perfect work, that you may be perfect and complete, lacking nothing" James 1:2-4.

We must remember there is always a positive reason for any trial that comes our way, be it discipline for unconfessed sin, or another God given opportunity to grow in that ongoing process of sanctification—being conformed to the image of Jesus Christ.

The more we experience the discipline of our Heavenly Father, the more we shall understand it, humbly accept it, and prayerfully learn and grow because of it. The natural tendency is to resist it, and, like the knot in a wet rope, the more tension applied, the tighter it becomes. "My son, do not despise the chastening of the LORD, nor be discouraged when you are rebuked by Him"—this is often the hardest attitude to accept, for we may not think we need the discipline, but remember, God knows our heart better than we do. He deals with not only our thoughts and actions, but also the intent of our heart.

He is our Father, He loves us beyond measure, and will achieve His grand purpose of conforming every one of His adopted children to the perfect image of Jesus.

Puritan Quote:

"As long as there is sin to be mortified and a grace to be fully cultivated, do not treat it [discipline] lightly and do not faint" John Owen—1616-1684.

CLOUDY DAYS

Reading: Psalm 13:1-6
"How long shall I take counsel in my soul,
having sorrow in my heart daily? Psalm 13:2

The previous two meditations have considered the Fatherly discipline of God to His children—discipline that is required for every true believer so they might be continually conformed to the image of Jesus Christ. Now, I would like to share some thoughts on a different aspect of spiritual growth as a child of God, the hand of God working to prepare us for service in His kingdom.

A friend of mine who lives in Denmark recently wrote in his internet ministry: *"Let me ask you a question, a tabooed one really: Is your soul in darkness? Is the Lord hiding Himself from you? Are your prayers just getting nowhere? Are you going through a dry desert panting for living water? Unless your problem is unconfessed sin (Oh, we can't be too sensitive to sin in all its forms), do take courage. As a child of God you are a child of light, but you may still go through experiences of darkness seeing no light. Please read Isaiah 50:10—these are times when our "fair weather faith" should give way to "cloudy weather trust."*

"You are in good company with men like Spurgeon, Luther, John Bunyon, David Brainerd, and many, many others who went through similar experiences which God used to make them a blessing to others. God is doing that right now with your life too" Jørn Nielsen.

To the experienced believer, when he or she goes through such a dark period in their spiritual life, they will hopefully recognize it for what it is—the hand of God training them for a work He has planned for them. We all have to participate in God's Boot Camp; the place where we are trained for His service, training that is unavailable anywhere else. Both my friend Jørn and I went through missionary training in the New Tribes Mission Boot Camp—it was no picnic, but rather strict training in both spiritual and practical issues. We were taught biblical principles, as well as how to kill, gut and prepare chickens, pigs and cows—things that are necessary for those called to serve the Lord in contacting and ministering in previously unreached tribes throughout the world: Invaluable training.

God has His Boot Camp where He trains individuals to do the work to which He has called them. God will never ask us to do something for which we are unprepared. If part of the training requires us to experience dark and troublesome times, then He will take us through them so we might be able to help others who experience similar things. There is a huge difference between sympathy and empathy, and we can be of greater help to others when we know from experience what another might be undergoing.

Some of these times are very difficult to bear, even to the point where we ask God "Where are You? Where have You gone?" David asked the same questions:

"How long, O LORD? Will You forget me forever? How long will You hide Your face from me? How long shall I take counsel in my soul, having sorrow in my heart daily? How long will my enemy be exalted over me?" Psalm 13:1-2.

These are five very legitimate questions that, while in the depths of despair and discouragement, our Heavenly Father will respond to in love, and not chastening for a lack of faith. Our Father is constantly working in our life by His Spirit and looks for us to remain in constant contact with Him, not only during the "good" times, but also in the "dark" times. Besides, we have the guarantee of scripture that

"God is faithful, who will not allow you to be tempted beyond what you are able, but with the temptation will also make the way of escape, that you may be able to bear it" 1 Corinthians 10:13.

Instead of crawling into a corner and feeling sorry for himself, David turned to God and spoke to Him about his situation: "Consider and hear me, O LORD my God; enlighten my eyes." Show me, my Father, what it is You are teaching me. Open my eyes that I may know Your will. Help me to remain steadfast, without wavering, knowing that You are in complete control of everything that happens in my life.

It is a total misconception that all our Heavenly Father asks of us is it curl up at His feet and listen to Him tell us He loves us. While this is true, and we all are in need of such times, God has a plan for each of His children, a plan that involves us in the work of His kingdom. None are exempt from this, therefore all will go through His Boot Camp training.

Although we are made one in Christ Jesus we remain individuals, and He uses us as individuals. We are a part of the Body of Christ, some hands, some feet, some eyes, etc. Read again Paul's wonderfully clear explanation of this concept in 1 Corinthians 12:12-31. We all have different roles to play; the role is not the important matter, rather it is how we function in the work to which God calls us:

"Are all apostles? Are all prophets? Are all teachers? Are all workers of miracles? Do all have gifts of healings? Do all speak with tongues? Do all interpret?" 1 Corinthians 12:29-30.

I would love to be a Spurgeon, or a David Brainerd, or maybe a Billy Graham, but God chose others to fill those shoes. God has given me a ministry of sharing His Word through the media of writing, and my prayer is that I will draw constantly on His strength to fulfill with all faithfulness and commitment that role to which He has called me and prepared me.

Father, give me the wisdom to know the difference between Your discipline and Your Boot Camp training. I pray I will always, in every situation, sing with David, "But I have trusted in Your mercy; my heart shall rejoice in Your salvation. I will sing to the LORD, because He has dealt bountifully with me."

Puritan Quote:
"If the work of the Lord be not soundly done upon your own hearts, how can you expect that he will bless your labours for effecting it in others?" Richard Baxter (1615-1691).

ALL THINGS

Reading: Romans 8:28-32
"How shall He not with Him also freely give us all things?" Romans 8:32

Most of us have scriptures that we enjoy quoting and even believing, yet are not quite sure what they mean. Such is the above text. What does "all things" mean? It certainly does not mean everything with no qualification. If someone owns something I have always wanted, I cannot just walk into his house and take it because the bible tells me "all things" are mine. That is called stealing.

In this passage from his letter to the believers in Rome, Paul is speaking of the incredible gift God has given us, His Son Jesus Christ. His Son is the dearest thing to His heart, yet, in order that His divine eternal purpose might be fulfilled, He sent Him to earth to die. If this is true, Paul's logic dictates, "how shall He not with Him also freely give us all things?" There is no reason for Him to withhold anything less since He has given us the greatest of all gifts that encompasses "all things." This most wonderful of gifts cannot be exceeded or superseded. Jesus Christ and all that He is, and all that He possesses and represents, is ours. To the Ephesian believers Paul wrote something similar:

"Blessed be the God and Father of our Lord Jesus Christ, who has blessed us with every spiritual blessing in the Heavenly places in Christ" Ephesians 1:3.

Here the apostle defines these "things" as "spiritual blessings," yet still designates them as "every" or "all." Neither of these words leave room for exceptions or exclusions—they are all inclusive. Our Heavenly Father, in all His sovereignty and power, is withholding nothing. The day will never dawn when He says, "Oops, I forgot something," or "I never saw that happening—I wish I had included this or that along with the other things I have given my children." No, our Father has provided everything His children need, or will

31

ever need, in order that His will and purpose be fulfilled in and through them.

A few of the essential things God provides for His children include the complete forgiveness of sins, Christ's imputed righteousness, unchallenged pardon, total removal of guilt, unqualified acceptance by God, unlimited access to Him—all this, and so much more, is summarized by Paul when he wrote, "you are complete in Him" (Colossians 2:10). Nothing lacking:

"For all things are yours: whether Paul or Apollos or Cephas, or the world or life or death, or things present or things to come—all are yours. And you are Christ's, and Christ is God's" 1 Corinthians 3:21-23.

Paul, Apollos and Cephas (Peter) were preachers of the gospel and were accepted by believers as one of them and not elevated to a higher level because of their calling. God calls each of His children to serve Him in some capacity—preachers, teachers, authors, musicians, factory workers, office staff, doctors, nurses, farmers, retired persons, disabled individuals and yes, even lawyers and tax auditors—the issue is not to which vocation He has called us but how we approach that work and our attitude in it. What has the "all things" got to do with our vocation? It means that God makes all of His resources available to us to assist us in whatever capacity He calls us. God will not ask you to do that for which He does not prepare you or provide for you. Remember—all things are yours. Do not misunderstand me, I am not advocating the "name it and claim it" teaching that prevails in certain elements of the church today, but I am saying that when God's children need anything to help them in fulfilling the calling of God in their lives or for their spiritual benefit, it is there for their use.

Not most things, not almost everything, but "all things are yours," all that God has and is—all is yours—unqualified. This is what God has given that His purpose will be fulfilled—the "adoption of His children into His family:

"For it was fitting for Him, for whom are all things and by whom are all things, in bringing many sons to glory, to make the captain of their salvation perfect through sufferings" Hebrews 2:10.

Don't you just love these two words "All things?" We have been made one with Him for whom all things were created and by whom all things were created and by whom all things are maintained. They belong to Him and He will use whichever of these things are needed on behalf of and for the benefit of His children.

The goal and motive of every believer must be the glory of God. This is what was in the forefront of Jesus' mind:

"Now My soul is troubled, and what shall I say? 'Father, save Me from this hour'? But for this purpose I came to this hour. Father, glorify Your name" John 12:27
"Now the Son of Man is glorified, and God is glorified in Him" John 13:31
"Father, the hour has come. Glorify Your Son, that Your Son also may glorify You" John 17:1.

Jesus told His followers to do something that was impossible—to glorify Him and their Heavenly Father:

"By this My Father is glorified, that you bear much fruit" John 15:8
"Let your light so shine before men, that they may see your good works and glorify your Father in heaven" Matthew 5:16.

We must all agree that we cannot please God in our own strength or by using our own abilities, but we can when we learn to draw on those "all things" He has graciously given us. Did not Jesus say, "Without Me you can do nothing?" But Paul says, "I can do *all things* through Christ who strengthens me" Philippians 4:13. There are those two words again!

Puritan Quote:

"And so Paul draws an argument from the greater to the less, that as he had nothing dearer, or more precious, or more excellent than his Son, he will neglect nothing of what he foresees will be profitable to us" John Calvin,1509-1564.

JOINT HEIRS

Reading: Romans 8:12-17
"And if children, then heirs—heirs of God and joint heirs with Christ"
Romans 8:17

If being adopted by God into His family is not glorious enough, how about being made joint-heirs with Jesus Christ? How much better can this thing called salvation get? To be saved from God's wrath by His undeserved grace, and to be loved by the Sovereign Creator of the universe, is unbelievable—unless the Spirit of God makes it real to us:

"He who did not spare His own Son, but delivered Him up for us all, how shall He not with Him also freely give us all things?" Romans 8:32.

Everything is centered in and around Jesus Christ. Without Him we have no salvation and no hope; without Him we would be lost in our sins and prime candidates for God's judgment. Saved—what a wonderful concept.

As adopted sons and daughters of God we have an inheritance—God Himself is our inheritance: "O LORD, You are the portion of my inheritance and my cup; You maintain my lot. . . . Yes, I have a good inheritance" (Psalm 16:5-6). Our right to this inheritance lies strictly with Jesus Christ. If it were not for Him and our union with Him we would be outcasts and not inheritors of an eternal estate.

God is the Owner of the estate and He wrote the will in which His Son Jesus Christ is the beneficiary, the One "whom He has appointed heir of all things" (Hebrews 1:2). Now, here is the amazing thing—through our adoption into God's family we have been made joint heirs with Jesus. That is correct, that which Jesus has inherited He now shares with every child of God, His kin. He is the "first born of many brethren" Romans 8:29.

The will of God is valid—signed, sealed and delivered. It contains no flaws for it was devised and written by God. If any flaw was to be found it would affect Jesus as well as us, for it is the same will. If it was to be challenged and a loophole discovered, every inheritor would be affected similarly.

"*If Satan accuses one of God's children he does so to Christ Himself for our union with Him is so bound in the court of heaven that no charge, accusation or challenge can be made against the one that it does not affect the other*" C.H. Spurgeon. If God's will is disproved then it is jointly disproved.

If, after the will is declared and delivered, it is discovered to be void of money or property, it is void to Jesus also—no heaven for us, and no heaven for Him; no treasure for us, then no treasure for Jesus. I mention this only to emphasize the unity, the bond, the oneness we have with our Elder Brother, our Savior Jesus Christ. This fact must not be passed over lightly for it is the crux of our relationship with our Heavenly Father.

There is nothing to fear for the Father has accepted the work of Christ and rewarded Him with a kingdom, one that will not pass away (Daniel 7:14). Our bond with Jesus is unbreakable for the Father looks upon all His children as one. There is no flaw in the will of God, and there is no distinction of treasures between His children. There are no grounds for grumbling or mumbling with the way in which the Father's estate is distributed, for we are the recipients of "all things," one not more than another. We will all be satisfied with our portion:

> "*As for me, I will see Your face in righteousness; I shall be satisfied when I awake in Your likeness*" Psalm 17:15
> "*They are abundantly satisfied with the fullness of Your house*" Psalm 36:8
> "*My people shall be satisfied with My goodness, says the LORD*" Jeremiah 31:14.

Satisfaction with God is guaranteed for the child who walks closely with his Father, and the more His Spirit reveals Him to us, the more satisfied we become. Our portion cannot be slender or narrow, for it is Jesus' portion also.

If you are pardoned it is through His blood; if you are justified it is through His righteousness; if you are sanctified it is because He is made to you sanctification; if you are taught in His ways it is because He is made to you Wisdom; if you are kept from falling it is because you are preserved in Jesus Christ; if you are perfected it is because you are complete in Him; if you are glorified it is because His Father has glorified Jesus. Jesus is the forerunner for us.

Please take time to meditate on the reality that, as an adopted child of God, you are a joint heir with the King of Kings and Lord of Lords, the Divine Counselor, the Mighty God, the Everlasting Father, and the Prince of Peace. The Lion of Judah is your Brother by His choice: "Father, I desire that they also whom You gave Me may be with Me where I am, that they may behold My glory which You have given Me" John 17:24.

There is another aspect of this joint heirship that must be considered:

"And if children, then heirs—heirs of God and joint heirs with Christ, if indeed we suffer with Him, that we may also be glorified together" Romans 8:17.

We are joint heirs, not only of His treasures, but His sufferings and afflictions also; this is a necessary part of our union with Jesus. We are called upon to carry our cross as He did: "If anyone desires to come after Me, let him deny himself, and take up his cross, and follow Me" (Matthew 16:24). "For to you it has been granted on behalf of Christ, not only to believe in Him, but also to suffer for His sake, having the same conflict which you saw in me and now hear is in me" (Philippians 1:29-30). The crown and the cross cannot be separated—no cross, no crown. If we reject the sufferings we reject the treasures, for they are all part of the estate.

Our inheritance includes three things: treasures, affliction, and temptation, all three are a part of Jesus' inheritance, therefore a necessary part of ours.

"I now send you, to open their eyes, in order to turn them from darkness to light, and from the power of Satan to God, that they may receive forgiveness of sins and an inheritance among those who are sanctified by faith in Me" Acts 26:17-18.

Puritan Quote:

"The man who can truly say, 'The Lord is mine,' hath an inheritance which death cannot wither, which space cannot compass, which time cannot limit, which eternity cannot explore" Charles H. Spurgeon—1834-1892.

FULLNESS OF TIME

Reading: Galatians 3:26-4:7
"But when the fullness of the time had come, God sent forth His
Son . . . that we might receive the adoption as sons" Galatians 4:4-5.

In 1926, a patent was granted on the slogan for the phonogram or talking machine. The slogan is still in use today, although applied to various and sundry products. The slogan is "The gift that keeps on giving." I am taking the liberty of applying these words to describe how I feel about the subject we have been considering—Spiritual Adoption. The more time I invest in searching the scriptures and researching the commentaries on this marvelous subject, the more I believe it could consume our thoughts for years. One thought leads to another, and that thought is intrinsic to so many doctrines. It is like a biblical centipede—one body with numerous legs. I trust, as we continue with this subject, you have been and will continue to be blessed and challenged to dig deeper into its glorious truths and ramifications.

The words "In the fullness of the time" have been on my mind a lot recently, and have strengthened my belief that nothing takes place in a believer's life until it is the time appointed by God. It is not a time when certain things fall into place and God sees the circumstances are optimum and acted in response. For instance, the Greek language was dominant and was the most favorable to carry the gospel message, and the road technology developed by the Romans made it easier to travel than ever before. Judaism had reached a point where the introduction of the prophesied Messiah was most advantageous. God does not act in response to human circumstances, but is the Sovereign God who appoints and accomplishes the events in time. Time does not control God, God controls time—He is the Creator of time; time is not merely a clock but an element created by and controlled by God.

The sense to which it is applied by Paul in our reading today sheds great light on the adoption of God's elect to the status of sons. The chapter break, in my opinion, is unfortunate, for the thought continues uninterrupted from

3:26 to 4:7. Remember, the chapter and verse divisions in the bible are not claimed to have been inspired by the Holy Spirit.

The Old Testament saints were also children of God, chosen and loved by Him, yet did not enjoy the same status as you and I, that os New Testament saints. A Father of wealth would designate, in most cases, his eldest son as the inheritor of his estate. However, that son would be unable to take possession of the estate until he reached a certain age. Under Jewish law that age was 13 years plus one day for males, and 12 years plus one day for females. If the expected signs of maturity were not evident in the child, the guardian could extend the years according to his choosing. Roman law stated that the age of accountability was 25 years. It is a procedure practiced today when a father places his estate into a trust naming his child as the beneficiary. The trust states that the child cannot have access to the contents of the trust until he has reached a certain age, often referred to as the age of accountability. Until that time arrives, provision for the child is met by a trustee or guardian named by the father who has access to the contents of the trust. The age of access is determined by the father, and his will cannot be broken unless certain emergency circumstances occur.

Paul draws on this practice to illustrate the analogy of spiritual adoption:

> *"Now I say that the heir, as long as he is a child, does not differ at all from a slave, though he is master of all, but is under guardians and stewards until the time appointed by the father" Galatians 4:1-2.*

Under the law there is no difference between a son and a slave as far as the inheritance is concerned—neither one has access to it. The point Paul is making is that Old Testament saints were like children who had not achieved the age of accountability. They were children of God but had no access to their inheritance because they had not yet reached spiritual maturity. They were still under the guardianship of a school teacher:

> *"Therefore the law was our tutor to bring us to Christ, that we might be justified by faith. But after faith has come, we are no longer under a tutor" Galatians 3:24-25.*

The tutor or guardian was the law. When Christ came He fulfilled the law—the tutor was released of his responsibility, his function had ended. He was no longer needed. In other words, God's appointed time had arrived and God's children now had access to their inheritance.

One important thing to understand is that the very moment Mary conceived by the Holy Spirit, and all that took place in the life, death and resurrection of Jesus Christ, was appointed by the Father. Circumstances did not control the coming of Christ, but God appointed and controlled the circumstances.

This was the time appointed by God whereby His adopted children were qualified to have access to "all things" made available in their inheritance. This availability was first granted to God's Only Begotten Son, and then to all who by faith believe in Him:

"Therefore you are no longer a slave but a son, and if a son, then an heir of God through Christ" Galatians 4:7.

The age of accountability has been reached because we are in Christ. Whatever is available to God's children in their inheritance is available now. Some things promised are withheld only because God's appointed time for them is still in the future, such as our domain in heaven and final glorification. These things are guaranteed as part of our inheritance, things that our Elder Brother is already enjoying.

"In the fullness of time"—what marvelous truths are contained in these words—words that should comfort, encourage and strengthen every child of God.

Puritan Quote:
"What is God's remedy for dejection at apparent failure in our labours? This—the assurance that God's purpose cannot fail, that God's plans cannot miscarry, that God's will must be done. Our labours are not intended to bring about that which God has not decreed" Arthur W. Pink, 1856-1952. (Puritan in heart if not in history)

IDENTIFICATION

Reading: Genesis 17:9-14

"Every male child among you shall be circumcised . . . and it shall be a sign
of the covenant between Me and you" Genesis 17:10-11.

Ever since God called out a people for Himself they have been separated from others by a mark. The first form of identification was established by God Himself when He made a covenant between Himself and the descendents of Abraham. It was important to God and to His chosen people that they be identified as belonging to Him and separate from the nations among whom they dwelt. "I will be their God" He promised (Genesis 17:8), a promise that was reiterated time and time again throughout their turbulent history.

Even though children of God by faith in Jesus Christ are spoken of as "Abraham's seed" (Galatians 3:29), the ritual of circumcision is no longer required by God as the means of identification. This was a concept Peter initially had difficulty grasping (Galatians 2:11-16). Commentators seem to consider this difference of opinion as being between the Jews and the gentiles; while this is true, it is more between the law and the gospel. The law said that God is served by obeying its statutes, while the gospel is so much better and, I might add more difficult, in that it requires obedience from the heart. Even in the Old Testament this was the intent behind the law, for the time came when the Law-giver Himself was offended by an outward obedience when the heart continued in its wickedness:

> *"I will give you a new heart and put a new spirit within you; I will take the heart of stone out of your flesh and give you a heart of flesh. I will put My Spirit within you and cause you to walk in My statutes, and you will keep My judgments and do them" Ezekiel 36:26-27.*

But I stray—circumcision was the indentifying mark by which God's people were known. The gospel of Jesus Christ brought with it a new requirement, a spiritual requirement, one that involves the heart. The new heart and the new spirit is the difference that God spoke of in Ezekiel. God's people, His adopted children, are now to be known by the outward evidences of this inward change. God does not renew or refurbish our wicked heart which is born in sin and is at enmity with God, instead, He gives us a new heart and a new spirit, one that is in accord with Him, and one with which He can have communion and fellowship.

The new heart is the new way by which the Heavenly Father's children are identified whether they are Jew or Gentile: "For in Christ Jesus neither circumcision nor uncircumcision avails anything, but a new creation" (Galatians 6:15). The gospel is all about new things. Nothing used was good enough for Jesus who fulfilled the law and the prophets, and established a new law which God places in the new heart when He makes us new creatures in Christ. A new heart will behave differently than the old heart with which we were born:

> *"Let your light so shine before men, that they may see your good works and glorify your Father in heaven" Matthew 5:16.*
> *"He who abides in Me, and I in him, bears much fruit . . . By this My Father is glorified, that you bear much fruit; so you will be My disciples" John 15:5, 8.*

Wilhelmus à Brakel (1635-1711), a Dutch Reformed Pastor, suggests three marks on sonship—1) "saving faith, 2) bearing the Father's image, and 3) having inner motions which only belong to a child of God." Another Puritan offers these marks of a child of God: 1) a spirit of faith and dependency (2 Corinthians 4:13; 2) a spirit of prayer (Acts 9:11), 3) a spirit of evidence (Romans 8:16), 4) a spirit of liberty (2 Corinthians 3:17), 5) a spirit of waiting (Romans 8:23), and 6) a spirit of love (1 John 5:2)—Robert Drake ((1608-1669).

The children of God are a marked people. Others should see a difference in the way we behave—a noticeable difference. Our inward circumcision will be evidenced by our outward behavior. Not only will others note the difference, but the child of God himself will also. Paul says to "Examine yourselves as to whether you are in the faith. Test yourselves. Do you not know yourselves, that Jesus Christ is in you?" 2 Corinthians 13:5.

Tragically, there are many who call themselves Christians but do not carry the required marks of identification. Surely you will know whether or not you have been given a new heart? Satan will do his best to cast doubt in your mind, but you can always assure yourself of your spiritual adoption by examining yourself to see if the "marks" are there. The Holy Spirit, who was given to you when you were made a son of God, will always confirm your spiritual status.

"For you did not receive the spirit of bondage again to fear, but you received the Spirit of adoption by whom we cry out, 'Abba, Father.' The Spirit Himself bears witness with our spirit that we are children of God" (Romans 8:15-16). If you have been circumcised "by the circumcision of Christ" (Colossians 2:11) you will know it—the Spirit of God will confirm it. Therefore,

"Do all things without complaining and disputing, that you may become blameless and harmless, children of God without fault in the midst of a crooked and perverse generation, among whom you shine as lights in the world, holding fast the word of life" Philippians 2:14-16.

Will we ever make mistakes? Of course we will. This is one of the marks of God's children—that we are conscious of our mistakes and are troubled by them. If we sin and it does not trouble us, we need to examine ourselves to make sure we have indeed been reconciled to God.

Puritan Quote:

"When a sinner is born again and brought into God's family, he discovers that worldly people no longer understand him. Believers and unbelievers live in different worlds, in different kingdoms and in different families. This separation brings consequences; nevertheless, God will uphold His adopted children" John Cotton (1585-1652).

RESPONSIBILITIES & OBLIGATIONS

Reading: Colossians 3:1-11

"If then you were raised with Christ, seek those things which are above"

Colossians 3:1

Previously we have examined what it means to be an adopted child of God—how and why it happened, as well as some of its benefits. I am sure you agree with me that to be adopted into the family of God, where God is our Father and Jesus Christ our Elder Brother, is a blessing far exceeding the comprehension of sinful man. God, by His Spirit, has made this real to us so, as far as is possible this side of glory, we have an understanding of the truth. Even so, as wonderful as it is to those who are participators of this act of grace, we still "see in a mirror, dimly, but then face to face. Now I know in part, but then I shall know just as I also am known" 1 Corinthians 13:12.

Along with the privileges and benefits of our adoption come responsibilities and obligations. When a child is adopted into a new family he is expected to abide by the rules of the family; it is not only expected but demanded of him. In the Roman courts, when the child to be adopted is of a mature age, he is asked if he agrees to the terms of the adoption, which include obeying the rules of his prospective family. As adopted sons and daughters of God, it is required of us that we live by His rules. We are not free to live as we did in our previous family where the devil was our father; new family, new rules, new demands.

Paul addressed this letter (Colossians) to "the saints and faithful brethren in Christ," to his brothers and sisters in Christ, to his fellow adoptees into the family of God. As such, he exhorts them to "seek those things which are above, where Christ is, sitting at the right hand of God" (3:1).

Over the next few verses he explains what that means:

1) "Set your mind on things above, not on things on the earth" vs 2;
2) "Put to death your members which are on the earth" vs 5;
3) "Put on tender mercies, kindness, humility, meekness, longsuffering" vs 12;

4) "Let the word of Christ dwell in you richly" vs 16;
5) "And whatever you do in word or deed, do all in the name of the Lord Jesus, giving thanks to God the Father through Him" vs 17.

The following verses give instruction to wives, husbands, children, fathers, bond servants, and masters—no matter our station in life, we are united as children of God, and therefore are to abide by the same family rules—no exceptions.

He concludes by exhorting his brethren to:
6) "Continue earnestly in prayer" 4:2;
7) "Walk in wisdom" 4:5.

Space does not permit us to examine each of these exhortations individually, but most of them speak for themselves. One thing that stands out is that we are responsible for our behavior. In other words, we cannot rely on God to do it for us. Yes, we have previously given thought to the fact that it is the work of the Holy Spirit to conform us to the image of our Elder Brother, but this is a joint work with each of us. If we are hard headed, He will chastise and discipline us in order to achieve this goal. The bottom line is:

"Work out your own salvation with fear and trembling; for it is God who works in you both to will and to do for His good pleasure" Philippians 2:12-13.

The impetus is on us: "Set your mind," "Put to death," "Put on," "Let the word," "What ever you do," "Pray," "Walk," etc. These are indicative of our responsibilities and obligations as children of God.

"There is nothing done in secret but thy Father seeth it. There is no heart-pride, no heart-earthlyness, but thy Father seeth it. There is never a time thou prayest, hearest the Word, but thy Father seeth with what form of spirit it is. Oh therefore, if thou be a son of God, thou wilt discover it in thy whole carriage: a son feareth the frowns of his Father; I dare not do this; my Father will be offended; and I, whither shall I go? Thus the Apostle Peter, "if ye call Him Father, pass your sojourning here with fear" Anthony Burgess, (c1609-1664).

Another obligation of those who love their adoptive Parent is to obey and imitate Him:

"Therefore be imitators of God as dear children" Ephesians 5:1.

Make every effort to be like Him; to be holy as He is holy, to be loving as He is loving. When the Spirit of God shows you something from the scriptures, open your heart to embrace it. This is hard for adopted children to do because by nature we are members of a different family, and we tend to follow the traits of that family. However, when God adopts us into His family, we are endowed with a new nature and the power to cast aside the old traits and accept the new.

A child of God will find pleasure in communing with Him and learning more about Him. He will love His Word and have a desire to obey Him. When he falls down he has confidence that His Father will pick him up. When discouraged he will look for His encouragement and know He will give it; when saddened he knows He will be comforted, and when all seems lost he will discover His Father to be there in whatever capacity He is needed. The Great "I Am" is exactly that—He is whatever is needful for His child's encouragement and growth.

Life as an adopted child of Almighty God is not a life of cup cakes and cloudless skies, but one where we must "fight the good fight," "run the race that is set before us" and "walk worthy of the calling with which you were called, with all lowliness and gentleness, with longsuffering, bearing with one another in love, endeavoring to keep the unity of the Spirit in the bond of peace. There is one body and one Spirit, just as you were called in one hope of your calling; one Lord, one faith, one baptism; one God and Father of all, who is above all, and through all, and in you all" Ephesians 4:1-6.

Puritan Quote:
"Abdicate and abandon all bad company, all your former sins and lusts, never to resume or take them into your practice again. [It is] a shame for us, who are heirs apparent of the kingdom of heaven, to be groveling among things of this life along with others" Thomas Hooker (1586-1647).

OUR BODIES ALSO

Reading: Romans 8:18-25
"Even we ourselves groan within ourselves, eagerly waiting for the adoption, the redemption of our body" Romans 8:23

Right in the middle of this wonderful passage of scripture that speaks of our adoption into the family of God, we are told there is more to come. We have previously discussed that the full measure, the full experience of our adoption, will not be enjoyed until we are completely conformed into the image of our Elder Brother, Jesus Christ. Everything we have discussed has been in the spiritual arena, but now our bodies are brought into the picture.

It is amazing to me how few believers have a clear vision of their eternal future. For many years I bought into the picture of floating around in heaven as a bodiless spirit, perhaps sitting on a fluffy cloud playing a harp. How boring is that? The bible clearly teaches otherwise—we are to be given new bodies. Jesus is spoken of as the Firstborn of many brethren (Romans 8:29). He is first of all we are to become. It is written that we died with Him (Galatians 2:20; 2 Timothy 2:11), we have been raised with Him (Colossians 2:12), seated with Him in Heavenly places (Ephesians 2:6). So Jesus is the forerunner in the bodily resurrection—He was the first to be raised from the dead and given a new body, a body that was recognized by His friends, yet different in its capabilities and functions.

The resurrected body of Jesus could pass through walls (John 20:19) and suddenly appear and disappear at will (Luke 24:15, 32; John 21:1, 4).

The blood of Jesus not only redeemed our soul, but our body also:

"For you were bought at a price; therefore glorify God in your body and in your spirit, which are God's" 1 Corinthians 6:20.
"For our citizenship is in heaven, from which we also eagerly wait for the Savior, the Lord Jesus Christ, who will transform our lowly body that it may be conformed to His glorious body, according to the

working by which He is able even to subdue all things to Himself"
Philippians 3:20-21.

When the bible says "But we all, with unveiled face, beholding as in a mirror the glory of the Lord, are being transformed into the same image from glory to glory, just as by the Spirit of the Lord" (2 Corinthians 3:18), it is speaking not only of our soul but also of our body.

Another exciting aspect of the resurrection of Jesus concerns the new creation. John wrote: "Now I saw a new heaven and a new earth, for the first heaven and the first earth had passed away" (Revelation 21:1). That new creation is when heaven and earth are joined together, and is inhabited by God's people in their new resurrection bodies—not disembodied spirits. Their conformation to Jesus will finally be complete in both soul and body. God began His new creation when He raised Jesus from the dead, and added to it when He made us new creatures in Christ Jesus by our new birth and adopting us into His family. The new heaven and new earth, the next great act of creation, is not something to be accomplished sometime in the future, but was initiated by the resurrection of Jesus, is being continued by the adoption of children into the family of God, and is to be finalized at the appearing of Jesus when these children will be given their new bodies.

"In and through Jesus of Nazareth the Creator God achieved what He set out to achieve which is to deal with the problem of evil and particularly the problem of death itself and to launch a project which we can call New Creation" N.T. Wright, Bishop of Durham.

In our reading we read that the children of God, "even we ourselves groan within ourselves, eagerly waiting for the adoption, the redemption of our body." I concur with the apostle. What a day that will be. Our salvation, as we understand it today, is wonderful, but remember,

"Eye has not seen, nor ear heard, nor have entered into the heart of man the things which God has prepared for those who love Him" 1 Corinthians 2:9.

Everything that was affected by sin is corrected by redemption—curses, death, sadness, sickness, and all unpleasantness, will have no place when our adoption is completed and the new creation is finalized.

"Now I saw a new heaven and a new earth, for the first heaven and the first earth had passed away . . . And I heard a loud voice from heaven saying, 'Behold, the tabernacle of God is with men, and He will dwell with them, and they shall be His people. God Himself will be with them and be their God. And God will wipe away every tear from their eyes; there shall be no more death, nor sorrow, nor crying. There shall be no more pain, for the former things have passed away.'"

"So also is the resurrection of the dead. The body is sown in corruption, it is raised in incorruption. It is sown in dishonor, it is raised in glory. It is sown in weakness, it is raised in power. It is sown a natural body, it is raised a spiritual body. There is a natural body, and there is a spiritual body" 1 Corinthians 15:42-44.

Puritan Quote:
"Our earthly bodies without sin and infirmity shall inherit the kingdom of God. Sin and corruption has made a mad work in our bodies and souls. But, in glory there shall be no lame legs, no crumpled shoulders, no blurred eyes, and no wrinkled faces—He will transform our lowly body to be like His glorious body (Phil 3:21)" John Bunyan (1628-1688).

OUR BROTHER'S PRAYERS

Reading: Romans 8:31-35

"It is Christ . . . who also makes intercession for us" Romans 8:34

When we consider the "all things" (#11 in this series) it is hard to separate them as to their value to the child of God—it would be unwise to do so. Each aspect of salvation, although unique in their individuality, is dependent on one other. Salvation is like a chain—one link, or even two or three, cannot be classified as a chain, but string several together and you have a qualified chain. In the eighth chapter of Romans, Paul strings together spiritual links in the chain known as salvation, with each link having equal strength and importance. Remove one link and the chain collapses; one such link is the intercession of our Elder Brother. This, along with spiritual adoption, is an aspect of our adoption that, to a great extent, is neglected.

What does the intercession of Christ mean to us? Just before He died on the cross, Jesus, "knowing that all things were now accomplished" said, "It is finished" (John 19:30). If "all things were now accomplished," why are the prayers of Jesus important, if not necessary, for the welfare of God's children?

John Owen, the great 17th century Puritan writer calls the intercessory work of Christ the *"center of our faith, hope and consolation."* Yes, everything necessary for our salvation was accomplished by the death and resurrection of Jesus, but His prayers are important in that He prays for *"the application of the fruits of His oblation unto all those for whom He offered Himself in sacrifice, according as their conditions and occasions do require"* John Owen. In other words everything is in place; there is nothing left to do but to conform us to the image of Jesus Christ. This, in itself, has its detractors and enemies. The prince of darkness and liars, take great delight in accusing the children of God before Him, and, standing between the devil and our Father is Jesus Christ:

"For there is one God and one Mediator between God and men, the Man Christ Jesus" **1 Timothy 2:5.**

Satan does not have direct access to the Father for he is waylaid by our Great High Priest, Jesus Christ. The prayers of Jesus on behalf of His brothers and sisters are like the walls of a mighty fortress, impenetrable and unscalable. They are the protection every child needs; the security upon which we base our faith and hope, and glean both comfort and consolation. Without the intercessory intervention of Jesus we would have no hope in His promises, for we would be left alone to face the devices of the devil, therefore Jesus said, "Without Me, you can do nothing" John 15:5, but, says Paul, "I can do all things through Christ who strengthens me" Philippians 4:13. Why? How? Because of the prayers of Jesus:

"Also there were many priests, because they were prevented by death from continuing. But He, because He continues forever, has an unchangeable priesthood. Therefore He is also able to save to the uttermost those who come to God through Him, since He always lives to make intercession for them" **Hebrews 7:23-25.**

This ministry of Jesus is beautifully portrayed in the Old Testament. The High Priest typifies Jesus Christ as he was the mediator between God and man. The offering he made once a year was to include incense (Leviticus 16:12-13), which was to be fired by burning coals taken from the altar of burnt-offerings. The "sweet smell" of the incense was to fill the Holy of Holies, "that the cloud of incense may cover the mercy seat." The sacrifice had been made, but the incense (typifying the prayers of Jesus) was also required. Jesus is currently fulfilling the burning of incense by His prayers of intercession that fills the nostrils of our Heavenly Father.

This ritual was practiced once a year on the Day of Atonement, but was also practiced daily at the morning and evening sacrifice. Incense was made by pounding specified spices into a fine dust, then, when burned with fire, produced a sweet smelling incense acceptable and pleasing to God. The prayers of Jesus are the incense produced by the beating and death He endured for God's children. The fact this was required every day speaks of the continual intercessory ministry of Jesus, a ministry that makes effective the one perfect sacrifice He offered once for all.

Fear not, no person, not even Satan himself, can bring any effective charge against you to your Heavenly Father:

"Who shall bring a charge against God's elect? It is God who justifies. Who is he who condemns? It is Christ who died, and furthermore is also risen, who is even at the right hand of God, who also makes intercession for us. Who shall separate us from the love of Christ?" Romans 8:33-35.

It is Christ who died. It is Christ who rose from the dead. It is Christ who sits at the right hand of God. It is Christ who makes intercession for us. It is Christ—it is all of Him, by Him, and through Him. His prayers are effective, and He is committed to His ministry. Is there any wonder that He could say with the utmost confidence, "I give them eternal life, and they shall never perish; neither shall anyone snatch them out of My hand. My Father, who has given them to Me, is greater than all; and no one is able to snatch them out of My Father's hand" John 10:28-29.

"Who shall separate us from the love of Christ? Shall tribulation, or distress, or persecution, or famine, or nakedness, or peril, or sword? . . . For I am persuaded that neither death nor life, nor angels nor principalities nor powers, nor things present nor things to come, nor height nor depth, nor any other created thing, shall be able to separate us from the love of God which is in Christ Jesus our Lord" Romans 8:35-39.

Jesus said: "I will build my church and the gates of hades shall not prevail against it." He is accomplishing this through His ministry of intercessory prayer.

Puritan Quote:
"So great and glorious is the work of saving believers unto the uttermost, that it is necessary that the Lord Christ should lead a mediatory life in heaven, for the perfecting and accomplishment of it" John Owen (1616-1683).

THE GARMENTS OF SALVATION

Reading: Isaiah 61: 1-11
"He has clothed me with the garments of salvation" Isaiah 61:10

That day in September, 1967, is one that is forever inscribed in my memory—it was the day we adopted my eldest son. The sun was shining and my wife and I had a smile on our faces and great expectation and joy in our hearts. We were about to be introduced to our son for the very first time. We waited in the lady's office while she went to get the newest member of our family. When she opened the door she held in her arms the most adorable little boy you have ever seen. After signing the final paperwork, we walked out into the sun drenched day with our son in our arms, and the sunshine in our hearts. The first thing we did was drive to Fred Meyer's and bought our son some clothes.

Although God does not shop at Fred Meyers, He does clothe His newly adopted children in garments only He can provide—the garments of salvation. Isaiah speaks of God's children as "the posterity whom the LORD has blessed" (v 9). Yes, all who are in Christ are Abraham's seed (Galatians 3:29), and are the posterity of the Lord.

Would you prefer to be clothed otherwise? God's children are identified by the clothing they wear. It does not matter how you are clothed, for when He first adopts you He outfits you with the garments of salvation. When we adopted our baby he was dressed in a beautiful canary yellow outfit, but we still bought him new clothes. Whether God's newly adopted child comes clothed with a life of good works and pleasing personality, or whether he has been convicted of bank robbery or murder, in God's eyes his clothing is nothing but filthy rags:

"But we are all like an unclean thing, and all our righteousnesses are like filthy rags; we all fade as a leaf, and our iniquities, like the wind, have taken us away" Isaiah 64:6.

A wonderful account in the Old Testament (Zechariah 3:1-5) describes perfectly what God has done for us. Joshua, a High Priest, was standing before the Lord and Satan was busy accusing him. Joshua, instead of being clothed in his beautiful High Priestly garments, stood before the Lord in "filthy garments." Instead of listening to Satan's accusations the Lord told His angel:

> *"'Take away the filthy garments from him.' And to him He said, 'See, I have removed your iniquity from you, and I will clothe you with rich robes'" Zechariah 3:4.*

What very rich robes our Heavenly Father has dressed us in. The Levite priests were clothed in "white linen robes" and, as priests to the Lord, we also are clothed in the purest and brightest of all white clothing, the righteousness of Jesus Christ. Ever since our first ancestors sinned, God has provided clothing for His people (Genesis 3:21), and will do so until the end of time (Revelation 19:14). The only antidote for sin is the righteousness of Christ which is made available to us by the shedding of His blood. As heirs of the Living God we rejoice in our Father's declaration: "'This is the heritage of the servants of the LORD, and their righteousness is from Me,' says the LORD" (Isaiah 54:17). The righteousness with which we are clothed is a gift from God (Romans 5:17), and praise God for it, for our righteousness, such as it is, is "like filthy rags" (Isaiah 64:6), or putrid bandages, like those removed from the sores of a leper.

The message is that the very best we can produce is loathsome to God, and is a stench in His nostrils. This is the condition we are in before God adopts us into His family. There is no litmus test He puts us through, "for all have sinned and fall short of the glory of God" (Romans 3:23). We are each one putrid in His eyes—loathsome when compared to His holiness.

While our new Father does not take us shopping at Fred Meyer's for new clothes, He does clothe us. The Psalmist put it this way:

> *"You have turned for me my mourning into dancing; You have put off my sackcloth and clothed me with gladness" Psalm 30:11.*

Jesus promised to those who are called overcomers:

"He who overcomes shall be clothed in white garments, and I will not blot out his name from the Book of Life; but I will confess his name before My Father and before His angels" Revelation 3:5.

This is how He presents His brethren to His Father—in white garments, pure white garments, with no smears or stains. One of the analogies the Spirit of God uses to describe the relationship of Jesus and the saved is that of Husband and spouse:

"And to her it was granted to be arrayed in fine linen, clean and bright, for the fine linen is the righteous acts of the saints" Revelation 19:8, see also Ezekiel 16;10-14.

When the God who created the gorgeous plumage of birds, and the brilliant colors of tropical fish, when the Divine Artist who painted the evening sky with its multitude of pastel colors, and places the arc of color in the sky, when He designs and produces the garments for His children to wear, nothing can match their design and beauty. When viewed by God and through His eyes, the white linen robes in which the saints are clothed are perfect in design, and are a perfect blend of color with no flaws, no smudges and no blemish of any kind.

May God be praised for His magnificent workmanship seen in the garments of salvation with which He clothes each of His adopted children.

Puritan Quote:

"Oh then, what matter of joy must it be to a sincere Christian to have the rich and royal garment of Christ's righteousness cast upon him! (Isaiah 28:16). A sincere Christian rests on the righteousness of Christ as on a sure foundation: "Surely shall one say, In the Lord have I righteousness and strength" (Isaiah 45:24) (Thomas Brooks—1608-1680).

NOURISHMENT

Reading: 2 Samuel 9:1-13
"So Mephibosheth dwelt in Jerusalem, for he ate continually
at the king's table" 2 Samuel 9:13

If you have read the scripture reading for today's thought, you have read one of the greatest illustrations of spiritual adoption in the bible. David asked if his good friend Jonathan had any relatives left to whom he could show kindness, and was told of Mephibosheth. The only problem was he was a cripple, he was "lame in both his feet" (v 13). Ziba, a servant in the house of Saul, felt it necessary to inform the king of the young man's infirmity, for what good would a cripple be to him? David was not interested in Mephibosheth's usefulness; he just wanted to be kind to him.

When some of the circumstances in this story are applied to our adoption into God's family, it opens our understanding even more to the glorious beauty of this act of the King of Heaven.

1) Mephibosheth was a cripple (v 13)
2) He was called by the king (v 5)
3) He was as one of the king's sons (v 11)
4) He ate continually at the king's table (v 3).

Let us consider specifically the fact that "He ate continually at the king's table." This was an important thing, for it is mentioned three times in the space of four verses. This was no Bed & Breakfast establishment into which this young man was invited—enjoy your breakfast but you are on your own for lunch and dinner—no, he was invited to participate in every meal that was prepared for the royal family.

David could have shown Mephibosheth kindness by bringing him into his household as a servant, and could have fed him and provided for his every need. What a blessing this would have been, something beyond his wildest dreams, but no, he accepted him as one of his sons, therefore he joined the king's family and ate with them at the same table. He ate the same food and consumed as much as he wanted. Oh, precious Father, is this not a picture of what You have done for me?

"I sat down in his shade with great delight, and his fruit was sweet to my taste. He brought me to the banqueting house, and his banner over me was love" Song of Songs 2:3-4.

A son is fed a better quality of food than a servant and, instead of serving it to others, he himself is served. A son can eat until he is satisfied—his rations are not limited. A son can eat whenever he wants to, even between meals. When the prodigal son returned to his father he was accepted as a son, not a servant, and was fed the choicest of food, the fatted calf (Luke 15:11-22).

But what is the food that our Heavenly Father provides for His children? Our human diet usually consists of a variety of foods including breads, meat, fruit, and drinks. A variety is not only necessary to our health, but without it our eating habits would become very boring. The same things are true for our spiritual nutrition. However, instead of shopping at Safeway's where we can walk up and down the aisles picking and choosing which items we desire, God points us to a Man, His Son Jesus Christ. Jesus is not only the Source of our spiritual food, He is our spiritual food:

"And Jesus said to them, 'I am the bread of life. He who comes to Me shall never hunger, and he who believes in Me shall never thirst'" John 6:35.

In Jesus there is great variety, and the more we draw our nutrition from Him, the greater the variety of food and drink we experience. It cannot be said of the life of God's children that it is boring. The more we feast on Him through prayer, meditation and the reading of His Word, the more He excites us with both familiar and new refreshing samples. Our souls cannot be truly satisfied by imitating the world with its bingo, dances, drums and guitars, and various entertainment, but only in desiring Him who is the "Desire of All Nations" (Haggai 2:7).

"There is a tendency about us all to get away from Jesus, and to look rather to the streams than to the Fountain-head. Why are we more taken up with bits

of glass that sparkle in the light than with the sun himself? That tree of life, in the midst of the Paradise of God-we forget to eat of that; and we wander to the borders of the garden, to pluck the fruit of the forbidden tree of the knowledge of good and evil" Charles H. Spurgeon.

Jesus is not only Bread but "Living Bread." The bread we buy from the store is dead already—its main ingredient had to die before it could be made into bread. Jesus is "living Bread" and as such can give life to that which was dead:

"This is the bread which comes down from heaven, that one may eat of it and not die. I am the living bread which came down from heaven. If anyone eats of this bread, he will live forever" John 6:50-51.

From these words it can readily be seen that in Jesus there is everything the child of God requires for both growth and maturity. When a person is born again he is given a new life with new needs and desires, and Jesus is there to meet all those needs: "He is also able to save to the uttermost those who come to God through Him" (Hebrews 7:25). The child of God will never present to his Father a need that cannot be met in Jesus Christ. He is also well aware of what we need, and responds to the child who asks: "So I say to you, ask, and it will be given to you; seek, and you will find; knock, and it will be opened to you. For everyone who asks receives, and he who seeks finds, and to him who knocks it will be opened" Luke 11:9-10.

"Jesus, thou joy of loving hearts! Thou Fount of life! Thou Light of men! From the best bliss that earth imparts we turn unfill'd to thee again. We taste thee, O thou living Bread, and long to feast upon thee still! We drink of thee, the Fountain-head, and thirst our souls from thee to fill." Bernard of Clairvaux (1090-1153).

Puritan Quote:
"It was himself, my brethren, that our Lord set before his hearers as the bread of life; he did not mention anything of doctrine, or of precept, or of ordinance, but himself. He says "I am that bread of life." Of him, therefore, let us think" (C.H. Spurgeon 1834-1892)

CONCLUSION

Reading: Jude 20-25
"But you, beloved . . . keep yourselves in the love of God" Jude 21

Over the past nineteen meditations we have considered some of the most glorious aspects of being adopted children of God. Our adoption into the family of Almighty God gives us a deeper understanding of our relationship to our Father and Jesus, than if we considered only our new birth. Do not misunderstand me, our new birth projects such wonderful and amazing concepts of what God has accomplished in reconciling sinners to Himself, that it beyond human comprehension. Can a person be born again without being adopted by God? Of course not—neither can one be adopted into the family of God without being born again.

To conclude our thoughts in this series I would like to quote what some of the Puritans said on this matter. Joel Beeke, in his lovely little book "Heirs with Christ," suggests five motives for pursuing the consciousness of adoption, and I quote freely from his book:

1) Peace and comfort. "If we would have true peace and comfort in every estate, whether adversity or prosperity, let us labor for the knowledge of our adoption. This will be our joy in want, in wealth, in bondage, in freedom, in sickness, in health, in life and in death" William Perkins (1558-1602).

A sense of adoption provides "peace of conscience—a rest from those troubled and unquiet thoughts which otherwise would perplex us" Thomas Manton (1620-1677).

2) Experience of God's love. "God did not adopt us when we were bespangled with the jewels of holiness, and had the glory of angels upon us; but when we were black as (spades), diseased as lepers, then it was the time of love" Thomas Watson (1620-1886).

"How the love of the Father ought to motivate us toward a greater realization of our adoption! People on earth often adopt children because they have none or because those they have are not pleasing them so that their name will not be perpetuated well. But why did the Father condescend from all eternity to choose you, a mere worm at best, yes. An enemy by nature, when He had a perfect, devoted Son from eternity?

"Here is love the like was never heard of, that the Lord should rear poor worms, and let a work pass on them, to make them the sons of God" Stephen Marshall (1594?—1655).

3) Readiness for duty. When believers know they are adopted of God "they serve God with a free spirit; the holy life is carried on with more sweetness and success; not by compulsion, but by a ready mind.

But by the grace of adoption, "when the heart is suited to the work, there needs no other urgings; but if we force a course of religion upon ourselves, contrary to our own inclination, all is harsh, and ingrate, and cannot hold long" Thomas Manton (1620-1677).

4) Liberty in prayer. The Spirit of adoption provides unspeakable help in prayer (Zech 12:10). "That Spirit which comes from the grace and free favor of God, stirs up child-like addresses to God, Rom 8:26; Jude 21. Without this our prayers are but a vain babbling" Thomas Manton.

5) Victory over Satan. "The devil's drift is to overthrow this persuasion [of being adopted by God], and therefore our endeavor must be to confirm and settle our hearts herein (2 Peter 1:10). We cannot do the devil a greater pleasure than to neglect the getting of this assurance; for hereupon he will take occasion (specially in time of distress) fearfully and dangerously to seek to break the neck of our souls; he cares not otherwise what men profess, and what knowledge and other common gifts of the Spirit they have, so that they want this blessed assurance" William Perkins (1558-1602).

We must live by hope, not by "present sense," remembering "It is the delight of Satan to be keeping the thoughts of the children of God looking and pouring upon their present sinful and sorrowful condition, that they may be held under discouragement by thinking themselves miserable, but we live by hope" Samuel Willard (1640-1707).

End of quotes.

Personally, I have been greatly blessed as the Holy Spirit has guided throughout these considerations of Spiritual Adoption. To know that it was nothing in me that qualified me to be adopted into God's family, but is nothing less than His perfect love and unmerited favor.

Grace! 'tis a charming sound,
Harmonious to the ear;
Heav'n with the echo shall resound,
And all the earth shall hear.
'Twas grace that wrote my name
In life's eternal book;
'Twas grace that gave me to the Lamb,
Who all my sorrows took.
Oh, let that grace inspire
My heart with strength divine;
May all my powers to Thee aspire,
And all my days be Thine.
Philip Doddridge (1702-17510
Augustus Toplady (1740-1748)

Puritan Quote:

"Be always comforting of yourselves with the thoughts of your adoption: Draw your comforts at this tap, fetch your consolations from this relation; be therefore often chewing on the precious privileges of it, and make them your rejoicing. Let this joy outstrip the verdure of every other joy. Let this joy dispel the mists of every sorrow, and clear up your souls in the midst of all troubles and difficulties as you await Heavenly glory, where you will live out your perfect adoption by forever communing with the Triune God. There you will dwell at the fountain, and swim forever in those bankless and bottomless Oceans of Glory" Samuel Willard (1640-1707).

WHAT IS JUSTIFICATION?

Reading: Galatians 2:14-21
"We might be justified by faith in Christ and not by the works of the law; for by the works of the law no flesh shall be justified" Galatians 2:16

Today, I would like to begin a series on the wonderful doctrine of Justification, a doctrine gravely misunderstood by a large number of those who call themselves Christians.

Robert Bragge, an 18th century puritan, said of Galatians 2:16, "*These words are like an alabaster box of precious ointment, which, if rightly opened and applied, will, under the influences of the Spirit, fill every believer's soul with the perfume thereof.*"

Since the day that Adam blatantly disobeyed God and brought divine wrath upon himself and his progeny (for we were all represented in him), mankind, in God's eyes, have been considered "ungodly" (Romans 4:5). As such we are "guilty before God" (Romans 3:19), and justly placed under the condemnation of His wrath. Try as we might, and many have and do, we can offer no excuse that is acceptable to God (Romans 1:20; 2:1). Our works, life style and behavior are unacceptable to God, no matter how righteous, gallant, and successful they may be in the eyes of our fellow man. This fact alone leaves every man and woman guilty in the court of heaven.

There are primarily two court systems in our legal system—family or civil court and judicial or criminal court. Heaven is also presented as having similar courts, and the relationship and status man has with God is determined in these courts. Our previous series of thoughts concerning our adoption into the family of God falls into the declaration made in heaven's family court, but the determination of our guilt before God is the decision of the judicial court of heaven. The bible clearly states that we are "guilty before God" (Romans 3:19; Galatians 3:22), and are worthy of death (Romans 3:23; 6:23). Left to ourselves we are in a helpless situation, with no hope of ever being reconciled to our Creator. In this court there is no appeal. The judgment is final. But there is good news:

"Having no hope and without God in the world. But now in Christ Jesus you who once were far off have been brought near by the blood of Christ" Ephesians 2:12-13.

Justification is the way and means whereby a person without hope, and without God, obtains acceptance with God with a right and title to a Heavenly inheritance. Guilty men and women can be declared "not guilty," thereby being reconciled to God and being qualified for adoption into His family. This is such wonderful news, you say, but how can this happen? Read again the verse quoted above—"by the blood of Christ." There is your answer. Jesus suffered and died for our justification. Apart from His death and resurrection we would all still be in our sins with no hope of redemption, forever in our sins and forever under God's condemnation. "There is therefore now no condemnation to those who are in Christ Jesus" (Roman 8:1). The news just keeps getting better and better.

"Justification by faith is like Atlas, it bears the world on its shoulders. The entire evangelical knowledge of saving grace—the doctrines of election, effectual calling, regeneration, repentance, adoption, etc. etc., all have to be interpreted and understood in the light of Justification by faith. When Atlas falls, everything that was resting on his shoulders comes crashing down" J.I. Packer.

Unless we understand what it really means to be justified, to be declared "not guilty" in the judicial court of heaven, where God Himself is the Judge, then our concept of salvation is awry, incomplete, and lacking; our joy cannot be full and our praise to the glory of His name will be weak and apathetic.

"Justification is the account whereof God pardons all their sins, receives them into His favour, declares or pronounces them righteous and acquitted from all guilt, removes the curse, and turns away all His wrath from them, giving them right and title unto a blessed immortality or life eternal" John Owen, 1616-1683.

This divine, eternal act of heaven's Righteous and Holy Judge, sets upon all whom this right is conferred, a distinction that separates them from all others, and the world unto God. There are only two categories of persons on this earth—justified and unjustified, guilty or not guilty, reconciled to God and non-reconciled, enemies of God and friends of God. Every person is one or the other. Jesus made this distinction clear when He said:

"No servant can serve two masters; for either he will hate the one and love the other, or else he will be loyal to the one and despise the other. You cannot serve God and mammon" Luke 16:13.

Paul told the Corinthian believers:

"Do not be unequally yoked together with unbelievers. For what fellowship has righteousness with lawlessness? And what communion has light with darkness? And what accord has Christ with Belial? Or what part has a believer with an unbeliever? And what agreement has the temple of God with idols? 2 Corinthians 6:14-16.

The destiny of every man and woman is to stand before the "Judge of all the earth" (Genesis 18:25), where He will declare each one individually either guilty or not guilty. Will we be found in the camp of the justified or the unjustified? Then it will be too late to plead our perceived innocence, for our Judge sees all and knows all. The things done in secret are open before Him, and our good works count for nothing, and carry no influence in His final judgment. To the truly born again, adopted child of God, justified by the righteousness of Jesus Christ, there is no fear in his heart, for God is his Father, and Jesus his Redeemer, Friend and Brother.

Only God can change the "guilty" verdict that faces us all to that of "not guilty." What an extraordinary God we have.

Puritan Quote:

"Once I was a slave but now I am a son; once I was dead but now I am alive; once I was darkness but now I am light in the Lord; once I was a child of wrath, an heir of hell, but now I am an heir of heaven; once I was Satan's bond-servant but now I am God's freeman; once I was under the spirit of bondage but now I am under the Spirit of adoption that seals up to me the remission of my sins, the justification of my person and the salvation of my soul" Thomas Brooks (1608-1680)

MOTIVES

Reading: Romans 4:163-32
"They are without excuse" Romans 1:20

There has to be a motive or reason for every action taken whether the person performing the action is God or man. God is the Source of Justification, so what is His motive? God has only one motive and that is to bring glory to Himself. If any human was to make such a claim he/she would be considered extremely arrogant and self-centered, but God is not human—He is God. In this scenario the big difference between God and man is that He is worthy to receive all glory and honor, whereas man is not. The declaration of heaven says it all:

"You are worthy, O Lord, to receive glory and honor and power; for You created all things, and by Your will they exist and were created" Revelation 4:11.

This is all we need to know. God is worthy because He is perfect in His Holiness, Justice, and Truth. There is no element or attribute of God that is or ever has been tainted by sin. Sin is what makes man unworthy, "for all have sinned and fall[en] short of the glory of God" (Romans 3:23). Sin is the reason salvation is needed, and salvation can only be provided by the power of God. What is the means by which God provides sinful, unworthy man, salvation from the wages if sin?

"For I am not ashamed of the gospel of Christ, for it is the power of God to salvation for everyone who believes" Romans 1:16.

There is no greater example of God's power than the salvation He has provided in the gospel—and that includes the creation of the universe. How readily we take the gospel for granted. Over the years man has watered down the gospel to the extent that the power of God is often replaced by the whims and fancies of sinful man.

The secondary motive for Justification is the welfare of believers. I suggest this is secondary only because when a person is saved and justified, God is automatically glorified. This is true of every doctrine associated with salvation. For example, as believers are sanctified by the Holy Spirit, God is glorified. Justification is a one time event in the life of every believer, whereas sanctification is progressive, yet they both bring glory to the name of God.

Justification, as most other doctrines, cannot be fully understood without considering several others. When those other doctrines are ignored or denied, Justification cannot be grasped in faith, or maintained as the life blood of the children of God. It is a rare instant that a doctrine can stand alone. For us to better understand a doctrine it needs to be placed in context.

One of the truths that place the doctrine of Justification in context is the nature of God.

"The doctrine of Justification is what it is because God is Who He is." A.N. Martin. The study of any doctrine must always begin with God, not man. Perfection must be held forth as the standard, so that anything that follows can be compared to and contrasted with it.

Three attributes should be considered to bring Justification into context: God's Holiness, God's Justice, and God's Truth. These are intrinsic to our understanding of this glorious doctrine.

a) God's Holiness has always been at the forefront of everything He has ever done, and that includes before He created heaven and earth:

"Who is like You, O LORD, among the gods? Who is like You, glorious in holiness, fearful in praises, doing wonders?" Exodus 15:11.

Jehovah is incomparable. There is none like Him: "'To whom then will you liken Me, or to whom shall I be equal?' says the Holy one" (Isaiah 40:25). The choirs of heaven have one thing on their lips and in their hearts, "Holy, holy, holy is the LORD of hosts; the whole earth is full of His glory!" (Isaiah 6:3; Revelation 4:8-11). God's holiness rules and is the standard by which every other thing is judged.

Holiness basically means to be separate from. God, by nature, is separate from all that is not Him. The slightest degree of difference is classified as falling short of His glory (Romans 3:23). Even though man knew God, he fell short of the standard He has set, because he failed to glorify Him as God (Romans 1:21-23). *"God cannot be indifferent or complacent toward that which is in contradiction to Himself"* Professor Murray. What is an utter contradiction of Himself?—sin, unholiness, and uncleanness. God's perfection demands He deals with any contradiction with a holy wrath and justice. God's wrath is the response of righteous indignation against all that differs from His perfect nature.

b) God's Justice. As with His holiness, so it is with His Justice—infinite, eternal, and unchangeable—the qualities of everything God is. Abraham's declaration after pleading with God on behalf of his brother, is like an umbrella covering both the Old and New Testaments: "Shall not the Judge of all the earth do right?" (Genesis 18:25) and "Righteousness and justice are the foundation of His throne" Psalm 97:2.

Remove God's righteous justice and His throne collapses. No one can ever justly convict the Almighty of making an incorrect decision. No soul clothed in the righteousness of Jesus will be found in hell, and no one found clothed in his own righteousness will set foot in the eternal kingdom of Jesus Christ.

c) God's Truth. Put simply, God says what He means and means what He says. Tragically, truth has become a rare commodity in today's society. From the President of the United States to leaders in the church to the every day man and woman in business and the home, lying is practiced without conviction. There is no remorse until a liar is caught in his lie, or unless the Holy Spirit convicts the child of God. "The works of His hands are verity and justice; all His precepts are sure. They stand fast forever and ever, and are done in truth and uprightness" (Psalm 111:7-8). This is who God is, and it is from this high and lofty throne that men and angels are judged.

Puritan Quote:
"The whole work of justification, with all that belongs thereunto, is represented after the manner of a juridical proceeding before God's tribunal" *John Owen—1616-1683.*

GOD'S TRIBUNAL

Reading: Psalm 143:1-8
"Do not enter into judgment with Your servant, for in Your sight no one living is righteous" Psalm 143:2

Please read the following words written by John Owen slowly and carefully: *"Wherefore I cannot but judge it best (others may think of it as they please), for those who would teach or learn the doctrine of justification in a due manner, to place their consciences in the presence of God, and their persons before his tribunal, and then, upon a due consideration of his greatness, power, majesty, righteousness, holiness,—of the terror of his glory and sovereign authority, to inquire what the Scripture and a sense of their own condition direct them unto as their relief and refuge, and what plea it becomes them to make for themselves. Secret thoughts of God and ourselves, retired meditations, the conduct of the spirit in humble supplications, deathbed preparations for an immediate appearance before God, faith and love in exercise on Christ, speak other things, for the most part, than many contend for."*

Now, if you will, read them again. They are so important to a correct understanding of this glorious doctrine of justification. Owen's writings are not always easily understood, but I find that such as above are well worth the effort. Let us meditate on them as Ezekiel was told what to do with the scroll God gave him—Ezekiel 3:1-3.

If we today should be in the presence of God, and find ourselves standing "before His tribunal," what would be our first impression? Surely it would be an immediate awareness of His "greatness, power, majesty, righteousness, [and] holiness." We would need to shade our eyes at the brightness exceeding that of the sun that radiates from His very Person. Even the Seraphim covered their faces when before His throne—Isaiah 6:2.

Next, we would immediately fall on our face because we are filled with the terror of His glory and sovereign authority. One thing of which I am sure, we would not stand before Him unfazed as we see a chubby Judge smiling at us and blowing kisses our way. Neither would we walk up to Him, sit on His lap, look into His loving eyes and say, "Hello daddy."

Do not misunderstand me. I am not belittling the relationship born again believers have with their Heavenly Father. I shudder, however, when I hear the words, "Jesus is my buddy, my pal, and we hang out together." It saddens me when I hear a church elder refer to God as "the old man upstairs."

"A son honors his father, and a servant his master. If then I am the Father, where is My honor? And if I am a Master, where is My reverence? says the LORD of hosts" Malachi 1:6.

A close and loving relationship with God does not come with a lack of respect and reverence; rather, it is always accompanied with awe, wonder and honor. Our God is the King of Kings and Lord of Lords, not only to the unsaved but to the saved. He is our Friend, yes, but He is still our King and Ruler. Justification is that divine act of grace whereby the Judge of all the earth declares us "not guilty." The question remains, whereby can the all seeing, all searching eye of God penetrate the very depths of my soul and find nothing whereby He can declare me "not guilty," when everything associated with me, and of which I am charged, says I am guilty?

It is important that every true believer sees God's relationship to him in the following three ways: 1) as Creator—whereby we owe Him our existence, 2) as Lawgiver—whereby we owe Him our implicit obedience, and 3) as Judge—whereby we stand before Him and give a personal account.

1) We are God's unique and sovereign creation (Genesis 1:26-27; Psalm 139:13-16). If God is not our Creator, why be concerned about a right standing with Him? If we are but a product of slime, when did we gain an interest in One greater than ourselves? Where does Paul start in presenting the doctrine of Justification? With the wrath of God revealed from heaven on His creation—against man created by God (Romans 1:18-25, see also Acts 17:22-29). God is my Creator and I owe my existence to Him.

2) God is my Lawgiver, and I owe my allegiance to Him (Genesis 1:28; 2:15-17; Exodus 20:1-17). Israel's downfall was rebellion against the Law of God. Man's downfall was, and continues to be, disobedience to God's mandates. Disobedience equals sin, sin equals death, death equals

judgment. Mankind is condemned because he refuses to acknowledge God as his Lawgiver.

3) God is my Judge, and I will stand before Him and give a personal account. God said, "If you walk in My statutes and keep My commandments, and perform them, then I will . . . ," and "If you do not obey Me, and do not observe all these commandments, . . . I also will do this to you" (Leviticus 26:3-16). Both Testaments contain this divine principle: "If you will, then I shall." The Divine Creator, Lawgiver and Judge, has no obligation to Himself, but He does have the obligation to uphold the integrity of His own character. He must be true to His word. His word says He will judge His creation with the final pronouncement of "guilty" upon all, with the one exception of those whom He has declared Justified.

"What that is upon the account whereof God pardons all their sins, receives them into his favour, declares or pronounces them righteous and acquitted from all guilt, removes the curse, and turns away all his wrath from them, giving them right and title unto a blessed, immortality or life eternal?" John Owen.

This sevenfold statement by John Owen is the most concise yet complete description of Justification I have ever read. My prayer is these thoughts will open our hearts to the greatness of our God, and the magnitude of what He has accomplished for His children in and through the Person of His Son, Jesus Christ.

Puritan Quote:
"This is the righteousness [Christ's] in which alone a sinner can stand acquitted at God's bar? There he must make mention of this righteousness, even of this only: for none but this can answer the demands of the law, and expiate the curse of it, and this righteousness can be made his by no other way than by God's imputing it to him" William Romaine, 1714-1795.

SINS PARDONED

Reading: Numbers 14:11-25
"Then the LORD said:'I have pardoned, according to your word; but . . ."
Numbers 14:20-21

"*What that is upon the account whereof God* **pardons all their sins**, *receives them into his favour, declares or pronounces them righteous and acquitted from all guilt, removes the curse, and turns away all his wrath from them, giving them right and title unto a blessed, immortality or life eternal?" John Owen.*

The first act of God mentioned in Owen's definition of Justification is His pardoning of sins. The pardoning of misspoken words, misdeeds and crimes committed, is familiar to all of us—each of us at some time in our life have either been the benefactor of pardon or the grantor. A child says he is sorry for stealing five dollars from his mother's purse, a father apologizes for reacting too severely to his child's disobedience, a husband begs the forgiveness of his wife for a certain discretion—all the way to a presidential pardon for crimes committed. Sometimes, if it were not for the pardon, the offender would spend many years behind bars. Degrees of violation require varying degrees of pardon. Many are personal and confined to the welfare of the family, while others are social or political and may affect the welfare of a nation.

The nation of Israel had violated the promises to which they had agreed with Almighty God:

"*[They] have not heeded My voice, [they have] rejected Me . . . they shall be consumed, and there they shall die" Numbers 14:22-23, 35.*

Moses, their leader, a type of our great Mediator, Jesus Christ, pleaded with God to pardon the iniquities of the people (Numbers 14:19), and He heard him and answered Him:

"Then the LORD said: "I have pardoned, according to your word; but . . . ' Numbers 14:20-21

Oh, that little yet all important word "but." God forgave them, but there were consequences for their actions. As a father may forgive his son for his disobedience but ground him for a month, so God forgave His people yet administered a consequence. His 'grounding for a month' was a lot more severe, "they certainly shall not see the land of which I swore to their fathers, nor shall any of those who rejected Me see it" (Numbers 14:23-24). The only exceptions to this consequence were two men, Joshua and Caleb (Numbers 25:65). Why did God make an exception for these two men? "Because he has a different spirit in him and has followed Me fully" (Numbers 14:24). God rewarded their obedience to His Word:

"All the paths of the LORD are mercy and truth, to such as keep His covenant and His testimonies. For Your name's sake, O LORD, pardon my iniquity, for it is great" Psalm 25:10-11.

Is this account from the Old Testament a good description of New Testament Justification? Only to a point; only as far as pardon is a part of Justification. In Justification there is no *"but,'* it is either *all* or nothing. When a child of God is the recipient of Justification there are no negative consequences attached or involved. God's forgiveness of the sinner's iniquity is full and complete. As someone has simply put it, "Justification is just as if I'd never sinned." While this is true as far as the recipient is concerned, it is not accurate as far as God is concerned.

In order for God to justify His children, His Only Begotten Son had to die. God's holiness and justice demanded the wages of sin be paid. The wages of sin is death, separation from God, in other words, hell. We will speak of this aspect of our Justification later in this series of thoughts.

Was it necessary for Jesus to die for God to pardon us? No. God is Supreme and Just. He could pardon every one of us as a sovereign act. But, in order for Him to justify us in all of its meaning and applications, the wages of sin had to be paid, and Jesus paid the price.

Justification is more, far more, than pardon, yet, without God's pardoning of our sin, Justification could not achieve the purpose of God in the redemption of His children.

Puritan Quotes:

"*My conscience has deserved damnation, and my repentance is not sufficient for satisfaction; but most certain it is that thy mercy aboundeth above all offense*" *Anselm, 1033-1109.*

"*[Justification is] the doctrine by which the church stands or falls.*" *Martin Luther, 1483-1546.*

RECEIVED BY GOD

Reading: Romans 4:16-5:5
"Therefore, having been justified by faith, we have . . . access by faith into this grace in which we stand" Romans 5:1-2.

"*What that is upon the account whereof God pardons all their sins, receives them into his favour, declares or pronounces them righteous and acquitted from all guilt, removes the curse, and turns away all his wrath from them, giving them right and title unto a blessed, immortality or life eternal?*" John Owen.

Which gospel is this of which we speak? Is this some new revelation that God receives us? Do we not hear at the conclusion of a gospel message, "Come to the front and receive Jesus as your Savior?" This is the message of nearly all modern day evangelists—"Come to Jesus and open your heart and let Him in." Unfortunately, Warner Sallman's painting of Revelation 3:21 where Jesus stands outside a bramble covered door that has no handle, has been interpreted as Jesus pleading at the door of our heart to be granted entrance. Scripture does not present Jesus as a pathetic person standing at the door of our heart, helpless to do anything but beg for us to unlatch the door from inside and grant Him entrance. The words of Jesus in Revelation 3:21 is addressed Christians, not the unsaved, but that's a different thought.

This is not the gospel message I read of in the scriptures. There, I read:

"No one can come to Me unless the Father who sent Me draws him"
"All that the Father gives Me will come to Me, and the one who comes to Me I will by no means cast out" John 6:37, 44.

It is both a privilege and honor to be received by God. Sin has made us totally unacceptable to God, and His holiness demands that His wrath be poured out in the fullest measure upon us. As sinners we have no access to God, and no hope He will ever receive us into His presence. There is also no way, however ingenious our method and persistent our effort, whereby we can get Him to change His mind. The bible declares us to be dead in our sins (Ephesians 2:1,5), and I have never heard of a dead man being capable of doing anything but remain in his dead condition.

Did Lazarus, dead for four days and already rotting in the tomb, suddenly decide to walk out of the tomb? It was not until the Son of God demanded him to do so that life entered his body, his rotting flesh became whole, and his organs and brain began to function properly. Lazarus responded to the Divine voice of God—so it is spiritually. Unless God calls us, we have no desire or power to accept Him, for WE ARE DEAD IN OUR TRESSPASSES AND SINS.

Our salvation is not the result of anything we can do or have done:

"The wages of sin is death, but the gift of God is eternal life in Christ Jesus our Lord" Romans 6:23.
"For by grace you have been saved through faith, and that not of yourselves; it is the gift of God, not of works, lest anyone should boast" Ephesians 2:8-9.

Our salvation is a gift from God—nothing requested and nothing earned. When God calls us, He does so through the conviction of sin in our heart. The Holy Spirit is not only our Comforter, but also the One who convicts us. It is His work that brings about a reconciliation with God. There is no other way. The process of salvation begins with the calling of God and the Holy Spirit's conviction. Our response is not one of receiving Jesus as our Savior, but falling before God under that conviction and repenting of our sins. There is no salvation without repentance (Acts 2:38; 3:19). The message is the same as that of God to the Israelites:

"Repent, and turn from all your transgressions, so that iniquity will not be your ruin. Cast away from you all the transgressions

which you have committed, and get yourselves a new heart and a new spirit" Ezekiel 18:30-31.

There is no new heart and new spirit without repentance. This is God's way. Salvation is a gift from God, and so is our justification, for it is a part of our salvation:

"For if by the one man's offense death reigned through the one, much more those who receive abundance of grace and of the gift of righteousness will reign in life through the one, Jesus Christ" Romans 5:17.

Justification does not happen after some time has passed, for when you are saved you are justified. When you are saved you are reconciled to God, you have access to Him, and the age old question "How can man have a right standing with God?" is answered. Now He can receive you. There are no more cherubim wielding flaming swords barring you from God's presence. You can now "come boldly to the throne of grace" (Hebrews 4:16) without fear of rejection. This is because you have been justified. That which barred your access to Almighty God (sin) has been removed, and replaced with the righteousness of Jesus Christ. You have been received by God.

Puritan Quote:

"But some others there are amongst us, that regard not Christ and his satisfaction alone, but join faith and works together in justification; they will have other priests, and other intercessors than Christ. Alas! beloved, how are these men fallen from Christ to another gospel, as if Christ were not an all-sufficient Saviour, and able to deliver to the uttermost! What is the gospel but salvation and redemption by Christ alone?" Thomas Goodwin, 1600-1679.

ACQUITTED FROM ALL GUILT

Reading: Jude 24-25

"Now to Him who is able to keep you from stumbling, and to present you faultless before the presence of His glory with exceeding joy" Jude 24

"*What that is upon the account whereof God pardons all their sins, receives them into his favour, **declares or pronounces them righteous and acquitted from all guilt,** removes the curse, and turns away all his wrath from them, giving them right and title unto a blessed, immortality or life eternal?*" John Owen.

Imagine standing in heaven's court of Justice awaiting the decision of the jury on the charges made against you. You know you are guilty, and no defense has been offered on your behalf. You stand there fully convinced you will be found guilty. You can tell by the look in their eyes. They want to say otherwise, but they are the jury in the court of the Judge of all the earth, and are bound to consider the evidence.

The box is passed around the jurors and each one drops in a stone, for that is the way it was done during the time when the Judge walked the earth. Each juror holds two stones, a white one and a black one. If, in his opinion, the accused is innocent, he will place the white stone in the box, if guilty he places in the black one.

When each juror has placed his stone in the box the court administrator carries it to the bench and hands it to the Judge who empties it on his desk. Your heart is beating wildly as He counts the stones. His face does not reveal the decision. The court room is silent as He takes one stone and stands up.

"The decision of the jury is evenly divided," He said. "I counted six black stones and six white ones. Therefore it falls upon me to cast the deciding stone."

The Judge, known for His fairness and absolute compliance with the law, walks toward you with His hand outreached. You open your hand to receive His verdict. He places His stone in your hand and you dare not look down for His decision will seal your fate for eternity.

"You must look at the stone," He said calmly.

You do so, fully convinced it will be black. But no, it is white. The Judge, who has never made a mistake, has given you His white stone. Your knees weaken, and the Judge reaches out and holds you up.

"Thank you," you whisper, "but why?"

"The day when My Holy Spirit convicted you of your sin and you repented and believed on Me to forgive you, that is the day when your eternal future was sealed. It was then that I did several things for you. I forgave your sins, and presented you to My Father who adopted you into His family. You became a son of God, and I became your Brother. The Holy Spirit entered your heart, and you and I became one. The reason I have given you My white stone is, at that very moment, a great transaction took place—My righteousness was imputed to you and your sin and guilt was imputed to Me. When I died on the cross I died because I accepted your sins and guilt as My own, and therefore I had to be punished. The punishment you deserved, I suffered instead. The law says that the same crime cannot be punished twice, and, seeing as I was punished for your crimes, you cannot be also. In My eyes you are therefore innocent—hence I gave you My white stone."

The Judge smiled, took you by the hand and walked you out of the courtroom to freedom. You are a free man; enter into the kingdom prepared for you from the foundation of the world:

"To him who overcomes I will give some of the hidden manna to eat. And I will give him a white stone, and on the stone a new name written which no one knows except him who receives it' Revelation 2:17.

Yes, I have taken some liberties with this description of Justification, and I, along with you, can pull it apart. It is, however, how I feel about this wonderful act of God to this undeserving sinner. The great thing is I do not have to wait until I stand before the Bar of God to know my status before the Almighty Judge. Because of His grace, I know the color of the stone in His hand.

Justification is so much more than pardon—it is the removal of all guilt. I can understand pardon, but how can guilt be removed? If I commit a crime, I am for ever guilty of it even if I am pardoned. The removal of guilt is something only God can accomplish, and He does so for every one of His born again, adopted children.

Father God, Judge of all the earth, thank You for Your white stone. To many it is just a white stone, but to me it is Your way of reminding me I am innocent of all guilt in Your eyes. When You search my heart You see Jesus, not my sin; instead of guilt You see innocence; instead of black You see white. My soul cannot praise You enough for this incomprehensible act of Your love and grace. Keep me always conscious of Your sacrifice that was required for me to stand guiltless before You, and thereby acceptable in Your sight. Because of this I am Your child, and fully justified in Your sight, because of this I will spend eternity with You. Thank You. Thank You.

Puritan Quote:
"*There is no difference amongst believers as to their justification; one is no more justified than another, for every justified person hath a plenary forgiveness of his sins, and the same imputation of Christ's righteousness*" *Thomas Brooks, 1608-1680.*

DECLARE YOU FAULTLESS

Reading: Jude 24-25

"Now to Him who is able to keep you from stumbling, and to present you
faultless before the presence of His glory with exceeding joy" Jude 24

THE ROOM . . . . (Anon)

In that place between wakefulness and dreams, I found myself in the
room. There were no distinguishing features except for the one wall
covered with small index card files. They were like the ones in libraries that
list titles by author or subject in alphabetical order. But these files, which
stretched from floor to ceiling and seemingly endlessly in either direction,
had very different headings.

As I drew near the wall of files, the first to catch my attention was
one that read "Girls I have liked." I opened it and began flipping through
the cards. I quickly shut it, shocked to realize that I recognized the names
written on each one. And then without being told, I knew exactly where I
was. This lifeless room with its small files was a crude catalog system for my
life. Here were written the actions of my every moment, big and small, in a
detail my memory couldn't match.

A sense of wonder and curiosity, coupled with horror, stirred within
me as I began randomly opening files and exploring their content. Some
brought joy and sweet memories; others a sense of shame and regret so
intense that I would look over my shoulder to see if anyone was watching.

A file named "Friends" was next to one marked "Friends I Have Betrayed."
The titles ranged from the mundane to the outright weird. "Books I Have
Read," "Lies I Have Told," "Comfort I Have Given," "Jokes I Have Laughed
at." Some were almost hilarious in their exactness: "Things I've Yelled at My

Brothers". Others I couldn't laugh at: "Things I Have Done in My Anger," "Things I Have Muttered Under My Breath at My Parents."

I never ceased to be surprised by the contents. Often there were many more cards than I expected. Sometimes fewer than hoped. I was overwhelmed by the sheer volume of the life I had lived. Could it be possible that I had the time in my 20 years to write each of these thousands or even millions of cards? But each card confirmed this truth. Each was written in my own handwriting. Each signed with my signature. When I pulled out the file marked "Songs I have listened to," I realized the files grew to contain their contents. The cards were packed tightly, and yet after two or three cards, I hadn't found the end of the file. I shut it, shamed, not so much by the quality of music, but more by the vast amount of time I knew that file represented.

When I came to a file marked "Lustful Thoughts," I felt a chill run through my body. I pulled the file out only an inch, not willing to test its size, and drew out a card. I shuddered at its detailed content. I felt sick to think that such a moment had been recorded. An almost animal rage broke on me. One thought dominated my mind: "No one must ever see these cards! No one must ever see this room! I have to destroy them!" In insane frenzy I yanked the file out. Its size didn't matter now. I had to empty it and burn the cards. But as I took it at one end and began pounding it on the floor, I could not dislodge a single card. I became desperate and pulled out a card, only to find it as strong as steel when I tried to tear it.

Defeated and utterly helpless, I returned the file to its slot. Leaning my forehead against the wall, I let out a long, self-pitying sigh. And then I saw it. The title bore "People I Have Shared the Gospel With." The handle was brighter than those around it were, newer, almost unused. I pulled on its handle and a small box not more than three inches long fell into my hands. I could count the cards it contained on one hand.

And then the tears came. I began to weep; sobs so deep that the hurt started in my stomach and shook all through me. I fell on my knees and cried. I cried out of shame, from the overwhelming shame of it all. The rows of file shelves swirled in my tear-filled eyes. No one must ever, ever know of this room. I must lock it up and hide the key.

But then as I pushed away the tears, I saw Him. No, please not Him. Not here. Oh, anyone but Jesus. I watched helplessly as He began to open the files and read the cards. I couldn't bear to watch His response. And in the moments I could bring myself to look at His face, I saw a sorrow deeper than my own. He seemed to intuitively go to the worst boxes. Why did He have to read every one?

Finally He turned and looked at me from across the room. He looked at me with pity in His eyes. But this was a pity that didn't anger me. I dropped my head, covered my face with my hands and began to cry again. He walked over and put His arm around me. He could have said so many things. But He didn't say a word. He just cried with me. Then He got up and walked back to the wall of files. Starting at one end of the room, He took out a file and, one by one, began to sign His name over mine on each card. "No!" I shouted rushing to Him. All I could find to say was "No, no," as I pulled the card from Him. His name shouldn't be on these cards. But there it was, written in red so rich, so dark, so alive.

The name of Jesus covered mine. It was written with His blood. He gently took the card back. He smiled a sad smile and began to sign the cards. I don't think I'll ever understand how He did it so quickly, but the next instant it seemed I heard Him close the last file and walk back to my side. He placed His hand on my shoulder and said, "It is finished."

I stood up, and He led me out of the room. There was no lock on its door. There were still cards to be written. "I can do all things through Christ who strengthens me." Phil. 4:13.

Puritan Quote:
"There is not a doctrine in the gospel but it may be abused: but a work of grace on the heart cannot: that is like a running spring, which breaks through all opposition, and works out all filth" Robert Bragge, 1665—?

IMPARTED OR IMPUTED?

Reading: Acts 13:36-41

"By Him everyone who believes is justified from all things from which you could not be justified by the law of Moses" Acts 13:39.

Ever since the days of the early church there have been those who have failed to make the distinction between Sanctification and Justification. To most, who have been raised with this distinction clearly taught, it is readily and easily understood, but, to those who were raised in the non-evangelical churches, it may remain a clouded issue.

One thing that both doctrines have in common is that their effect in the heart of all believers originates from God in and through Jesus Christ:

"But of Him you are in Christ Jesus, who became for us wisdom from God—and righteousness and sanctification and redemption" *1 Corinthians 1:30.*

Apart from the Beloved Son of God there is neither Sanctification nor Justification. No person is worthy in themselves to qualify for such blessings, neither can they earn them. Both are acts of God applied to those He has saved and adopted into His family.

One distinction concerns their status—Justification occurs once in the life of every believer at the moment he or she is born again by the Spirit of God. An unsaved person is never justified in the eyes of God, while every true believer is. In this all believers are alike. On the other hand, sanctification is a process begun at a believer's new birth. While it is true that God sees every believer as he is in His Son, which is fully sanctified, in reality God's children are always in the process of being conformed to the image of Jesus Christ:

"But we all, with unveiled face, beholding as in a mirror the glory of the Lord, are being transformed into the same image from glory to glory, just as by the Spirit of the Lord" 2 Corinthians 3:18.

Another distinction lies in the fact that justification is a change in our position and condition in the eye of the law, whereas sanctification is conformity to the will of the Lawgiver. Justification changes us from being guilty in the eyes of the Divine Judge, to being righteous and faultless. Sanctification is the process that changes us from being filthy to holy. The first changes us from enemies of God to children of God, while the second changes the sinner's heart from enmity against God and His law, to one that loves His law and desires to keep it as a loyal subject and child.

Our children are no less our children when they are born than when they older, but many years will pass before they mature and learn to apply the lessons we have taught them.

Yet another distinction is the application by which these truths are reality to every believer. As we have seen in previous weeks, Justification means the forgiveness of sins and the removal of guilt by God. But, as marvelous as this is, there is more, much more. Paul tells us:

"Blessed be the God and Father of our Lord Jesus Christ, who has blessed us with every spiritual blessing in the Heavenly places in Christ" Ephesians 1:3.

The scriptures are filled with descriptions of the multitude of blessings and benefits that are ours because we now have a right standing before God. These blessings and benefits differ from justification in that they are not imputed to us. They are imparted to us, whereas justification is imputed. This is an important distinction.

Justification is something we have become. We were sinners and are now saints; enemies now children, haters of God now lovers, our heart has been changed, we are new creatures in Christ; all this because the righteousness of Christ is imputed to us. We are now one in and with Him (Romans 4:5-6). Being justified does not necessarily mean we have anything more. A pardoned man is not guaranteed new clothes, new car, or new home. He has escaped the penalty his crime warrants by law, and is a free man, but there are many who have freedom but nothing else. The homeless man who begs for a coin or two has his freedom, but needs to either beg or steal in order to live. Not so with the one who stands justified before God.

Along with the declaration "Not guilty" comes the promise:

"He who did not spare His own Son, but delivered Him up for us all, how shall He not with Him also freely give us all things?" Romans 8:32-33.

The point is that the "all things" are imparted to every believer and not imputed, as is our justification. The righteousness of Jesus Christ is within us, and cannot be separated from us. The blessings with which we have been blessed are ours for the taking. It is up to us to reach out and grasp these blessings. They are available to us because we have been justified completely and are not simply a part of it. How many believers have their sins pardoned, yet do not know how to take advantage of the benefits that are theirs. Many do not even know what they are.

Paul speaks of that "peace that surpasses all understanding" (Philippians 4:7) yet how many believers have never experienced it. Do not pray for God's peace—it is already yours, reach out and grasp it. So much for which we pray we already have—they are among the "all things" that are ours because we are in Christ and He in us. They have been imparted to us, they are already ours. What a tragedy to leave the courthouse having had your sins pardoned, and to not hear that "all things" are now yours. Believers are not destitute. Believers are rich beyond measure. Believers have been made one with Him who owns the "cattle on a thousand hills" Psalm 50:10.

The "all spiritual blessings" are ours to assist us in our daily walk with God. By them we are able to grow in Christ Jesus. We are told to "workout your own salvation with fear and trembling" (Philippians 2:12), and these are to help us. I would suggest it is impossible to see true spiritual growth (sanctification) without drawing on the spiritual blessings that are ours in Christ Jesus.

Puritan Quote:

"He has made Him to be sin for us, who knew no sin, that we might be made the righteousness of God in Him" Romans 10:4, which is the amazing account we have in scripture of a sinners justification before God; which to be sure, is the wonder of angels, that man fallen so low in the first Adam, should be raised so high in Christ the second" Robert Bragge, 1665—?

JESUS IN HEAVEN'S JUDICIAL COURT

Reading: Daniel 7:9-14

"The Son of Man . . . came to the Ancient of Days, and they brought
Him near before Him" Daniel 7:13

In my opinion, our reading is one of the most exciting passages in
scripture. I will never forget the moment God opened my eyes to the
relevance of these words. I was in the Faroe Islands preparing a message
for a meeting the following day, and turned to this passage as a reference to
the kingdom of Jesus Christ. After reading these words, the subject of my
message changed dramatically.

The writer of the Epistle to the Hebrews refers to Jesus as "the
forerunner" (Hebrews 6:20), in particular as our Priest He has entered
beyond the veil, a place we, as born again believers, are privileged to go.
Jesus, as the Forerunner and our Representative, is the first to experience
everything His followers are to experience under the plan of redemption.
He was resurrected, as will all His followers; He ascended into heaven; He
is seated at His Father's right hand, etc.

When Jesus died, He not only bore our sins but He became sin (2
Corinthians 5:21). When He became sin His Father turned His face from
Him and, for the first time in eternity, Jesus was separated from Him, an
agony that made the Son of Man scream out in pain and sweat drops of
blood. When, after three days He rose from the dead, He did so free of
sin.

At the tomb an interesting event took place. Mary Magdalene went
to the tomb where she met the risen Christ (John 20:11-18). When she
realized Jesus had risen and stood before her, she wanted to hug Him, but
Jesus said, "Do not cling to Me, for I have not yet ascended to My Father;
but go to My brethren and say to them, 'I am ascending to My Father and
your Father, and to My God and your God.'" A short time after, He revealed
Himself to His disciples, and invited Thomas, "Reach your finger here, and
look at My hands; and reach your hand here, and put it into My side" (John

20:27). The question might well be asked, "What changed between Jesus' meeting with Mary and later with the disciples?"

The question is answered, I believe, in our reading from Daniel 7. Jesus ascended into heaven to stand before His Father, the Ancient of Days, and present Himself as our Forerunner in the judicial court of heaven. Remember, when Jesus died, He did so full of sin, our sin, requiring His Father to separate Himself completely from Him. Now, as will we all, He stands before His Father to be judged. Verses 9-10 describe both the Judge and the courtroom:

"And the Ancient of Days was seated; His garment was white as snow, and the hair of His head was like pure wool. His throne was a fiery flame, its wheels a burning fire; a fiery stream issued and came forth from before Him."

His white garment and wool-like hair speak of the purity and righteousness of the Judge. The "fiery flame" reminds us that "Our God is a consuming fire" (Hebrews 12:29,) and no unrighteousness can survive in His presence. The courtroom is made ready (Daniel 7:10) and Jesus, the Son of Man, is brought to stand before the Judge. If one iota of sin remained in Jesus He would have been immediately condemned and sentenced to hell. However:

"To Him was given dominion and glory and a kingdom, that all peoples, nations, and languages should serve Him. His dominion is an everlasting dominion, which shall not pass away, and His kingdom the one which shall not be destroyed" Daniel 7:14.

Jesus was the first to stand trial in the Judicial Court of Heaven and be declared "Not Guilty." There is no sign of the sin that made Him experience death. He is clean, pure, spotless, without blemish of any kind—He is as His Judge—completely righteous. Our Forerunner, indeed, for it is this righteousness that is imputed into every born again child of God. We are made one with Him and in Him. As He is, so are we. He is no longer the "Only Begotten Son of God" but is now the "First Begotten of the dead" (Revelation 1:5), the "firstborn from the dead" (Colossians 1:18), and He is the "the firstfruits of those who have fallen asleep" (1 Corinthians 15:20). Indeed, He is the "first to rise from the dead" (Acts 26:23). We are justified sons of God, and Jesus is the Forerunner.

Imagine, to stand before, and be scrutinized by the intense holiness of Almighty God, and be declared "not guilty" of any sin and wrongdoing—it is an amazing thing. How completely did Jesus deal with our sins? So completely that even the eyes of the all consuming God, whose eyes search even the thoughts and intents of the heart, can find no trace. This is the result of that great and wonderful transaction when our sins were imputed to Jesus Christ, and His righteousness to us. When we stand before our Judge in the Judicial Court of Heaven we, just as was Jesus, will be declared "not guilty," for we will be found to be without sin. Our reward, even though it is not from any good we have done, is to spend eternity with Jesus in His kingdom that will never pass away, and which can never be destroyed.

Puritan Quote:

"Grant, Almighty God, I pray thee, may we be so directed towards life eternal, until after the performance of our course in this present life, and the removal of all obstacles which Satan places in our way, either to delay or turn us aside, we may at length arrive at the enjoyment of that blessed life in which Christ, thine only begotten son has preceded us. May we thus be co-heirs with him, and as thou hast appointed him sole inheritor, so may he gather us unto the secure inheritance of a blessed immortality. Amen." John Calvin, 1509-1564.

DEBTS PAID

Reading: Galatians 3:1-14
"Christ has redeemed us from the curse of the law,
having become a curse for us" Galatians 3:13

It is one of the hot topics of the day reported by every kind of media: The United States of America is almost one and a half trillion dollars in debt. This number is unimaginable to most of us, far beyond our realm of understanding. This same statement can be made of the debt we, as individuals, are held accountable to God. It is beyond our comprehension. We, as human beings, are incapable of knowing exactly what sin means to God. We do know God's holiness is so great that He cannot look at sin:

"You are of purer eyes than to behold evil, and cannot look on wickedness" Habakkuk 1:13.

As we have seen in previous thoughts, our justification places us in a right standing with God. Sin no longer stands in the way of a personal relationship with Him. Something wonderful has happened—God can now embrace us because, in His eyes, we are pure and perfectly righteous. If but one little sin remained unpaid for and unforgiven, our text above (Habakkuk 1:13) would still be in effect. The slate has been wiped clean. Jesus Christ has paid all our debt.

There is a two-fold debt for which, as unredeemed sinners, we are held responsible. One is the debt of obedience to the law, and the other is the debt of punishment for our sins. Jesus paid the debt of our disobedience of the law by "fulfilling all righteousness" (Matthew 3:15). The important word here is "all," not most, not ninety-nine percent, but every single facet of righteousness; the same righteousness that God is. Jesus lived the life of a man and remained sinless throughout.

The second debt, that of punishment for our iniquity or wickedness, has been paid by Jesus by the shedding of His blood on the cross:

"He was wounded for our transgressions, He was bruised for our iniquities"
"He has put Him to grief. When You make His soul an offering for sin"
"He poured out His soul unto death, and He was numbered with the transgressors, and He bore the sin of many" Isaiah 53:4,10,12.

We have been "bought at a price" (1 Corinthians 6:20; 7:23), and Jesus is spoken of as our "Ransom" (Matthew 20:28; 1 Timothy 2:6). The Greek word translated "ransom" indicates a "valuable price laid down for another's ransom." The blood of Jesus was indeed a valuable price, valuable in the sight of His Father. Not only was it valuable, it was sufficient to pay the enormous price. Nothing needed to be added to it; it was sufficient to pay whatever debt(s) for which God held us accountable.

"The blood of Christ . . . was as much as would take off all enmities. And take away all sin, and to satisfy divine justice, and, indeed, so it did; and therefore you read that "in His blood we have redemption, even the forgiveness of our sins" Eph 1:7; Col 1:14, 20. His death was such a full compensation to divine justice, that the apostle makes a challenge to all, "who shall lay anything to the charge of God's elect" and "who is he that condemneth? It is Christ that died" Rom 8:33-34 (KJV). Thomas Brooks, 1608-1680.

The scapegoat in the Old Testament is a wonderful picture of what Jesus has done for us, a picture that helps us understand, to some degree, the out-workings of Christ's sacrifice:

"Aaron shall lay both his hands on the head of the live goat, confess over it all the iniquities of the children of Israel, and all their transgressions, concerning all their sins, putting them on the head of the goat, and shall send it away into the wilderness by the hand of a suitable man. The goat shall bear on itself all their iniquities to an uninhabited land; and he shall release the goat in the wilderness" Leviticus 16:21-22.

The iniquity was symbolically transferred from the people to the scapegoat. It was then led out into the wilderness, an unoccupied place, and released. The first goat was killed, representing the sacrificial death of the Son of God. Together, the goats represent the entire gambit of the work of Jesus Christ, providing reconciliation to God, and a relationship with Him. As a result, the saved are redeemed and justified:

"There is therefore now no condemnation to those who are in Christ Jesus" Romans 8:1.

This is the bottom line. God sees us and accepts us in His Son, Jesus Christ. "Love has been perfected among us in this: that we may have boldness in the day of judgment; because as He is, so are we in this world" 1 John 4:17.

Many years ago, 1964 to be exact, I wrote the following words in the front of my bible. I do not know who wrote them originally:

I owed a debt I could not pay.
Jesus paid a debt He did not owe.

Puritan Quote:
"Now, what a singular support, what a wonderful comfort is this, that we ourselves are not to make up our accounts and reckonings between God and us. Therefore it is said that, "in His blood we have redemption, even the forgiveness of our sins. Ephesians 1:7." Thomas Brooks, 1608-1680.

JUSTIFICATION BY FAITH

Reading: Romans 1:16-21

"The righteousness of God is revealed from faith to faith; as it is written,
'The just shall live by faith'" Romans 1:17

It was June, 1954 when my uncle took me to London to listen to Billy Graham speak at Wembley Stadium. I had just turned 13 years of age and it was a day of "firsts" for me. One first was that I had never before seen such a large crowd—the stadium was packed to the rafters. Billy preached on John 6:47-48, "Most assuredly, I say to you, he who believes in Me has everlasting life. I am the bread of life." At the close of the meeting he invited all who wished to "accept Jesus as their Savior" to leave their seats and walk to the space in front of him. I remember thinking why had they set apart such a large area when only two or three people would "come forward?" You can imagine my amazement when thousands of people filled that entire area.

So, what happened to all those new Christians? If this was typical of every meeting he held, it would not be long before every person in England would be saved. Of course, while the numbers responding to every "altar call" were similar, the percentage of Christians in England increased very little.

In our text Paul quotes words spoken by Habakkuk in his Prophecy about 650 years previous, "the just shall live by faith" Habakkuk 2:4. (Rom:1:7, Gal 3:11, Heb 10:38). A statement as important as this requires an answer to the question, What then is this "faith" to which these men of God referred?

Let me begin by saying what it is not. The faith of which Paul speaks is not that which thousands of persons receive when they respond to an evangelist's or preacher's call to the front of an arena or church. Now, some have received genuine faith on such occasions, but not most. Well then, you might well ask, "Is there more than one kind of faith?" To which I answer, "Yes."

Scripture makes mention of two kinds of faith whereby men and women receive the gospel. There is the faith whereby we are saved and therefore justified, for justification is received by all who are saved. This faith is that which makes us a new creation in Christ Jesus (2 Corinthians 5:17; Galatians 6:15) and, by so doing forgives our sins, removes the guilt those sins have brought, and cleanses our heart while reconciling us to God.

The other "faith" of which scripture speaks does none of the above. It is said of Simon the magician, "Then Simon himself also believed; and when he was baptized he continued with Philip, and was amazed, seeing the miracles and signs which were done," yet he remained "poisoned by bitterness and bound by iniquity" (Acts 8:13, 23). Simon's faith or belief was not saving faith—his heart was not changed, he was not made a new creation in Christ Jesus. In other words he continued to live the life he had before he believed.

There were many who, like Simon, believed when they saw the miracles of Jesus and the apostles:

"Now when He was in Jerusalem at the Passover, during the feast, many believed in His name when they saw the signs which He did. But Jesus did not commit Himself to them, because He knew all men" John 2:23-24.

They did not believe on His name with the same faith as those to whom He gave the

"right (power—KJV) to become children of God, to those who believe in His name: who were born, not of blood, nor of the will of the flesh, nor of the will of man, but of God" John 1:12.

Remember the Parable of the Sower where Jesus speaks of some seed that fell on rock, and "the ones on the rock are those who, when they hear, receive the word with joy; and these have no root, who believe for a while and in time of temptation fall away" Luke 8:13. These people "receive the word with joy," it is the answer to all their needs and problems so they respond to the invitation with gladness," but, says Jesus, "they have no root," they are easily swept away when faced with temptation. Therein is the difference between genuine justifying faith and spurious faith. The one receives the gospel message in their heart and a new creation is born, while the other receives it in their head where no difference is made.

Jude has analogies of apostates—he describes them as "clouds without water, carried about by the winds; late autumn trees without fruit" Jude 12.

The expectation of those with genuine faith is made clear by Paul:

"As you therefore have received Christ Jesus the Lord, so walk in Him, rooted and built up in Him and established in the faith" Colossians 2:6-7,
"That Christ may dwell in your hearts through faith; that you, being rooted and grounded in love, may be able to comprehend with all the saints what is the width and length and depth and height—to know the love of Christ which passes knowledge; that you may be filled with all the fullness of God" Ephesians 3:17.

The new life of those whom God has justified is a real, life-changing, fruit bearing one. James speaks of spurious faith as "dead." "What does it profit, my brethren, if someone says he has faith but does not have works? . . . Thus also faith by itself, if it does not have works, is dead" James 2:14-17.

Solomon, in his God given wisdom, wrote, "A man is not established by wickedness, but the root of the righteous [justified ones] cannot be moved" and "the root of the righteous yields fruit" Proverbs 12:3, 12.

When the bible speaks of justification by faith, it is speaking of a saving, justifying and overcoming faith, not that when a person believes temporarily. Let us take the words of Paul seriously: "Examine yourselves as to whether you are in the faith. Test yourselves. Do you not know yourselves, that Jesus Christ is in you?—unless indeed you are disqualified" 2 Corinthians 13:5.

Puritan Quote:

"We allow no faith to be justifying, or to be of the same kind with it, which is not itself, and in its own nature, a spiritually vital principle of obedience and good works" John Owen.

JUSTIFICATION BY WORKS

Reading: James 2:14-26
"You see then that a man is justified by works, and not by faith only"
James 2:24

We previously considered the scriptural fact that God's children are justified by faith and nothing but faith. Nothing we do or can do adds to our acceptance by God—the merits of Jesus Christ are our only means of reconciliation with God. So, why do Paul and James say different things? Or do they? Actually, they do not. Faith and works are not diametrically opposed. It is not a question of faith or works. Paul dogmatically states "The just shall live by faith" (Romans 1:17), and James "A man is justified by works, and not faith only (James 2:24).

Once again, as we have done numerous times, we must take into account the context of any statement. False doctrines are conceived when statements are considered as stand-alone proclamations and the context ignored. James is dealing with people who glibly make a profession of faith, but their so-called faith makes no difference in their lifestyle. When a soul is saved it is saved from something and to something. It is saved from condemnation and judgment to righteousness and complete acceptance by God. Scripture defines such a person as something "new."

> *"Therefore, if anyone is in Christ, he is a new creation; old things have passed away; behold, all things have become new" 2 Corinthians 5:17.*
> *"For in Christ Jesus neither circumcision nor uncircumcision avails anything, but a new creation" Galatians 6:15.*

The expectation of a new believer (born again) is that he should "walk in newness of life" and "serve in the newness of the Spirit" (Romans 6:4; 7:6), Things have changed:

"I will give you a new heart and put a new spirit within you; I will take the heart of stone out of your flesh and give you a heart of flesh. I will put My Spirit within you and cause you to walk in My statutes, and you will keep My judgments and do them" Ezekiel 36:26-27.

This is James' argument—"Faith without works is dead" (James 2:17, 20). He points back to when God created man—first He created a body which was still a part of the ground. It had no life; it was useless and could not function. It was not until God "breathed into his nostrils the breath of life; [that] man became a living being" Genesis 2:7.

So it is with justification—the breath or Spirit of God creates a new, living creation, out of which corresponding works will be evidenced. A body dies when its spirit (life) leaves. Faith is not saving faith without a new life to prove it. To say you believe in God is not enough, for "even the demons believe—and they tremble."

"Show me your faith without your works, and I will show you my faith by my works" James 2:18.

What are the properties of Justification? What is the impact of Justification in the life of a true believer? Justification is the act of God, instantaneous, wrought by free grace alone, based on Christ's righteousness and received by faith alone. The overriding purpose of a believer's justification is the glory of God—"That in all things He might be glorified through Jesus Christ" (1 Peter 4:11). One important way in which God is glorified is through the good works of His people, or, as the bible says in one place, "By this My Father is glorified, that you bear much fruit" (John 15:8) and

"Let your light so shine before men, that they may see your good works and glorify your Father in heaven" Matthew 5:16.

Our good works are not to stroke our own ego but to bring glory to our Heavenly Father. Our good works are not so we can gain "brownie points" thereby establishing an advantageous position in heaven (as some sects believe and practice), but are the natural outworking of our justification in Christ. The works Jesus performed were the natural result of who He was, and therefore solely that His Father may be glorified. Everything Jesus said and did was for the glory of His Father—John 12:28; 17:1, 5; 21:19.

Our salvation, including our justification and sanctification, is all for the glory of God. If this is so, and I strongly believe it is, our lives must be lived with this purpose in mind. This includes listening to the Holy Spirit as He seeks to communicate God's will to us, and then to live in obedience to His will, word, and purpose.

This all sounds well and good, but we have an enemy whose purpose is to thwart the purpose of God in our lives. Millions of so called Christians spend their lives doing good works without the knowledge and experience of justification. These are those of whom Jesus spoke when He said:

"Not everyone who says to Me, 'Lord, Lord,' shall enter the kingdom of heaven, but he who does the will of My Father in heaven. Many will say to Me in that day, 'Lord, Lord, have we not prophesied in Your name, cast out demons in Your name, and done many wonders in Your name?' And then I will declare to them, 'I never knew you; depart from Me, you who practice lawlessness!" Matthew 7:21-23.

In contrast to this Peter wrote:

"If anyone speaks, let him speak as the oracles of God. If anyone ministers, let him do it as with the ability which God supplies, that in all things God may be glorified through Jesus Christ, to whom belong the glory and the dominion forever and ever. Amen" 1 Peter 4:11.

Puritan Quote:
"Holiness is required, that we may not be a disgrace to God and a dishonor to him. The sin of God's people stains his honor and profanes his name. When men profess to be a people near God, and live carnally and loosely, they dishonor God exceedingly by their conversation" Thomas Manton—1620-1677.

THE HOLINESS OF GOD

Reading: Psalm 22:1-8
"But You are holy, enthroned in the praises of Israel" Psalm 22:3

"If God puts no trust in His saints, and the heavens are not pure in His sight, how much less man, who is abominable and filthy, who drinks iniquity like water!" Job 15:15-16.

The holiness of God must be approached with the understanding that it is something that cannot be conceived in our mind or expressed in any form of language. It is something with which we are unfamiliar. In comparison we are "abominable and filthy," and "drink(s) iniquity like water," "a maggot," "a worm," and anything else that describes that which is foul and distasteful to the Holy One.

But God is Holy. He never learned how to be holy, for He never changes. He is no more holy now than He was, and He will never be more holy than He is now or ever has been. God is Holiness.

Eternal Light! Eternal Light! How pure the soul must be
When placed within Thy searching sight, it shrinks not, but with calm delight
Can live and look on Thee.

The spirits that surround Thy throne may bear the burning bliss;
But that is surely theirs alone, since they have never, never known
A fallen world like this.

Oh, how shall I, whose native sphere is dark, whose mind is dim,
Before the Ineffable appear, and on my natural spirit bear
The uncreated beam?

There is a way for man to rise to Thee, sublime Abode;
An Offering, and a Sacrifice, a Holy Spirit's energies,

An Advocate with God.

These, these prepare us for the sight of Holiness above;
The sons of ignorance and night may dwell in the eternal Light,
Through the eternal Love.
Thomas Binney, 1798-1874

This is He before whom every man and woman must eventually stand. Only those who are found in Christ, made righteous in His righteousness, made holy in His holiness, will be able to withstand being exposed to the Holy One. "The uncreated beam," the fire with which The Holy One is surrounded, consumes all that is not prepared and guarded by the sinless perfection of their Savior. We should then approach Him boldly yet reverently, boldly yet with fear, boldly yet with awe and wonder.

There He sits upon His throne surrounded by spirits and fire,
Unapproachable, unseen by man, in dreams he may aspire.

One sits there at His right hand, whose penetrating eye
Searches all approaching life, to live with Him or die.

How can I, a lowly worm, stand now before my Creator?
Sinful man, filthy rags, without hope—death is now the order.

Those made white by the blood of the Lamb alone can pass the test,
The redeemed of the Christ, made one with Him, invited now to rest.

Seated with Him in places high to reign with Him for ever,
Eternal home, eternal light, alive in holy splendor.
DTP

This is what justification has done for those who truly believe in His name. No longer clothed in the filthy rags of our own righteousness, but in the glorious robe of the righteousness of Jesus Christ—therefore acceptable to God our Father.

Puritan Quote:

"The principle or heart of holiness is within, and consists in the love of God, his Word, his ways, his servants, his honour and his interest in the world. It consists in the soul's delight in God, and the ways of God" Richard Baxter, 1615-1691.

ALL THINGS

Reading: 2 Peter 1:1-4
"His Divine power has given to us all things that pertain to life and godliness" 2 Peter 1:3

A young man and his wife, raised in poverty in Ireland, had scrimped and saved for several years to try to purchase passage to the United States. They desired to immigrate to this country. Where they lived, it seems there was no opportunity, so they desired above everything else to come to the land they had heard so much about, the United States of America.

They finally scraped together enough funds to purchase the least expensive ticket on a ship coming to this great country. The voyage was almost over, and one of the Stewards on the ship happened to walk by their little cabin. As stated, they had the least accommodating quarters. The door was open, so he stopped to chat with them for a few moments. He saw crumbs on the bed, and asked what it was?

The man answered, "That's our lunch."

The Steward retorted by saying, "What do you mean, your lunch?"

The man answered, "Yes, that's our lunch. We had enough money for passage, but we didn't have any money left over for food. So we packed what little we could, and by now it's getting stale and very difficult to eat."

The Steward stood there looking at them for a few moments, and said, "Do you mean to say that you have been eating this type of food the entire voyage?"

Again the man answered, "Yes! We simply didn't have money for anything else."

The Steward looked at them and said, "The ticket you purchased also paid for your food. In fact, there are several restaurants on this ship, and you have access to all of them. You can eat all the food you like, as many times a day as you desire."

The man and his wife stood there looking at the Steward and finally said, "You mean the ticket we purchased, also paid for our food, which means we have been needlessly eating this stale bread?"

"That's exactly what I've stated," the Steward answered!

That little illustration describes very well, I think, the plight of many Christians. That new creation that Jesus purchased for us by His divine power includes everything that is needed for the believer to live the life of godliness—nothing is excluded. If we are not enjoying the abundant life Jesus promised us, the fault cannot be laid on Him. He has provided everything we need. The above illustration is a sad story, yet to how many of us does it apply spiritually?

"For the LORD God is a sun and shield; the LORD will give grace and glory; no good thing will He withhold from those who walk uprightly" Psalm 84:11.

But the truth is, most Christians, even though they have "more abundant life," by reason that they belong to Jesus Christ, simply aren't enjoying "more abundant life." As a result, our Spiritual Life, which flows into every other aspect of our being, is so much less than what it ought to be and can be:

"He who did not spare His own Son, but delivered Him up for us all, how shall He not with Him also freely give us all things?" Romans 8:32.

In other words, due to a dearth of understanding concerning the Cross of Christ, which is the means by which Christ gives us everything, most Christians simply do not know how to live for God.

Puritan Quote:

"Thy Word is full of promises,
Flowers of sweet fragrance,
Fruit of refreshing flavor
When called by faith.

David T. Peckham

May I be rich in its riches,
Be strong in its power,
Be happy in its joy,
Abide in its sweetness,
Feast on its preciousness,
Draw vigor from its manna.
Lord, increase my faith.
Puritan Prayer.
The Valley of Vision.

THE RIGHTEOUS MAN

Reading: Proverbs 10:1-32
"The righteous will never be removed, but the wicked will not inhabit the earth" Proverbs 10:30.

Over the past meditations we have been considering the doctrine of justification, and, if we have learned little else, it is that justification and righteousness are permanently yoked—one cannot exist without the other. For every true believer righteousness is the outworking or fruit of their justification.

Recently, while meditating in the Book of Proverbs, I was impressed by the Holy Spirit's use of the Hebrew word 'tsaddiyq,' translated righteous or just. This word is used on 205 occasions in the Old Testament, 62 times in Proverbs, and 13 times in the tenth chapter alone. If we seek to understand some specifics of righteousness, such as how God blesses the righteous, and how a righteous person behaves, a reading of Proverbs will enlighten us—this could be material for an entire book, but let us take a brief look in this tenth chapter.

It would be a freak of nature should an apple tree produce oranges, or tulip bulbs grow into sunflowers. We rightfully expect like to produce like, a principle clearly taught in the scriptures:

> *"Can the Ethiopian change his skin or the leopard its spots? Then may you also do good who are accustomed to do evil" Jeremiah 13:23.*

The behavior of a righteous person is described by Jesus as "light" (Matthew 5:16), and "fruit":

> *"For a good tree does not bear bad fruit, nor does a bad tree bear good fruit. For every tree is known by its own fruit. For men do not gather figs from thorns, nor do they gather grapes from a bramble*

bush. A good man out of the good treasure of his heart brings forth good; and an evil man out of the evil treasure of his heart brings forth evil" Luke 6:43-45.

Our behavior depends upon the condition of our heart. If our heart has been made pure and righteous by the justifying grace of God, it will produce that fruit which brings glory to our Heavenly Father.

The two categories of persons in God's eyes are the righteous and the wicked. When Proverbs speaks of the righteous, it often does so by comparing them with the wicked—"The righteous . . . but the wicked." The wicked are not necessarily defined as those who commit adultery and murder, but as those who are not righteous.

Righteousness affects the whole person—his soul (10:3), head (6), memory (7), mouth (11, 31), labor (16), tongue (20), lips (21, 32), desire (24) and hope (28)—all this in one chapter. If we branch out into the entire Book of Proverbs we will discover that justification (the changing of a wicked person into a righteous person) influences his entire life, even his treatment of animals:

"A righteous man regards the life of his animal, but the tender mercies of the wicked are cruel" Proverbs 12:10.

Does this mean that every unjustified person is cruel to animals? Of course not, but it does mean that the righteous will be kind to them. If a Christian treats his dog with cruelty, it will be wise for him to examine himself and see if he is truly in the faith (2 Corinthians 13:5).

Will a righteous person never lose his temper, lie, kick his dog, have lustful thoughts, etc.? No, we are still influenced by the "old man" that dwells within us, however, when he does sin, he will be sensitive to the conviction of the Holy Spirit who also dwells within him. The justified person will seek His Heavenly Father's forgiveness by confessing it to Him with the knowledge that He is faithful and just to forgive us our sins (1 John 1:8-10).

Other attributes are associated with the righteous, such as wisdom, understanding, knowledge, instruction, kindness, generosity, compassion, love, respect, and many others. The righteous person will reflect the righteousness of Jesus Christ, after all, it is His righteousness with which you have been justified.

Not only will his actions manifest the condition of his heart, but so will his thoughts:

"Finally, brethren, whatever things are true, whatever things are noble, whatever things are just, whatever things are pure, whatever things are lovely, whatever things are of good report, if there is any virtue and if there is anything praiseworthy—meditate on these things" Philippians 4:8.

We must always remember the promises that God has given to those who are righteous in His sight—they are varied and numerous. Let us close with two wonderful promises:

"And the desire of the righteous will be granted. When the whirlwind passes by, the wicked is no more, but the righteous has an everlasting foundation" Proverbs 10:24-25.

"The effective, fervent prayer of a righteous man avails much" James 5:16.

Puritan Quote:

"Christ will be master of the heart, and sin must be mortified. If your life is unholy, then your heart is unchanged, and you are an unsaved person. The Savior will sanctify His people, renew them, give them a hatred of sin, and a love of holiness. The grace that does not make a man better than others is a worthless counterfeit. Christ saves His people, not IN their sins, but FROM their sins. Without holiness, no man shall see the Lord" Charles Spurgeon, 1834-1892.

LET HIM BE YOUR FEAR

Reading: 1 Peter 1:13-25 (17)
"The LORD of hosts, Him you shall hallow; let Him be your fear,
and let Him be your dread" Isaiah 8:13.

In days past, our forefathers would describe a man who exhibited a certain degree of Godliness in his life as a "God-fearing man." One very astute Christian author wrote, *"The fear of God is the very soul of Godliness. When the soul is removed from a person's body it [the body] soon becomes a foul-smelling carcass. Take away the fear of God from any expression of Godliness and all you have left is a stinking carcass of Pharaseeism and barren religiosity"* Albert N. Martin.

The dominance of the fear of God throughout scripture cannot be ignored by one who is a devoted reader of God's Word. A quick visit to any good concordance will show that the word "fear" appears between 300 and 400 occasions depending on the particular version you use. Many other verses refer to the fear of God without actually using the words. A few references from both testaments will suffice to show the dominance, and therefore the importance, of this subject in God's Word:

> *"Unless the God of my father, the God of Abraham and the Fear of Isaac, had been with me, surely now you would have sent me away empty-handed" Genesis 31:42, see also 31:53.*

God's name is a revelation of His character. God gave an increasing understanding of who He was by the revelation of the names by which He identified Himself. Here, one of the names by which He revealed Himself to Jacob was "The Fear of Isaac." While the KJV does not capitalize these words, most other translations do. The "Fear of Isaac" is a name of God that reveals this aspect of His character. If our comprehension of the character of God does not cause us to fear Him, in whatever capacity that may be, then we have failed to correctly understand who God is. This understanding of God's character flies in the face of the modern day shallow, and God degrading thought, that God is our "Buddy," which leads not to a fear of God, but a lovey-dovey, non-sanctifying, unscriptural concept of who He really is.

In Exodus 18:21, when Jethro, Moses' father-in-law, suggested he choose men to assist him in the oversight of the Children of Israel, they must first and foremost be men that "fear God." This was a necessary component in any man chosen to be a judge in the nation of Israel. This is also a requirement for any who would become leaders in the church, the Body of Christ, today (1 Timothy 3:1-13). If a man's life and reputation does not qualify him as a God-fearing man, he fails to qualify as a leader among God's people in both the Old and New Testament.

When God gave His law to His people, He did so in a very demonstrative way: "There were thunderings and lightnings, and a thick cloud on the mountain; and the sound of the trumpet was very loud, so that all the people who were in the camp trembled" (Exodus 19:16-19). The people "shuddered with terror." Why would God cause such natural demonstrations that scared the 'living daylights' out them? It was to rid them of carnal fear and teach them of holy fear. The whole reason why He drew near in this manner was that His fear might be before them, "so that you may not sin." "That they may learn to fear Me" Deuteronomy 4:9-10.

The same thought is given when God required Abraham to sacrifice his son Isaac: "God tested Abraham" (Genesis 22:1). When Abraham raised the knife above his son to kill him, God stopped him and said, "Do not lay your hand on the lad, or do anything to him; for now I know that you fear God" Genesis 22:12.

Do you believe in the providence of God? I am sure we will all answer strongly, "Yes." But to what extent? Has God ever asked you to kill your Isaac, whatever or whomever that might be? Whenever God tests us and gives us trials that may seem impossible to overcome, He is testing us as to the level of our fear of Him. How much do you revere Him? Do you ever see Him as you read His Word, and simply stop and stand in awe of Him? God, the Almighty Yahweh, Jehovah of Hosts, is the only One before whom we should bow, call our Father, and give Him the reverence He warrants.

The only Reverend who deserves this title is Him who is filled with and surrounded with glory and majesty:

"They shall be My people, and I will be their God; then I will give them one heart and one way, that they may fear Me forever, for the good of them and their children after them. And I will make an everlasting covenant with them, that I will not turn away from doing them good; but I will put My fear in their hearts so that they will not depart from Me" Jeremiah 32:38-40.

The purpose for God putting His fear into His people's heart is that they may reverence Him. You may say that this is all Old Testament theology, but listen to the words of Paul:

"Men of Israel, and you who fear God, listen: . . . Men and brethren, sons of the family of Abraham, and those among you who fear God, to you the word of this salvation has been sent" Acts 13:16,26.

Paul's message was to those who fear God. Mary, Jesus' mother, in her wonderful song of praise said, "He who is mighty has done great things for me, and holy is His name. And His mercy is on those who fear Him from generation to generation" (Luke 1:49-50). From this time on, she said, men should fear God.

"Let us hear the conclusion of the whole matter: Fear God and keep His commandments, for this is man's all" Ecclesiastes 12:13.

Puritan Quote:
"Faith is always proved by action, and the fear of God by the fruits which flow from it" C.H. Mackintosh, 1820-1896.

FEAR HIM

Reading: Genesis 22:1-14
"The LORD of hosts, Him you shall hallow; let Him be your fear,
and let Him be your dread" Isaiah 8:13.

Let us continue with a subject that is given almost total silence today—the Fear of God. In days past, if a man was known to love God with all his heart and live by God's Word, he was known as a God-fearing man. The fear of God is the soul of Godliness.

Do not misunderstand me: There is nothing wrong with preaching and emphasizing the love of God, but it is not the God of the Bible when nothing but His love is advocated. Paul assured the Ephesian believers, "I have not shunned to declare to you the whole counsel of God" (Acts 20:27), and that included both the love of God and the fear of God. "Work out your own salvation with fear and trembling" Philippians 2:12.

There are two usages of the word fear:

1) Being afraid—having terror or dread; fear of potential harm; (Deuteronomy 2:25; Psalm 105:38; Luke 2:9): "So great fear came upon all the church and upon all who heard these things" Acts 5:11.

This is the fear and dread that the unsaved should have when the Holy Spirit convicts them of sin, and will have when they stand before the Righteous Judge at the Great White Throne of judgment. God is angry at their sin, and unless they repent and ask Him for forgiveness, they will perish as a result of the wrath of God. Paul tells us that those outside of Christ are at enmity with Him (Romans 8:7; James 4:4). God and unregenerate man are enemies, and only the mercy and grace of God can change that scenario by reconciling men and women to Himself by the death and resurrection of Jesus:

"Much more then, having now been justified by His blood, we shall
be saved from wrath through Him. For if when we were enemies we
were reconciled to God through the death of His Son, much more,

111

having been reconciled, we shall be saved by His life. And not only that, but we also rejoice in God through our Lord Jesus Christ, through whom we have now received the reconciliation" Romans 5:9-11.

2) Fear of veneration and respect, honor and awe (Leviticus 19:3):

"On that day the LORD exalted Joshua in the sight of all Israel; and they feared him, as they had feared Moses, all the days of his life" Joshua 4:14.

This is the fear every true believer should have toward God. The dread and terror man has of God in his unregenerate condition is exchanged for a reverend awe and respect for Him. Yes, Jesus is our Friend and Brother, but not to the point where He is not given the reverence and honor due Him as the King of Kings and Lord of Lords. He is the All-Conquering Hero of heaven whom His Father seated "at His right hand in the Heavenly places, far above all principality and power and might and dominion, and every name that is named, not only in this age but also in that which is to come. And He put all things under His feet, and gave Him to be head over all things to the church, which is His body, the fullness of Him who fills all in all" Ephesians 1:20-23.

This fear is the difference between running from God and submitting to Him.

Is it right to be afraid of God? The answer may surprise you—yes, if you have scriptural grounds to be so. Yes, if there is a reason to be so.

It did not take long for Adam to give us an answer to this question: "I heard Your voice in the garden, and I was afraid because I was naked; and I hid myself" (Genesis 3:10). Adam was afraid of God because he had sinned by disobeying Him. Disobedience was the reason, and "I hid myself" the effect of that sin. Since that day, every man finds himself in the same situation: "For all have sinned" (Romans 3:23). Therefore, every unrepentant person who is conscious of his sin before the Almighty God, his Creator, will be afraid of Him and His wrath.

When Moses explicitly explained the law God had given to him, it was basically summarized in the following words:

"So you shall put away the evil from among you . . . So all the people shall hear and fear, and no longer act presumptuously . . . So you shall put away the evil from among you, and all Israel shall hear and fear" Deuteronomy 17:7,13; 21:21.

Jesus told His disciples:
"And I say to you, My friends, do not be afraid of those who kill the body, and after that have no more that they can do. But I will show you whom you should fear: Fear Him who, after He has killed, has power to cast into hell; yes, I say to you, fear Him!" Luke 12:4-5.

But what about the child of God? Is there a place for him to fear Him who "so loved the world that He gave His Only Begotten son"? After all, there is no condemnation to those who are in Christ Jesus (Romans 8:1). The wrath of God has crushed His Son, our Savior. There is definitely a place when "My flesh trembles for fear of You, and I am afraid of Your judgments" (Psalm 119:120). The saved person has a more accurate understanding of the character of God than the unsaved, therefore, this aspect of the fear of God is not the dominant facet of the fear of God.

"Do not be haughty, but fear . . . Therefore consider the goodness and severity of God" (Romans 11:19-24, see also 2 Corinthians 5:9-11). There will be repercussions to the believer who knows the truth but does not live accordingly. A genuine fear of God will strongly influence the behavior of those who call Him Father.

Puritan Quote:
"As a malefactor trembles before the judge, and under the sense of his doom, but a child of God trembles under the sense of God's goodness and kindness to him" Jeremiah Burroughs, 1599-1646.

REVERENCE

Reading: Hebrews 12:25-29
"For our God is a consuming fire" Hebrews 12:29

"Therefore let us be grateful for receiving a kingdom that cannot be shaken, and thus let us offer to God acceptable worship, with reverence and awe" Hebrews 12:28, RSV.

In the light of who God is, "a consuming fire," we are to worship Him with reverence and awe. To the believer this consuming fire is not someone before whom we shudder and tremble with dread and terror (as should unbelievers), but before whom we bow in reverence and awe as the Spirit of God reveals to us His glory and majesty.

In order for us to reach this point of adoration we must review the primary ingredients of it. Of what does the "fear of the Lord" consist? Many elements of this important doctrine might be reflected on, but, when carefully considered, they fall into three primary ingredients:

1) One must have a correct understanding of who God is
2) One must have a constant awareness of God's presence
3) One must have a continuing understanding of their obligation to God.

1) Believers will not fear God unless and until they have a correct understanding of His character—His immensity, majesty, holiness, justice, and righteousness. His wrath and hatred of sin emanates directly from His holiness, and He has no option but to direct His wrath against that which violates His very nature, which is holy, pure, righteous, and sinless.

The God to whom you can snuggle up and sit quietly in His lap and purr like a kitten while ignoring His majesty and omniscience, is not the God of the Bible. That god is Satan's alternative god whom he has created in the hearts and minds of men and women to keep them from understanding that God is El Shaddai, God Almighty. Such a god is a false god, and compares to some of the Greek gods of mythology.

When Abraham was ninety-nine years old, God spoke to him and said, "I am Almighty God (El Shaddai), walk before Me and be blameless" (Genesis 17:1). The first thing God tells us to do is recognize who He is, the All-Powerful One who exercises His power in whichever direction He determines. Man cannot channel God's power for his own purpose or benefit; neither is El Shaddai his own personal Ouija board to be used at his discretion. He is the Supreme Ruler of the Universe who does what He wills, when He wills it, and to and for whom He wills:

> *"Our God is in heaven; He does whatever He pleases" Psalm 115:3.*
> *"All the inhabitants of the earth are reputed as nothing; He does according to His will in the army of heaven and among the inhabitants of the earth. No one can restrain His hand" Daniel 4:35.*
> *"With men this is impossible, but with God all things are possible" Matthew 19:26.*

2) One must have a constant awareness of God's presence. The presence of God with His people is pervasive. The definition of 'pervasive' is that which spreads throughout a given area, such as the fragrance of a flower or perfume. A modern example is the "plug-in" air deodorizer, whose fragrance pervades the entire room. The presence of God pervades our whole being; it extends throughout the entirety of our lives. Whatever place and circumstance in which we find ourselves we know God is "here"—in us and around us.

A child of God is perpetually aware of God's love for him, His mercy toward him, and his relationship with him. Jacob, Moses, Isaiah, Ezekiel, and John, reacted as they did to the presence of God because they knew that God was "here," with them, and not in the far distance disassociated from them:

> *"O LORD, You have searched me and known me. You know my sitting down and my rising up; You understand my thought afar off. You comprehend my path and my lying down, and are acquainted*

with all my ways. For there is not a word on my tongue, but behold, O LORD, You know it altogether. You have hedged me behind and before, and laid Your hand upon me. Such knowledge is too wonderful for me; it is high, I cannot attain it" Psalm 139:1-6.

This entire Psalm speaks of the Omniscience and Omnipresence of Jehovah. Even if I tried, I cannot escape from His presence. "Where can I go from Your Spirit? Or where can I flee from Your presence?" (Psalm 139:7). If I am living with this sense of His presence—this great, almighty, majestic, sovereign God, I will not dare to willfully sin against Him. The thought of disobeying and offending Him is unthinkable to one who walks in the fear of such a God. "The fear of the LORD is to hate evil" (Proverbs 8:13). "He is not far from each one of us; for in Him we live and move and have our being" Acts 17:27-28.

3) One must have a continuing understanding of his obligation to God. In the light of 1 & 2, we must know what our responsibility is to Him. What then, is the essence of our obligation to God? I would suggest the following three things:

a) To love Him supremely
b) To obey Him implicitly
c) To trust Him completely.

To love Him supremely means that we love nothing or no one more than we love Him—not even our mother or father. Jesus said, *"If anyone comes to Me and does not hate his father and mother, wife and children, brothers and sisters, in the event that they become hindrances to his supreme love for Me, yes, moreover also his own life in the same manner, he is not able to be My disciple" (Luke 14:26), The New Testament, an expanded translation, Kenneth S. Wuest.*

Peter told the High Priest and the High Council very simply, "We ought to obey God rather than men" (Acts 5:29). No ands, ifs, or buts.

Abraham is the ultimate example of completely trusting God. When asked to sacrifice his son, "He did not waver at the promise of God through unbelief, but was strengthened in faith, giving glory to God" Romans 4:20.

Puritan Quote:

"The holiness and jealousy of God, which is a cause of insupportable terror unto convinced sinners, driving them from Him, has towards believers only a gracious influence into that fear and reverence which causes them to cleave more firmly unto Him" John Owen, 1616-1683.

TESTING

Reading: Genesis 22:1-19
"Now I know that you fear God" Genesis 22:12

One cannot go too far into this marvelous subject of the fear of God without addressing the testing of Abraham's faith. At the conclusion of this awe inspiring experience, God tells Abraham, "Now I know that you fear God." Was God pleasantly surprised when His servant passed the test? Of course not; El Shaddai can never be taken by surprise, for He knows all things from the beginning of time to the end of time. The purpose of the test was not to prove to God that Abraham was a loyal, trustworthy servant, but to prove to Abraham that his faith was strong, and no matter what he was asked to do, he would do it. Our trials are not so God can take note of our response and put a check mark in His notebook where He records our growth in the process of our sanctification, but so we can grow in Him and be encouraged in our faith:

> *"My brethren, count it all joy when you fall into various trials, knowing that the testing of your faith produces patience. But let patience have its perfect work, that you may be perfect and complete, lacking nothing" James 1:2-4.*
> *"In this you greatly rejoice, though now for a little while, if need be, you have been grieved by various trials, that the genuineness of your faith . . . may be found to praise, honor, and glory at the revelation of Jesus Christ, whom having not seen you love" 1 Peter 1:6-8.*

When Abraham was an old man, God poured the foundation upon which he and all of his descendants (which includes every born again believer—Galatians 3:29) must build:

"When Abram was ninety-nine years old, the LORD appeared to Abram and said to him, 'I am Almighty God; walk before Me and be blameless'" Genesis 17:1.

If we are to ever hear the faith confirming words from God: "Now I know that you fear God," we must learn to "work out our [your] salvation with fear and trembling," and build upon this foundation laid by God to Abraham.

The first element of the fear of God is to recognize and accept the fact that "I am God Almighty." These words, when properly comprehended by His subjects, will cause them to fall on their face in awe, wonder and amazement in total reverence. Note the response of the Israelites—Leviticus 9:24; Ezekiel—Ezekiel 1:28; 3:23; Peter, James and John—Matthew 17:5-6, and John—Revelation 1:17. When God reveals Himself to us, our natural response should be one of awe and reverence. If men and women bow and curtsey to their human monarch, how much more ought God's subjects bow in obeisance to their Almighty Sovereign.

The second element of the fear of God is to "walk before Me." The words of Moses still ring true to all of God's people today:

"And now, Israel, what does the LORD your God require of you, but to fear the LORD your God, to walk in all His ways and to love Him, to serve the LORD your God with all your heart and with all your soul, and to keep the commandments of the LORD and His statutes which I command you today for your good?" Deuteronomy 10:12-13.

Paul prayed for the believers at Colosse "that you may walk worthy of the Lord, fully pleasing Him, being fruitful in every good work and increasing in the knowledge of God; strengthened with all might, according to His glorious power . . ." (Colossians 1:10-11). We can only "walk before Him" as we recognize and submit to His "glorious power," as we bow before our Sovereign God, then we will be able to say with confidence, "I can do all things through Christ who strengthens me" Philippians 4:13.

The third element of the fear of God is to "be blameless." This is extremely important as the believer walks and grows in Jesus Christ. While living on this earth, as we all know very well, it is impossible for any person to "be blameless" before God, or, as some translations put it, "be perfect." So, why does God demand it of His people? Perfection is a quality God requires of His chosen ones whether it is of Old Testament saints or New Testament saints:

"Do all things without complaining and disputing, that you may become blameless and harmless, children of God without fault in the midst of a crooked and perverse generation, among whom you shine as lights in the world" Philippians 2:14-15.

"Blameless and harmless," the condition required and expected of those who by grace have been made "children of God." John Calvin uses the word "unreprovable" when speaking of the qualifications for Elders and Deacons in the church (1 Timothy 3:2,10). The Amplified Bible reads, "A bishop (superintendent, overseer) must give no grounds for accusation but must be above reproach"; others use words such as "irreproachable," and "a man whose life cannot be spoken against." It comes from a word meaning "unable to be accused" or "without guilt under the law" (Matthew 12: 5,7). To be guiltless before men, which is the meaning of this word, and to be guiltless before God, are two different things. We must be as our Savior, who was the "Light of the Word," and "shine as lights in the world" (Philippians 2:15). Before men we must live lives where no person can point their finger at us, and rightfully accuse us of violating the law—man's or God's.

Jesus lived a life "without sin" (Hebrews 4:15), yet was accused, howbeit falsely, of blasphemy (John 10:33). Jesus is spoken of as "a lamb without blemish and without spot" (1 Peter 1:19). We also are called upon to live lives irreproachable by men. This is the life of one who fears God, who will do anything to live a life that exemplifies His Savior. We are to "walk in the light as He is in the light" 1 John 1:7.

Puritan Quote:

"Faith untried, unprobed, unproven, is faith uncertain. The quality of the metal is ascertained by what it can do and bear. The courage of the soldier is evidenced in the field" Henry Law, 1797-1844.

UNWAVERING FAITH

Reading: Genesis 22:1-19
"Now I know that you fear God" Genesis 22:12 (cont'd)

Paul wrote one of the most articulate statements concerning Abraham's obedience when God asked him to perform an act that went beyond all belief and logic. He was to sacrifice his son, the only one through whom God's promise and covenant with Abraham could be fulfilled. The promise of the birth of a son when he was one hundred years old and his wife ninety, was cause for laughter (Genesis 17:17). Yet God intended to give him a son by his barren wife who was far beyond the age of child bearing:

"And not being weak in faith, he did not consider his own body, already dead (since he was about a hundred years old), and the deadness of Sarah's womb. He did not waver at the promise of God through unbelief, but was strengthened in faith, giving glory to God, and being fully convinced that what He had promised He was also able to perform" Romans 4:19-21.

The miracle of the birth of Isaac was to be logged in the records of history as one of the greatest, yet now God asked his father to sacrifice him as the heathens sacrifice their children to their gods.

After travelling for three strenuous and agonizing days, father and son, along with their servants, still had a distance to go before they would arrive at Mount Moriah where the sacrifice was to be made. Each step taken must have been accompanied by thoughts of the torturous undertaking Abraham faced. The idle chatter that would normally have accompanied such a trip would be far from his lips as he contemplated his impossible task. As they made camp on the third day, the mountain of sacrifice loomed in the distance. At this point Abraham ordered his servants to remain with the pack mule while he and Isaac proceeded alone to worship Jehovah.

"And Abraham said to his young men, 'Stay here with the donkey; the lad and I will go yonder and worship, and we will come back to you." We can only speculate what was in Abraham's heart when he said these words. Did he say they both would return, believing that God would miraculously provide an alternative sacrifice, or was he shielding them and Isaac from the reality of the mission? We do not know for sure, other than what the writer to the Hebrews said:

"By faith Abraham, when he was tested, offered up Isaac, and he who had received the promises offered up his only begotten son, of whom it was said, 'In Isaac your seed shall be called,' concluding that God was able to raise him up, even from the dead"' Hebrews 11:17-19.

We do know for sure that, no matter what God told him to do, He would somehow keep His promise, that through Isaac Abraham would be a "father of many nations" (Romans 4:17-18). If Jehovah could create new life from two dead bodies (Romans 4:19) He could raise that new life from the dead and thereby keep His covenant to him.

An unwavering faith is a proof that a man or woman fears God: "Now I know that you fear God" (Genesis 22:12). Obedience to God and His Word is an indelible sign that a person fears the Lord:

"That you may fear the LORD your God, to keep all His statutes and His commandments" Deuteronomy 6:2.
"There was a man in the land of Uz, whose name was Job; and that man was blameless and upright, and one who feared God and shunned evil" Job 1:1.
"I will put My fear in their hearts so that they will not depart from Me" Jeremiah 32:40.
"The people, obeyed the voice of the LORD their God, and the words of Haggai the prophet, as the LORD their God had sent him; and the people feared the presence of the LORD" Haggai 1:12-13.

To know God is to love Him, and to love Him is to obey Him (John 14:24). It is readily learned from scripture that one who fears God will exhibit both of these characteristics; a confessing Christian whose life is void of these things does not fear God, and is therefore a Christian in word only, and does not have a saving relationship with Him. Do born again Christians ever disobey God? Of course, but when they do, sooner or later, the Holy Spirit, who dwells within them, will convict them. Conviction will be followed by confession, confession by forgiveness, and forgiveness by restored fellowship—1 John 1:6-10:

> *"Because they do not change, therefore they do not fear God" Psalm 55:19.*
> *"Do not let your heart envy sinners, but be zealous for the fear of the LORD all the day" Proverbs 23:17.*

The fear of the Lord is not a take-it-or-leave-it thing. As we grow in Christ and our knowledge of who God is developed (sanctification), so our regenerated spirit will respond in awe and reverence of Him who was slain, and has redeemed us to God by His blood . . . and has made us kings and priests to our God—Revelation 5:9-10:

> *"Let us hear the conclusion of the whole matter: Fear God and keep His commandments, for this is man's all" Ecclesiastes 12:13.*

Puritan Quote:

"Faith, without trouble or fighting, is a suspicious faith; for true faith is a fighting, wrestling faith." Ralph Erskine, 1685-1752.

A SOVEREIGN ACT

Reading: Jeremiah 32:38-41
"I will put My fear in their hearts" Jeremiah 32:40

Before we pursue this thought further, let me say that our text addresses both Jew and Gentile believers from whom God has "create(d) in Himself one new man from the two, thus making peace, and that He might reconcile them both to God in one body through the cross, thereby putting to death the enmity" (Ephesians 2:15-16). In other words, the only reason Gentile Christians can claim Old Testament promises originally made to the Jews, is because both Jew and Gentile believers are "Abraham's seed" (Galatians 3:29).

The prophets speak of an "everlasting covenant," the blessings of which are things "new." Another name for this covenant is the "New Covenant," the same one of which Jesus spoke when He inaugurated what we know as the Lord's Supper (Matthew 26:27). Our reading, plus several others, makes it clear that the fear of God is a distinct blessing of the New Covenant, the Covenant of Grace. While it was a characteristic of the Mosaic Covenant, it has not been discontinued under the New Covenant as some teach today. The fear of God has not been replaced by the love of God, as they are both blessings of the same New Everlasting Covenant:

> *"Behold, the days are coming, says the LORD, when I will make a new covenant with the house of Israel and with the house of Judah—not according to the covenant that I made with their fathers in the day that I took them by the hand to lead them out of the land of Egypt, My covenant which they broke, though I was a husband to them, says the LORD. But this is the covenant that I will make with the house of Israel after those days, says the LORD: I will put My law in their minds, and write it on their hearts; and I will be their God, and they shall be My people. No more shall every man teach his neighbor, and every man his brother, saying, 'Know the LORD,'*

for they all shall know Me, from the least of them to the greatest of them, says the LORD. For I will forgive their iniquity, and their sin I will remember no more" Jeremiah 31:31-34, see also Ezekiel 36:22-32 and Hebrews 8:7-13.

Not only is the fear of God a distinct blessing of the New Covenant, it is also a distinct undertaking of the Sovereign God. "I will make . . . I will put . . . I will be their God . . . I will forgive . . . I will remember no more . . . I will give them a new heart . . . I will put My fear in their heart . . . I will rejoice over them . . . I YAHVAH, JEHOVAH . . . I will," no one else, no substitute, none other than EL SHADDAIAH, God Almighty, the incomparable One. Do you consider your God Sovereign? I ask this because the behavior of so many who call themselves Christians belie this truth in their behavior before Him. Awe, reverence, honor, abeyance are all features of one who fears God and will be seen in their approach to and worship of Him who is surrounded by worshiping angels and seraphim. Every participant of the New Everlasting Covenant will experience and show evidence of the fear of God.

What is the basis or foundation upon which God implants the fear of God in the hearts of His people? "For I will forgive their iniquity, and their sin I will remember no more" (Jeremiah 31:34).

The LORD concludes this wonderful description of the New Covenant, not with another "and," but with "for." All of the preceding promises are because "I will forgive their iniquity, and their sin I will remember no more." Not one of the blessings we enjoy because of our status in Jesus Christ is apart from His forgiveness of our iniquity or sin. No forgiveness, no blessing. If God remembers our sin there is no salvation, no new covenant, and no everlasting life. Please note that God does not say He will forget our sin, but rather, He will remember our sin no more. This is a significant statement, because to forget implies a weakness, and there is no weakness or flaw in God; by His sovereign will He has determined to remember them no more. To forget leaves the door open to sometime remember, especially when we have an enemy that constantly accuses us before God. Satan can accuse all he wants, but he is no match for the sovereign will of El Shaddai who says, "I will remember no more" see also Hebrews 8:12; 10:17.

Take this wonderful truth to heart for we are all prone to sin. Sin does not miraculously disappear when we are born again and become children of God; the old man is still there, and will bug you until the day you die, BUT, "there is therefore now no condemnation to those who are in Christ Jesus, who do not walk according to the flesh, but according to the Spirit" (Romans 8:1). Sin can drive the believer down into the depths of depression unless he fully understands the wonderful grace of God shown in the words, "I will remember them no more."

David knew full well this truth:

"If You, Lord, should keep account of and treat [us according to our] sins, O Lord, who could stand? But there is forgiveness with You, that You may be reverently feared and worshiped" Psalm 130:1-4, Amplified Bible.

Oh, yes, there is an unbreakable bond between forgiveness and the fear of God. No person can know what it means to fear and reverence God unless and until he knows God's forgiveness. The only fear an unbeliever will ever know is that of dread and terror, either as the Holy Spirit convicts him of sin, or when he stands before God as his Judge.

Fellow believer in Jesus Christ, nurture the fear of God in your life. If you do not know how to worship Him with awe, amazement and wonder, ask Him to guide you down this path. You will find there are times when you cannot put your worship into words—you will be speechless before Him, but do not worry, He knows your heart, and rejoices in your silent worship and adoration.

Puritan Quote:

"How soon we are broken on the soft pillow of ease! Adam in paradise was overcome, when Job on the dunghill was a conqueror" Thomas Watson, 1620-1686.

THE ULTIMATE STANDARD

Reading: Leviticus 19:1-14
"You shall not cheat your neighbor, but shall fear your God: I am the
LORD. Leviticus 19:13-14.

The scriptures abound with illustrations and examples of what it means
to fear the Lord. To fear God was, and is, the ultimate standard by
which godliness is measured. Let's consider a few examples:

When Abraham moved south to Gerar (Genesis 20 1) with his
wife Sarah, the king of the area (more a local chieftain) whose name was
Abimelech, took her as his wife. He did not think he had done anything
wrong as Abraham had introduced Sarah as his sister. This was a half truth,
for Sarah and Abraham had the same father but a different mother. God
spoke to Abimelech and told him the truth, so he confronted Abraham as to
why he had lied. Abraham's answer is of interest here: "Because I thought,
surely the fear of God is not in this place; and they will kill me on account of
my wife" (11). Abraham was correct in his assessment of the situation, for
where there is no correct concept of God there will be no fear of God.

Before Joseph revealed who he was to his brothers, he sent them back
from Egypt to their father so they could take food to their family, and
bring his younger brother Benjamin to him. He demanded one of them
remain in Egypt as a guarantee they would return. The brothers were scared
this second in command to Pharaoh would not keep his words, so Joseph
basically said, "I can give you no better reason as to why my dealings with
you are honest and trustworthy, in that 'I fear God'. He knew this would
mean something to his brothers, so he employed the words that would
instill the greatest trust.

Let us consider the words of our text. God was laying out specifics of
the law when He said,

**"You shall not curse the deaf, nor put a stumbling block before the
blind, but shall fear your God: I am the LORD" Leviticus 19:14.**

If you curse a deaf man it does no good because he cannot hear you. Your words will not cause him to react in any way. If you place an object in the path of a blind man so he trips and falls, he will not blame you because he could not see who did it. God is saying that your curses and cruel acts may not be blamed on you because of the disabilities of the ones you seek to harm, but "fear God" because He both hears and sees your every action.

Our behavior toward men must not be governed by their ability or lack of ability to respond or retaliate, but because we fear God. Things done in secret are done openly before the ears and eyes of God. God took the prophet Ezekiel into the temple where the priests were worshipping idols, and said, "Son of man, have you seen what the elders of the house of Israel do in the dark, every man in the room of his idols? For they say, 'The LORD does not see us'" (Ezekiel 8:12). Jesus condemned the Pharisees because they made a public production of their prayers:

"But you, when you pray, go into your room, and when you have shut your door, pray to your Father who is in the secret place; and your Father who sees in secret will reward you openly" Matthew 6:6.

The student may get away with cheating, and the contractor with using inferior materials, but all behavior is observed by God, and those who truly fear God will not behave in such a manner because they are constantly aware of His presence. Men and women will be answerable to God for their behavior unless they repent and come under the forgiving grace of God.

"The fear of the LORD is to hate evil; pride and arrogance and the evil way and the perverse mouth I hate . . . By the fear of the LORD one departs from evil" Proverbs 8:13; 16:6.

Nehemiah offers a wonderful example of the effect of the fear of God. "Moreover, from the time that I was appointed to be their governor in the land of Judah, from the twentieth year until the thirty-second year of King Artaxerxes, twelve years, neither I nor my brothers ate the governor's provisions. But the former governors who were before me laid burdens on the people, and took from them bread and wine, besides forty shekels of silver. Yes, even their servants bore rule over the people, but I did not do so, because of the fear of God" (Nehemiah 5:14-15). In other words, Nehemiah did not use his position as governor for personal gain. The basis of his behavior was not to gain favor in the eyes of the people, but that he feared God. In this day of political corruption this example is very appropriate. Now to the New Testament:

"Therefore, having these promises, beloved, let us cleanse ourselves from all filthiness of the flesh and spirit, perfecting holiness in the fear of God" 2 Corinthians 7:1.

The promises previously spoken of by Paul, although taken from the Old Testament, apply to the New Covenant in Jesus Christ. "Therefore," he says, "perfect holiness in the fear of God." The motive and atmosphere for holiness is the fear of God. The process of sanctification cannot move forward outside of the acceptance and awareness of the fear of God. "Work out your own salvation with fear and trembling; for it is God who works in you both to will and to do for His good pleasure" (Philippians 2:12-13). The fear is the fear of God, and the trembling should be because we know "Thou God seest me" Genesis 16:13, KJV.

Another example is of the work the slave does for his master: "Bondservants, obey in all things your masters according to the flesh, not with eye service, as men-pleasers, but in sincerity of heart, fearing God" Colossians 3:22.

The slave is to do his work well, not to please the master of the house, but in the fear of God. His primary motive is his fear of God, not his fear of his earthly master's anger.

Today's moral decline is because man is trying to curb problems (drugs, immoral sex, murder, theft, divorce, etc.) apart from the fear of God. Apart from the fear of God all else will fail, for as Paul writes, "God gave them up" Romans 1:18-32.

From kings (2 Samuel 23:3) to slaves (Colossians 3:22) the governing standard for godliness is the fear of God.

Puritan Quote:
"Zeal without knowledge is as wild-fire in a fool's hand" Thomas Brooks, 1608-1680.

THE EYE OF THE LORD

Reading: Psalm 34:1-10
"Oh, fear the LORD, you His saints! There is no want to those who fear Him" Psalm 34:9.

"**B**less the LORD, O my soul, and forget not all His benefits" (Psalm 103:2), so the Psalmist reminds his own soul. It is easy to take for granted the blessings that God showers on us every day. Even when things are not going the way we would like them to, we do not have to look far to see how the Lord has and is blessing us. Temporal benefits are just that—temporary, and once this short life is over so are those benefits, but the spiritual blessings are ours for eternity.

Scripture tells us of many privileges (as John Bunyon calls them) of those who fear the Lord. Let us look briefly at some of these things mentioned by the Psalmist:

The one who fears the Lord is taught and guided by Him:

"Who is the man that fears the LORD? Him shall He teach in the way He chooses" Psalm 25:12.

Though there are many who attempt to lead you along paths differing from the one God has chosen for you, if you are walking in the fear of the Lord He will teach you those things necessary for your journey through life. It is clear that those who embrace falsehood and perverted angles of the truth are not walking in His fear. Some may say this is such a bold statement, yet it is exactly what the Word claims. If you hadn't noticed by now, the Word of God is packed with bold, uncompromising statements. The Lord will not leave us to wander along governed by our own ignorance. Spiritual wisdom is revealed to those to whom spiritual things are revealed: "The fear of the LORD is the beginning of wisdom" Proverbs 9:10.

The one who fears the Lord is constantly under the watchful eye of his Creator:

"Behold, the eye of the LORD is on those who fear Him, on those who hope in His mercy, to deliver their soul from death, and to keep them alive in famine" Psalm 33:18-19.

You have been granted eternal life, and God's eye is perpetually watching, and guarantees that He will be faithful to His promise, "they shall never perish." The eye of the Lord is upon us—not to take advantage of us or to destroy us for our sins, but to guide, help, and deliver us from death—spiritual death. He will also "keep them alive in famine." Did Jesus not say, "I am the bread of life. Your fathers ate the manna in the wilderness, and are dead. This is the bread which comes down from heaven that one may eat of it and not die. I am the living bread which came down from heaven. If anyone eats of this bread, he will live forever" John 6:48-51.

The one who fears the Lord has the armies of heaven to look after him, take charge of, to encamp about and deliver him:

"The angel of the LORD encamps all around those who fear Him, and delivers them" Psalm 34:7.

Some say this angel is Jesus Himself, while others believe each believer has his own angel assigned to him by God. One, or both of these thoughts gives us wonderful concepts upon which to meditate. One such angel was able to kill 185,000 men in one night (2 Kings 19:35). These are those who camped around Elisha like horses and chariots of fire when his enemy came to destroy him—2 Kings 6:17.

When Peter stood at the door and knocked after being miraculously released from prison, at first the believers inside said, "It is his angel" (Acts 12:15). Jesus said of the children that came to Him, "that in heaven their angels always see the face of My Father who is in heaven" Matthew 18:10.

The one who fears the Lord is the recipient of God's pity:

"As a father pities his children, so the LORD pities those who fear Him" Psalm 103:13.

The word "pities" means to have "compassion." God feels and sympathizes with us in all our afflictions: "In all their affliction He was afflicted, and the Angel of His Presence saved them; in His love and in His pity He redeemed them; and He bore them and carried them all the days of old" (Isaiah 63:9). God is not ignorant of our trials and temptations; our circumstances are fully known to Him. He does not sit in the heavens with a carefree, careless attitude: "For we have not an high priest which cannot be touched with the feeling of our infirmities" (Hebrews 4:15, KJV). A true comforter is one who has experienced and understands the depths of our affliction. "The Lord is very compassionate and merciful" James 5:11.

The one who fears the Lord is granted the privilege of knowing the Lord as his help and his shield:

"You who fear the LORD, trust in the LORD; He is their help and their shield" Psalm 115:11.

What a marvelous encouragement and comfort it is for the child of God who walks in the fear of the Lord, to have Him who is the Almighty Omniscient One, as his help and shield. He will be their help in all their weaknesses and infirmities, and their shield to defend them against all the assaults of the world, the flesh and the devil.

The one who fears the Lord is among His chief pleasures:

"The LORD takes pleasure in those who fear Him, in those who hope in His mercy" Psalm 147:11.

God takes pleasure in His Son, His works, and those who fear Him. He looks upon His children with great delight, and they bring joy to His heart. He takes pleasure in our well-being, spiritual growth, and worship: "They are abundantly satisfied with the fullness of Your house, and You give them drink from the river of Your pleasures" Psalm 36:8.

Puritan Quote:
"The highest heaven, the lowest heart, are the two places of God's most glorious residence" Jeremiah Burroughs, 1600-1646

A BELIEVER'S CONDUCT

Reading: 1 Peter 1:13-16
"Conduct yourselves throughout the time of your stay here in fear"
1 Peter 1:17.

Our scripture reading today presents us with a very acceptable summary of our thoughts on the fear of God. The fear of God is all about our conduct as believers during our stay (lifetime) here on earth. There is no question about our future, for when we see Him face to face in all His glory and majesty, we will be in that great eternal congregation whose song is perpetually "Holy, holy, holy" Isaiah 6:3; Revelation 4:8.

"The fear of God is that holy soil out of which a godly life grows. It is the atmosphere out of which a godly life breathes" Albert N. Martin. If you contaminate the soil the tree will die, or at least, will stop producing quality fruit. If you cut off the flow of oxygen to the heart the person will cease to breathe. The fear of God is vital to the spiritual life and growth of the believer, therefore Paul writes, "Work out your own salvation with fear and trembling" Philippians 2:12.

Paul lays out to the believers at Rome the matter of wickedness and unrighteousness in the life of all unbelievers—Jews and Gentiles. Then he goes on to prove his point by quoting several scriptures from Psalms and Isaiah, that "There is none righteous, no, not one" (Romans 3:10-12). He then uses the throat, and those parts that are used to express what is in the heart—tongue, lips, and mouth, "their throat is an open tomb . . ." (vss 13-14), and then feet (vss 15-17). He then concludes the whole matter with a statement that summarizes his argument, "There is no fear of God before their eyes" (vs 18).

The reason for their wickedness and corruption is that they do not fear God. That is the plain and simple truth. Where the fear of God is absent, true godliness is not to be found. The believer whose life is governed by his fear of God sees El Shaddai superimposed on every situation and circumstance with which he is confronted. As sunglasses temper the glare upon everything we look at, so the fear of God will influence all we see and do, from our waking moment to the closing of our eyes in sleep.

The fear of God must color every facet of life with which we come into contact—what we see, hear, say, and the decisions we make. Does the fear of God govern which television programs we watch, movies we pay to see, books we read, the company we keep? The desire to lose weight governs what we choose to eat. If we wish to excel in athletics we choose which exercises in which to participate, and so forth. If our desire is to grow in Christ and become "as He is," we will flood our hearts and minds with those things we know will achieve that result.

If we look back over the past twelve months and can see none or very little spiritual growth, then it is obvious we have not participated in those things that guarantee that result. Since their eyes do not see Him, their tongue and hands and feet act as if He does not exist.

"And if you call on the Father"—here is what millions of folk do, but only some fear Him; if you call on Him for any reason, it is your duty to "live in reverent fear of him during your time as foreigners here on earth" (NLT). You are a stranger to God if you call on Him Sunday morning, but live the rest of the week without His fear governing your behavior. As we have previously noted in this series of thoughts, the Christian life is not a walk in the park, but rather is a fight, a race, and exacting work.

Conversely, the ungodly person has no such fear of God before his eyes. He has no recognition of God's glory, majesty, authority and judgment. He knows nothing experientially of the love of God and His mercy, therefore his behavior is not governed or controlled by the holiness of the Almighty, or the fear of offending Him in any way.

The argument is given that there is a huge difference between the gangster who consistently commits heinous crimes and the one who, although not a believer, dedicates his or her life to doing good and caring for the poor and disadvantaged. It depends through whose eyes we are looking. If we judge the situation through human eyes, that statement is true, but if through the eyes of God, then we will agree with scripture that "all have sinned and fall short of the glory of God," hence the need for salvation and the requirement to be made a new creation in Christ Jesus. The only way to be transferred from one category into the other is by the transforming grace of God in the new birth. All the good deeds in the world cannot perform the new birth; we have to be made new creatures in Christ, not remodeled versions of the old:

> *"For by grace you have been saved through faith, and that not of yourselves; it is the gift of God, not of works, lest anyone should boast. For we are His workmanship, created in Christ Jesus for good works, which God prepared beforehand that we should walk in them" Ephesians 2:8-10.*

Without this new creation, the only fear of God available is that which makes the sinner tremble in dread and terror when the Holy Spirit convicts him of his sin and the judgment to come. There is no joy or peace in this fear, but the fear of God generated in the heart of the one who, through repentance and the grace of God, has become a member of God's family, will agree with the prophet that, "The fear of the LORD is His treasure" Isaiah 33:6:

> *"Now therefore, let the fear of the LORD be upon you; take care and do it, for there is no iniquity with the LORD our God, no partiality, nor taking of bribes . . . And he commanded them, saying, "Thus you shall act in the fear of the LORD, faithfully and with a loyal heart" 2 Chronicles 19:7, 9-10.*

Puritan Quote:
"Let none but the servants of sin be the slaves of fear" John Flavel, 1627-1691.

UNBLEMISHED SACRIFICE

Reading: Malachi 1: 1-14
"If I am a Master, where is My reverence?" Malachi 1:6

I am sure we have all experienced times when reading the scriptures, that the Holy Spirit explicitly personalizes the words to our own person. Such occurrences are often life changing in their impact; such a pivotal moment took place the other day as I was reading the first chapter of Malachi:

> *"A son honors his father, and a servant his master. If then I am your Father, where is My honor? And if I am your Master, where is My reverence? says the LORD of hosts."*

Ouch! Such questions make one think seriously when personalized, and not just considered as being asked of others. In order to answer these questions honestly we must have a scriptural understanding of what "honor" and "reverence" mean. When seeking the meaning of a word or statement, there is no better way than to consider the context in which they are found:

> *"You offer defiled food on My altar"* Malachi 1:7.

These few accusatory words uttered by Jehovah of Hosts say it all. Throughout the history of God's special people, they have gone from full compliance to God's law to complete rebellion against it and rejection of it. Fifty times the words "without blemish" are recorded in the Old Testament when sacrifices to Jehovah are spoken of, whether it be a single lamb on the initiation of the Passover (Exodus 12:5), the sacrifices of the Levitical law (Leviticus 1:3,10), or the new temple described in Ezekiel (43:22-25; 45:18,23; 46:12-18). The words "without blemish" describe the meaning of other words such as pure, holy, righteous, without spot and sinless.

God, who is the supreme example of these attributes, can have nothing to do with anything, or any person, that is blemished in any way, or even tainted with imperfection. "You are of purer eyes than to behold evil, and cannot look on wickedness" Habakkuk 1:13.

The only reason our Heavenly Father can have a relationship with His children and we with Him, is because the absolute righteousness of His Son Jesus has been imputed into us (Romans 4:23-25). God's chosen are made perfect in God's eyes even though our evil nature still resides in us. The righteousness of Jesus Christ imputed to us, assures us of eternal life and an unbroken relationship with God, nevertheless, sin does have an effect in the life of a believer. If allowed to continue, and not be confessed to Him, it can and will interrupt our fellowship with Him. This is the sense in which our text from Malachi challenges my own heart.

All the time I choose to allow unconfessed sin to have a part in my life it is the equivalent to offering a blemished sacrifice to God. A less than perfect animal was not acceptable to God under the old law, so a less than perfect life is unacceptable to God in the law of Jesus Christ. Does God toss us aside when we sin? Absolutely not, but our fellowship with Him will be interrupted, our worship of Him will be hypocritical, and our prayer life will suffer drastically; in other words, our fear of God will diminish and our enjoyment of Him will eventually disappear:

> *"When you offer the blind as a sacrifice, is it not evil? And when you offer the lame and sick, Is it not evil? Offer it then to your governor! would he be pleased with you? Would he accept you favorably?" says the LORD of hosts" Malachi 1:8.*

It is commanded that a child honors his mother and father (Exodus 20:10), and no less must the child of God honor and reverence (fear) his Heavenly Father. To present God with anything that is less than honorable is an offense to His Person. His perfection and holiness demands nothing that is less than perfect.

The challenge to every believer is for him to examine himself to make sure he is not offering God less than his best:

"I beseech you therefore, brethren, by the mercies of God, that you present your bodies a living sacrifice, holy, acceptable to God, which is your reasonable service. And do not be conformed to this world, but be transformed by the renewing of your mind, that you may prove what is that good and acceptable and perfect will of God" *Romans 12:1-2.*

Present your body and mind to God "a living sacrifice. holy, acceptable to God." Anything less than perfect and holy is unacceptable to Him. Does it seem like the heavens are made of steel when you try to pray? Do you search in vain for that abundant and joyful life Jesus promised His followers? Is the Holy Spirit silent when you read God's Word? Is the Christian life a chore and a heavy burden? Such a life is not that of one who fears God and who bows in worship and adoration in His presence—perhaps you are offering God less than your best:

"Take away all iniquity; receive us graciously, for we will offer the sacrifices of our lips" Hosea 14:1-2.
"Coming to Him as to a living stone, rejected indeed by men, but chosen by God and precious, you also, as living stones, are being built up a spiritual house, a holy priesthood, to offer up spiritual sacrifices acceptable to God through Jesus Christ" 1 Peter 2:4-5.
"Therefore by Him let us continually offer the sacrifice of praise to God, that is, the fruit of our lips, giving thanks to His name" Hebrews 13:15.
"'But cursed be the deceiver who has in his flock a male, and takes a vow, but sacrifices to the Lord what is blemished—for I am a great King," says the LORD of hosts, 'And My name is to be feared among the nations'" Malachi 1:14.

Puritan Quote:
"A man may be theologically knowing and spiritually ignorant" Stephen Charnock., 1628-1680.

THE BLESSED

Reading: Psalm 119; 1-8
"Blessed are the undefiled in the way, who walk in the law of the LORD!"
Psalm 119:1

Are you happy? Truly happy? Many of us are skilled in the art of putting on a 'happy face' when the truth is that we are not happy at all. So what does being happy have to do with being blessed? Both the Hebrew and Greek words translated 'blessed' are also translated 'happy.' Happiness is the direct result of being blessed or, perhaps it should be said that happiness should be the result of being blessed. Happiness is a part of the inheritance we have because we are "in Christ." Happiness is available to every true believer; the problem is that the happiness of many is squelched because their spiritual walk hinders its manifestation. The word "blessed" is usually qualified by some behavior or condition. Biblical happiness is not manifested by an uncontrollable giddiness, jumping up and down, dancing in the aisle, shouting, screaming, or howling like wolves. What is it then?

I would suggest the happiness spoken of in scripture includes that "peace of God, which surpasses all understanding" (Philippians 4:7), a joy that is known only by those who enjoy communion with God—"In Your presence is fullness of joy (Psalm 16:11), and yes, a joy that can be expressed audibly but is glorifying to God, and does not wreak of Phariseeism, which Jesus rebuked (Matthew 6:5-7). In other words, true happiness is the enjoyment of the fruit of the Spirit in the heart of that Believer who is dedicated to his Lord and Master, and whose spiritual arteries are not clogged by sin and disobedience to the Law of God. Consider our text:

"Blessed are the undefiled in the way, who walk in the law of the Lord."

If we wish to be blessed or happy we are told we must "walk in the law of the Lord." The law is the 'torah,' not just the Ten Commandments, but the entire 'law of the Lord.' To David this meant the law as revealed in the Pentateuch, but to us it is the law of God as it is in the law of Christ, the law of the Gospel. Christians are not required to keep the sacrificial laws, or the administrative laws, under which the nation of Israel were governed, but rather the law of the Spirit:

"The law of the Spirit of life in Christ Jesus has made me free from the law of sin and death" Romans 8:2 (8:1-8).

Sometimes, too much emphasis is laid on the freedom or liberty we as Christians have in Christ Jesus, to the neglect of the rule of the Spirit under which every believer is governed.

The law of the Spirit brings happiness to those who walk according to its mandates. It is not an oppressive law. The Spirit of God is not a ruthless dictator who governs so his maniacal ego is satisfied no matter how devastating the rules are to his subjects. It does, however, require sincere obedience, with the Divine promise that happiness will follow. To be a Christian does not in itself guarantee true happiness—that is guaranteed to believers who "walk in the law of the Lord."

Another reality for the believer that brings happiness is his freedom from the wrath of God, and, as we have recently seen, the removal of all guilt. Yes, we are guilty of sin and violating the law of God, but because we are in Christ, we are delivered from the condemnation we so richly deserve:

"He who hears My word and believes in Him who sent Me has everlasting life, and shall not come into judgment, but has passed from death into life" John 5:24.

The other part of our salvation is that we are reconciled to God. We are brought into a favorable relationship with Him. God could easily have withdrawn His wrath from us by laying our sin on His Son, but He completed the transaction by creating a personal relationship with us. All that was lost by Adam's sin in the Garden of Eden has been more than restored.

"You are My friends if you do whatever I command you" John 15:14.

Not only does God offer us happiness (blessedness) in this life, but promises His people more to come. We have been brought into an eternal covenant, one which gets even better and better.

"Beloved, now we are children of God; and it has not yet been revealed what we shall be, but we know that when He is revealed, we shall be like Him, for we shall see Him as He is" 1 John 3:2.

Are these blessings not incentive enough to "walk in the law of the Lord?" But there is so much more—have we not been blessed "with every spiritual blessing in the Heavenly places in Christ"?

The life of a Believer is spoken of as a walk, a walk along the path of God's law. We must walk as one "undefiled in the way," not sinless, for that is impossible, but as one who strives to

"Walk worthy of the Lord, fully pleasing Him, being fruitful in every good work and increasing in the knowledge of God; strengthened with all might, according to His glorious power, for all patience and longsuffering with joy; giving thanks to the Father who has qualified us to be partakers of the inheritance of the saints in the light" Colossians 1:10-12.

May God enable us so to walk as to please Him

"You will show me the path of life; in Your presence is fullness of joy; at Your right hand are pleasures forevermore" Psalm 16:11.

Puritan Quote:
"This which is begun in regeneration is continued and grows till it ultimately arrives at absolute perfection. That will be seen in the world to come; and oh, what a fulfillment of the law will be there!" C.H. Spurgeon—1834-1892.

THE WHOLE HEART

Reading: Psalm 119; 1-8

"Blessed are those who keep His testimonies, who seek Him with the whole heart!" Psalm 119:2

The importance and application of any biblical doctrine can readily be seen by its use in and throughout the scriptures. When it is used, how it is used, and what is the context in which it is used?

The word "blessed," which we considered previously, is a perfect example. It is a doctrine, for it is not an emotion in itself, even though it is the source of happiness when properly understood.

Two of the more prolific preachers quoted in scripture, can be used as examples. Jesus, the greatest of all preachers and teachers, began His public ministry by stressing the importance of being "blessed."

> *"Blessed are the poor in spirit, for theirs is the kingdom of heaven.*
> *Blessed are those who mourn, for they shall be comforted.*
> *Blessed are the meek, for they shall inherit the earth" Matthew 5:3-12*

And David begins his book of Psalms with this same thought:

> *"Blessed is the man who walks not in the counsel of the ungodly, nor stands in the path of sinners, nor sits in the seat of the scornful; but his delight is in the law of the LORD, and in His law he meditates day and night" Psalm 1:1-2.*

Forty-five times the word *'esher'* (blessed) is used in the Old Testament, and over half of those (26 times) are in the Psalms. It makes for a very rewarding study to research each occasion where it is used. I will guarantee the end result will tell us why most believers are not truly happy, and what we must do to correct that situation.

In the previous verse a blessed man is described by his actions, by the path he chooses to walk. Now, in the second verse, it is by the attitude of his heart, for our actions are conditioned by the condition of the heart: "For as he thinks in his heart, so is he" (Proverbs 23:7). Yes, a man may think one thing in his heart and do another, but eventually his lies and deceit will come to the forefront. A man cannot be happy while living a life contrary to his heart.

Our verse tells us those who keep close to God's testimonies are blessed. God's testimonies speak primarily of the Ten Commandments, those written by the "finger of God." In today's spiritual economy the "finger of God" is the Holy Spirit, as His ministry is to point the way the believer is to walk:

> *"But the Helper, the Holy Spirit, whom the Father will send in My name, He will teach you all things, and bring to your remembrance all things that I said to you"*
> *When He, the Spirit of truth, has come, He will guide you into all truth" John 14:26; 1613.*

The responsibility of each believer is to "seek Him with the whole heart." Good and worthy actions can fill our day, but, unless they are the result of a sincere, dedicated seeking of the Lord, they will not produce that happiness of which David and Jesus speak. A truly blessed and happy man is one who seeks the Lord "with his whole heart."

We might well ask, "For what do we seek?" Is it not union and communion with God? It is very sad when we hear of a child walking down the road to destruction and has cut off any contact with his or her parents. It is even more sad when a believer does not seek the Lord with his whole heart?

> *"Let the hearts of those rejoice who seek the LORD! Seek the LORD and His strength; seek His face evermore!" Psalm 105:3-4.*

There is no such thing as a half-hearted, happy Christian. William Cowper, the great poet and hymn writer of the eighteenth century suggests:

"We must remember six conditions required in them who would seek the Lord rightly:

1. We must seek him in Christ the Mediator. John 14:6.

2. We must seek him in truth. Jeremiah 10:10; John 4:24; Psalm 7:6.

3. We must seek him in holiness. 2 Timothy 2:19; Hebrews 12:14; 1 John 1:3.

4. We must seek him above all things and for himself.

5. We must seek him by the light of his own word.

6. We must seek him diligently and with perseverance, never resting till we find him, with the spouse in the Canticles"—*William Cowper, 1731-1800.*

The Psalmist sought God by the only means possible—the heart. Sight fails. Science fails. Reason fails. Only love and trust can be successful. Love can break through where all other avenues run into an impenetrable wall. There is no spiritual discovery without faith, and this is nowhere more true than when seeking and finding God. David learned that half heartedness seldom finds anything worth having. Half heartedness shows contempt for God, for, if He is who and what He claims to be, a less than whole hearted seeking for Him shows a disdain and disrespect for Him.

God will not reveal himself to half-heartedness. It would be putting the highest premium possible upon indifference.

Puritan Quote:

"Whosoever would have sound happiness must have a sound heart. So much sincerity as there is, so much blessedness there will be; and according to the degree of our hypocrisy, will be the measure of our misery. Richard Greenham, 1531-1591.

THE COMMAND

Reading: Psalm 119; 1-8
"You have commanded us to keep Your precepts diligently" Psalm 119:4.

When Joshua led the tribes of Israel into the Promised Land of Canaan, God required every male to be circumcised. At the time they were camped at Gilgal in preparation to begin their conquest of the Canaanite Kings, when Joshua "lifted his eyes and looked, and behold, a Man stood opposite him with His sword drawn in His hand." Not recognizing this man, he challenged him—"Are you for us or against us" (paraphrased) and the man answered, "No, but as Commander of the army of the LORD I have now come" (Joshua 5:13-14). In other words, "I am here to relieve you of command." Many believe this Man was the pre-incarnate Jesus Christ. The point is that God is the Commander of His army. A commander issues commands, and every soldier is expected to obey without question.

This is the purport of our text—God has commanded us, His people, to keep his commands, not just to keep them, but to do so "diligently," without question or debate. His Handbook of Engagement is the Bible.

Every true believer knows he should "keep the commandments," but there is a great tendency to apply a "take it or leave it" philosophy to God's commands. Christianity is not a part-time religion; it requires the utmost dedication and allegiance to our Commander's rules. It requires a twenty-four hour a day commitment. Yes, we are engaged in a battle, and are called upon to:

> *"Fight the good fight of faith, (to) lay hold on eternal life, to which you were (are) also called and have confessed the good confession in the presence of many witnesses . . . that you keep this commandment without spot, blameless until our Lord Jesus Christ's appearing" 1 Timothy 6:12, 14-15.*

Our verse clearly gives us the ground or reason for our obedience, which is the authority of God. He is the Commander and Law-giver:

"The LORD is our Judge, the LORD is our Lawgiver, the LORD is our King" Isaiah 33:22.
"There is one Lawgiver, who is able to save and to destroy" James 4:12.

God has commanded us; it is not left up to our arbitrary approval and acceptance. God has commanded, and we must recognize and kneel before His authority. Remember, these words are within the context of blessedness or happiness—true and lasting happiness comes only as we bow before God's power and keep His commands "diligently":

"Then it shall be, if you heed all that I command you, walk in My ways, and do what is right in My sight, to keep My statutes and My commandments . . . then I will be with you" 1 Kings 11:38.

This was an ongoing principle in the relationship between God and His chosen people Israel (Exodus 15:26; Deuteronomy 6:18, 12:25, 13:18; 1 Kings 11:33, 38; 2 Kings 10:30).

Obviously, the primary reason for us to keep God's commands diligently is because He has commanded it. However, there are other reasons:

1) Because our adversary the devil is diligent in his efforts to keep us from such a level of obedience; he goes about night and day seeking to devour us (1 Peter 5:8).

2) Because we, in and of ourselves, are weak: "The spirit indeed is willing, but the flesh is weak" (Matthew 26:41). We are no match against the onslaught of the devil. The only answer to the devil's diligence is God's strength: "Be strong in the Lord and in the power of His might. Put on the whole armor of God, that you may be able to stand against the Wiles of the devil" Ephesians 6:10-11.

3) Because of the tremendous loss we sustain every time Satan's diligence exceeds ours. We lose peace, confidence, and, as Psalm 119 says, we lose true happiness.

How are we to obey God's commands?
1. Not, partially, but fully.
2. Not doubtfully, but confidently.
3. Not reluctantly, but readily.
4. Not slovenly, but carefully.
5. Not coldly, but earnestly.
6. Not fitfully, but regularly.

When Jesus was challenged by the Pharisees, a lawyer in particular, as to which is the greatest or most important commandment, He replied:

"You shall love the LORD your God with all your heart, with all your soul, and with all your mind" Matthew 22:37.

In other words, "You shall love the Lord your God with the utmost of diligence," not half-heartedly, but with all your heart. A diligent, uncompromising obedience to the commands of our Sovereign Commander is the only way to true happiness.

Puritan Quotes:

"If you expect your Father's blessing, obey Him in whatever He commands, both in first and second duties. Obey your Heavenly Father, though He commands things contrary to flesh and blood. We act as God's children when we obey His voice and count not our lives dear so that we may show our love to Him" Thomas Watson, 1620-1886

"It is a course enjoined and imposed upon us by our Sovereign Law-giver. It is not in our choice, as if it were an indifferent thing, whether we will walk in the laws of God, or not; but of absolute necessity, unless we renounce the authority of God" Thomas Manton, 1620-1677.

THE CURE

Reading: Psalm 119; 9-16

"How can a young man cleanse his way? By taking heed according to Your Word" Psalm 119:9

It is always helpful when a question is asked and the answer is provided, especially when God is both the Examiner and the Teacher. If God asks the question there must be a good reason for it, and, if He provides the answer it must be both the correct and best one.

The question is an all important one, "How can a young man cleanse his way?" I do not wish to spend time discussing the question, "Why a 'young man' specifically?" because the answer is applicable to all persons no matter their age or gender.

The answer points in one direction—the Word of God—there is no substitute and no compromise. If God places such high importance and power to His Word, then why do so many of His people consider it worthy of such little attention? The Scriptures are God's chosen means of revealing Himself—His attributes and ways—and the condition of mankind—lost, wicked and unclean. They also contain the plan of the ages, the Plan of Salvation, the only way man can be cleansed from his woeful condition, from unrighteousness to righteousness, from filthy to clean.

The Word of not only reveals God's Plan of Salvation but His Plan of Sanctification. Who among us dare claim that he or she remains untainted by the world? Every believer, out of necessity, needs to be cleansed or washed every day. Sanctification is the process of being changed into the image of Jesus Christ. In what is called Jesus' High Priestly Prayer, He prays to His Father:

"Sanctify them by Your truth. Your word is truth" John 17:17.

Scripture analogizes itself in several different ways, two of which are a mirror and water. When we take heed to God's Word it is looking into a mirror—it reveals to us our condition:

"But be doers of the word, and not hearers only, deceiving yourselves. For if anyone is a hearer of the word and not a doer, he is like a man observing his natural face in a mirror; for he observes himself, goes away, and immediately forgets what kind of man he was. But he who looks into the perfect law of liberty and continues in it, and is not a forgetful hearer but a doer of the work, this one will be blessed in what he does" James 1:22-25.

When we look into this mirror we see our true status. Even though we have been made clean by the blood of Jesus and are clothed in His righteousness, this mirror does not hide the reality that we need daily washing. There is another mirror that shows us as we are in Jesus Christ, for we see "the glory of the Lord," a picture of what we will become once the Spirit of God has completed our transformation, for we are "being transformed into the same image from glory to glory":

"But we all, with unveiled face, beholding as in a mirror the glory of the Lord, are being transformed into the same image from glory to glory, just as by the Spirit of the Lord" 2 Corinthians 3:18.

The Bible also uses water as an analogy:

"Christ also loved the church and gave Himself for her, that He might sanctify and cleanse her with the washing of water by the word, that He might present her to Himself a glorious church, not having spot or wrinkle or any such thing, but that she should be holy and without blemish" Ephesians 5:25-27.

Is this not a glorious revelation from God? Christ died "that He Might sanctify and cleanse His people with the washing of water by the Word." The Word of God is so pure and powerful that, when applied as a cleansing agent, it purifies us of the every day sins by which we are infected.

This second eight verse stanza of Psalm 119 is dedicated to the cleansing of God's children, the secret to cleansing is to 'take heed' to God's Word. And we do this by:

1) Committing it to memory (vs 11)
2) meditating on it (vs 15)
3) testifying concerning it to others (vs 13)
4) delighting ourselves in it (vs 16).

Puritan Quote:

"He will take a constant pleasure in communion with God and obedience to him. It is not for a season that he rejoices in this light, but "I will still, I will for ever, delight myself in thy statutes, not only think of them, but do them with delight." David took more delight in God's statutes than in the pleasures of his court or the honours of his camp, more than in his sword or in his harp. When the law is written in the heart duty becomes a delight" Matthew Henry—1662-1714.

MEDITATION

Reading: Psalm 119; 9-16
"I will meditate on Your precepts, and contemplate Your ways"
Psalm 119:15

David speaks of the practice of meditation 11 times in the Psalms, 7 of which are in Psalm 119. The Hebrew word 'siyach' means 'commune, muse, pray, commune with oneself' and is a practice that obviously meant a great deal to the Psalmist. In today's world, some religions are known for their emphasis on meditation, but Christianity is not one of them. Religions such as Buddhism, Shintoism, Hinduism, most of the eastern religions, fall into this category. Within the realm of Christianity it is Catholicism that practices and writes more on meditation than does Protestantism, all the way from the Pentecostals to those who believe in what is called Reformed Theology.

When I wanted to read what Christian theologians had to say about meditation, I found myself reading books by Catholic Priests such as Thomas Merton; Henri Nouwen; Karl Rahner, and Morten Kelsey. Puritan writers of the sixteenth and seventeenth centuries also wrote many good thoughts on meditation, for example, Nathanael Ranew; Thomas Watson; William Fenner; Thomas Manton; Isaac Ambrose, and others.

To return to our text, "I will meditate on Your precepts, and contemplate Your ways," David turns from that which he has done, "I have sought" (vs10); "I have hid" (vs 11); "I have declared" (vs 13); "I have rejoiced" (vs 14), to what he will do, "I will meditate" and "I will contemplate" (vs 15).While our report of what we have done, and our testimony of what God has done for us. is very important, it cannot end there. We must set our minds on that which we will do from this day on. I have always been impressed with the words of Jesus when He said:

"I am the Alpha and the Omega, the Beginning and the End," says the Lord, "who is and who was and who is to come, the Almighty" Revelation 1:8.

Jesus spoke of Himself as He "who is" before He "who was." The present includes the future, because yesterday's future is today's present. So, when David says, "I will," he is saying "From today on I will . . ." Notice the progression here, in vs 14 he says, "I have rejoiced . . . in Your Testimonies," but now, "I will meditate" in and contemplate them," which takes him to the next level, "I will delight myself in Your statutes" (vs 15). How can we delight in that with which we are unfamiliar?

It is important for God's people to meditate on Him because He recommends it to us. He complains of the neglect of it: "Israel does not know, My people do not consider" (Isaiah 1:3). His people would not think upon Him, nor consider what great things he had done for them. When David could not sleep his thoughts turned to God—sometimes upon the works of God: "I meditate on all Your works; I muse on the work of Your hands" (Psalm 143:5); sometimes on His creation and providence; sometimes on the word of God (Psalm 1:2), and sometimes on the promises for support in a time of trial or temptation.

"Mary kept all these things and pondered them in her heart" (Luke 2:19). We ponder things when we consider the importance and meaning of them, so our hearts and actions may be affected with them. This was the thought when Moses told the Israelites: "Set your hearts on all the words which I testify among you today, which you shall command your children to be careful to observe—all the words of this law" (Deuteronomy 32:46). In other words, "Let these sayings sink into your ears and be seriously considered and thought of by you, and not be lost or vanish into the air, or stay in the brain. Our meditations will affect our actions:

"This Book of the Law shall not depart from your mouth, but you shall meditate in it day and night, that you may observe to do according to all that is written in it" Joshua 1:8.

The message of God to Joshua was "meditate that you may do." Paul offered the same advice:

"Finally, brethren, whatever things are true, whatever things are noble, whatever things are just, whatever things are pure, whatever things are lovely, whatever things are of good report, if there is any virtue and if there is anything praiseworthy—meditate on these things. The things which you learned and received and heard and saw in me, these do" Philippians 4:8-9.

"Meditate" then "do."

But what is meditation? First of all I do not believe it is the losing of one's self into a place of enlightenment to the exclusion of all the realities that surround us. It is not something to which monks dedicate themselves by existing in a monastery cut off from the world.

The meditation of which David speaks is a regular, consistent, submission to the Holy Spirit, with a heart open to His teaching and revelation. Meditation is not a means by which God reveals something new, although He might open up to our heart and understanding something that is new to us. Instead of doing our "duty" of reading a passage of scripture, and/or "Daily Meditations" written by someone else, we invest time with an open Bible and an open heart with the prayer on our lips, "Open my eyes, that I may see wondrous things from Your Law" vs 18.

Meditation is a discipline, it does not automatically happen. Just as in prayer, Satan will try to lead our thoughts down a different path.

Puritan Quotes:

"Meditation waters and cherishes the plants of Heavenly graces. It helps them to root deeper, shoot higher and grow stronger. Such Christians as meditate most will grow most, be growing to the end"

"Meditation is of that happy influence, it makes the mind wise, the affections warm, the soul fat and flourishing, and the conversation greatly fruitful" Nathanael Ranew, 1602(?)-1677.

WONDROUS THINGS

Reading: Psalm 119; 17-24
"Open my eyes, that I may see wondrous things from Your law"
Psalm 119:18

This verse might well be the first of this marvelous Psalm. The Word of God, as wonderful as it is, is nothing but words to him who is blind to spiritual things. Unless God heals our blindness we remain ignorant of Him, who He is, and what His Law contains. These words tell us several things about ourselves and the Law of God:

1) Spiritually we are blind to the "wondrous things" in God's Law
2) David desired the "wondrous things" in God's Law
3) Only God can open our eyes to see these "wondrous things."

God does not reveal the "wondrous things" in His Word simply because we may read His Word on a regular basis. It does no good to set a goal of reading through the Bible in one year if we are blind to its truths. Many, who study the styles of each writer and their usage of certain words and phrases, remain blind to the spiritual applications God's Word contains. To such persons the scriptures appear as shadows—they observe the outline or shape but are blind to the details. Tragically, many believers are in this category.

It is not that a believer's spiritual eyes are totally blind. David had a degree of spiritual discernment otherwise he would not have known God's Word contained "wondrous things." The dimness of his sight showed him enough to make him crave for the details, for a clearer and broader sight.

"David did not complain of the obscurity of the law, but of their own blindness. The Psalmist doth not say, ' Lord, make a plainer law,' but, ' Lord, open mine eyes.' Blind men might as well complain of God that he doth not make a sun whereby they might see. The word is 'A light that shineth in a dark place,' 2 Peter i. 19. There is no want of light in the scripture, but there is a veil of

darkness upon our hearts; so that if in this clear light we cannot see, the defect is not in the word, but in ourselves" Thomas Manton, 1620-1677.

David enlarges his prayer a little later in this Psalm when he said:

"Teach me, O LORD, the way of Your statutes, and I shall keep it to the end. Give me understanding, and I shall keep Your law; indeed, I shall observe it with my whole heart. Make me walk in the path of Your commandments, for I delight in it. Incline my heart to Your testimonies, and not to covetousness. Turn away my eyes from looking at worthless things, and revive me in Your way. Establish Your word to Your servant, who is devoted to fearing You. Turn away my reproach which I dread, for Your judgments are good. Behold, I long for Your precepts; revive me in Your righteousness" Psalm 119:33-41.

This entire stanza is a plea for God to open the Psalmist's eyes. He acknowledges his condition before God: "O Lord, teach me, give me understanding, make me walk, incline my heart, turn my eyes from looking at worthless things, establish Your Word to Your servant, revive me—O Lord, I long for Your precepts."

David desired the "wondrous things" in God's Law; he knew there was more than he could currently see. God had more for him, and he would not rest until God showed him what that was. The question we must ask as we self-examine our spiritual condition is, "Do I, beyond anything else, desire and crave a fuller and deeper understanding of those things God has set aside exclusively for His children?" Am I satisfied with what I know? Am I happy to continue looking at shadows when I know God wants to show me the details?

David was not seeking **to hear some new thing.** He didn't want a new or additional revelation. He desired with all his heart that his eyes would be opened to behold the "wondrous things" that have already been given. There is an abundance of treasure in God's Word that has never been exhausted. This is not the prayer of one that is satisfied with his current level of perception. He craves to go deeper and deeper into the Word, and discover the **"unsearchable riches of Christ."** He is not content to only drink milk, he desires the strong meat.

Why would one want to **"eat of the crumbs that fall from their masters' table,"** when there is a **wonderful feast prepared for their consumption?**

"And in this mountain the LORD of hosts will make for all people a feast of choice pieces, a feast of wines on the lees, of fat things full of marrow, of well-refined wines on the lees" Isaiah 25:6.

In his prayer, David acknowledged that he needed God to open his eyes—he was unable to see the "wondrous things" contained in God's Word by any effort of his own. Jesus asked the blind man, "What do you want Me to do for you?" and he answered, "Lord, that I may receive my sight" (Luke 18:41). The fault is in our eyes, not in the Word of God.

We may read it, study it, memorize it, and quote it, but unless the Holy Spirit opens our eyes, the "wondrous things" contained in the Word of God will forever remain but an outline.

God has given great and marvelous things in His word. Let us pray for Him to remove the cataracts that keep us from beholding, in all there Divine splendor, the "wondrous things" contained in His Law.

Puritan Quote:
"This further may be observed, that the Psalmist asks for no new faculty. The eyes are there already, and they need only to be opened. It is not the bestowal of a new and supernatural power which enables a man to read the Bible to profit, but the quickening of a power he already possesses" John Ker, 1877.

STRENGTH

Reading: Psalm 119; 25-32
"My soul melts from heaviness; strengthen me according to Your word"
Psalm 119:28.

Is David here speaking as a devout believer in God or has he yet to be delivered from his sins? Many, in today's understanding of what it means to be a child of God, believe God will keep and sustain them from dropping into such a condition as described here. But that is not true.

When a person is born again by the Spirit of God, he is reconciled to Him to such a degree that his senses are aware of that which pleases and displeases Him. Prior to salvation he neither knows these things, nor does he care. A true believer is sensitive to that which grieves the Spirit of God, therefore his heart aches when he sins, and that sin deprives him of that fellowship he so desperately needs with His Heavenly Father.

There are times when a child of God might think he is losing his spiritual sight, and will again become blind to the things of God. When he permits the burdens of life to sink him into depression and discouragement, out of necessity he cries out to the only One who can enlighten his eyes. Read of David's heart cry:

"How long, O LORD? Will You forget me forever? How long will You hide Your face from me? How long shall I take counsel in my soul, having sorrow in my heart daily? How long will my enemy be exalted over me? Consider and hear me, O LORD my God; enlighten my eyes, lest I sleep the sleep of death; Lest my enemy say, 'I have prevailed against him'; lest those who trouble me rejoice when I am moved" Psalm 13:1-4.

So great were the depths to which he had sunk that it appeared to him that God had forsaken Him. Had He? Of course not, but it seemed that way to him. We know, without any shadow of doubt, God will *"never leave us nor forsake us* (Hebrews 13:5). These are the very words Moses spoke to Israel. Their enemy was numerous, strong and intimidating, melting the hearts of Israel, but Moses turned them toward their God, the only One who could deliver them:

> **"Be strong and of good courage, do not fear nor be afraid of them; for the LORD your God, He is the one who goes with you. He will not leave you nor forsake you" Deuteronomy 31:6.**

"David pleas with God, "O Lord my God, enlighten my eyes, lest I sleep the sleep of death" (Psalm 13:3). The words of our text in the Hebrew, means *'to drop away.'* The Septuagint translates it, *'My soul fell asleep through weariness.'* Therefore, my God, open my eyes (vs 18), enlighten my eyes (13:3), restore me to that wonderful communion I have previously known with You.

These trials are such as are not experienced by the non-believer. He has no personal relationship with God other than that of Accuser and Judge, but, to those who have been reconciled to Him by the blood of Jesus Christ, He is Father, Shepherd, Priest and King.

When sin or the burdens of life drop us into depression, we must call out to God with the same plea, "Strengthen me according to Your word." Truly, it is weakness that causes us to fall when we should stand, to yield when we should "stand fast in the Lord" (Philippians 4:1). Therefore, our cry must be, "Strengthen me according to Your Word."

To what was David referring when he said, "according to Your Word?" Remember, he only had what to us is a small portion of God's Word. He would know of Moses' blessing to the tribe of Asher:

> **"Your sandals shall be iron and bronze; as your days, so shall your strength be" Deuteronomy 33:25**
> and
> **"Will he plead against me with his great power? No; but he would put strength in me" Job 23:6 (KJV).**

Here, David does not ask for deliverance from trials, but strength when he faces those things that bring him low. God's promise is not to keep us from the burdens of life and the onslaught of the devil, but to give us His strength to overcome them:

"He gives power to the weak, and to those who have no might He increases strength . . . But those who wait on the LORD shall renew their strength; they shall mount up with wings like eagles, they shall run and not be weary, they shall walk and not faint" Isaiah 40:29-31.

This is the promise of God to His children. It is not easy to call on God in the times of depression and weakness, but His promises remain firm and are ours for the taking. It is better by far to make it our daily prayer to *"be strong in the Lord and in the power of His might"* (Ephesians 6:10), and to *"Watch, stand fast in the faith, be brave, be strong"* (1 Corinthians 16:13), knowing with Paul that *"I can do all things through Christ who strengthens me"* Philippians 4:13.

Puritan Quote:

"God's children, before they go to heaven, will have their trials, they will have many burdens upon them: Heb. vi. 12, 'Be ye followers of them who through faith and patience inherit the promises.' There needs not only faith, but patience. There will be trouble. Now a heavy burden need have good shoulders. We pray for strength, that we may break through difficulties and afflictions that we meet in our passage to heaven" Thomas Manton, 1620-1677.

HOPE

Reading: Psalm 119:49-57
"Remember your promise to me, for it is my only hope"
Psalm 119:49 (NLT)

Do we really have to remind God of the promises He has made to His children? Is there any chance that our Sovereign God can be forgetful? Does He suffer from the malady so many of us experience as we get older—forgetfulness? Of course not. Would you place your faith and trust in one who could possibly forget He has redeemed you and adopted you as a son into His family?

David is not fearful that the Lord's memory will fail, but he uses His promise as the means for his own strength and comfort. *"He asks for no new promise, but to have the old word fulfilled. He is grateful that he has received so good a word, he embraces it with all his heart, and now entreats the Lord to deal with him according to it"* C.H. Spurgeon.

Is there one among us who, at one time or another, does not find himself in need of comfort in a time of stress? We call on God for strength in the time of trial, when it seems that God has forgotten us? These are times when we need to remember God's promises, promises such as:

"For the LORD will not forsake His people, for His great name's sake, because it has pleased the LORD to make you His people" 1 Samuel 12:22.
"I will never leave you nor forsake you." So we may boldly say: "The LORD is my helper; I will not fear, what can man do to me?" Hebrews 13:5-6.

The philosophy and advice of unregenerate man may be according to the text books studied in college, and offered with the sincerest of purpose, but so often they must be met with the same response as Job to one who would counsel him: *"How then can you comfort me with empty words"* (Job

160

21:34). How different from the Word of God: *"For all the promises of God in Him are Yes, and in Him Amen, to the glory of God"* (2 Corinthians 1:20). The promises of God are solid, and He can be trusted to keep them. There is no chance God will forget what He has promised, or to whom He has given them.

David refers to himself as God's "servant," and it is to those who serve Him that His promises are made. There is no comfort in the Word of God to one who does not know Him, but to those who know Him, how wonderful are those promises. That—

"through the knowledge of Him who called us by glory and virtue, by which have been given to us exceedingly great and precious promises, that through these you may be partakers of the divine nature" 2 Peter 1:3-4.

"Heavenly Father, I know I do not have to remind You of Your promises, for You are Faithful and True. Not once in Your Word can I find where You have broken Your promise or failed to live up to Your Word. How different is my experience with men and women—promises made with good intent are frequently broken, and yet I do not seem to learn from these experiences. Even Your people, my brothers and sisters in Christ, make sincere promises on the spur of the moment, yet fail in the keeping of them. I must not judge them too harshly for, unfortunately, I too fall into this category.

"The failure of people to keep their promises makes Your faithfulness all the more comforting. It is not to remind You of Your promises that I repeat these words, but to remind me that Your Word is the only thing upon which I can rely. Should I place my hope in anyone or anything other than You and Your Word, I am destined for disappointment and frustration. When I waver in my trust of You, I lose sight of Your promises, and this opens the door to Satan to play havoc with my mind, and my confidence in You dwindles.

"When I need comfort I can count on Your Holy Spirit; when I need strength I draw on Your strength; when I need wisdom I turn to You for You are the Wisdom of God; when I need direction I know that You are the Way. Whatever my need, I remember Your promises, for they are my only hope."

My hope is built on nothing less than Jesus Christ, my righteousness;
I dare not trust the sweetest frame, but wholly lean on Jesus' name.

When darkness veils His lovely face, I rest on His unchanging grace;
In every high and stormy gale, my anchor holds within the veil.

His oath, His covenant, His blood support me in the whelming flood;
When all around my soul gives way, He then is all my hope and stay.

When He shall come with trumpet sound, Oh, may I then in Him be found;
In Him, my righteousness, alone, faultless to stand before the throne.

On Christ, the solid rock, I stand; all other ground is sinking sand.
Edward Mote, 1797-1874.

"Through the LORD's mercies we are not consumed, because His compassions fail not. They are new every morning; Great is Your faithfulness. 'The LORD is my portion,' says my soul, 'Therefore I hope in Him!'" Lamentations 3:22-24.

Dear Lord, forgive me for my wavering trust in You and Your Word. Strengthen me when I am tempted to look elsewhere for comfort and encouragement. Remind me of Your Word and Your faithfulness, for Your promise revives me; it comforts me in all my troubles.

Puritan Quote:
"It would be all in vain for us if the promise were remembered to all others if it did not come true to ourselves; but there is no fear, for the Lord has never forgotten a single promise to a single believer" C.H Spurgeon, 1834-1892.

TO PONDER

Reading: Psalm 119:58-65
"I pondered the direction of my life, and I turned to follow your statutes"
Psalm 119:59 (NLT)

A message found throughout the scriptures is "Don't be an onlooker, but a participator." The caution is to be sure we are walking on the path of God's choosing. In our text today, the Psalmist does just that, he examined the path he was on, decided he was heading in the wrong direction, and made a choice—to follow God's Word. He compared his life, and the principles that governed it, with that found in God's law, and decided to make a change.

Throughout this psalm, the writer speaks of the path we should be walking. He refers to those who *"do not compromise with evil"* but *"walk only in His paths" (vs 3)*. He speaks of the Word of God being the light that enables him to stay on the right path (vs 105). He prays that the Lord will guide his steps by His Word (vs 133). It was very important that he walked only on God's path, because he knew that was the only way he would know God's blessings, and his happiness depended on it (vs 35).

Sometimes, when the promises of God are not evident in our life, we need to ponder the direction we are going. On which path am I traveling? The psalmist saw he was on the wrong path and decided to do something about it—*"I turned to follow your statutes."*

When the psalmist dedicates himself so completely to God's law, to what is he referring? Whatever it is, he meditated on it day and night:

"I will meditate on Your precepts, and contemplate Your ways. I will delight myself in Your statutes; I will not forget Your word" Psalm 119:15-16.

That which the writer had to delight in was the Pentateuch, the first 5 books of the bible and possibly Job. God explicitly laid out His law and commandments, and it was in this that the writer delighted. How excited are we when we read the 10 commandments? The rules and regulations, along with the offerings and sacrifices, seldom bring happiness when we read them—that is if we read them at all. I can imagine David, and the other Old Testament writers, reading passages like Deuteronomy 28, where God plainly emphasizes the need for absolute obedience to His commandments. Not only did they know the punishment for disobedience, but the wonderful blessings that would be theirs if they obeyed. They knew that God was faithful to His word, so that is why they committed themselves to it. Obedience to His Word brought happiness, but they approached it with fear and trembling:

> *"Now it shall come to pass, if you diligently obey the voice of the LORD your God, to observe carefully all His commandments which I command you today, that the LORD your God will set you high above all nations of the earth. And all these blessings shall come upon you and overtake you, because you obey the voice of the LORD your God" Deuteronomy 28:1-2.*

In the same breath the psalmist says, *"I love Your testimonies. My flesh trembles for fear of You, and I am afraid of Your judgments" (Psalm 119:119-120).* He loved God's Word because of the wonderful blessings He promised to those who obeyed, but, at the same time, he trembled because of the punishment for disobedience.

There is, of course, a more pertinent reason for walking in accord with God's Word—because we love Him and want to please Him. To receive His blessings should be considered the result of obedient living, not the reason. We want to obey because we love Him. To violate the Holiness of Him who has redeemed us by the sacrifice of His own life, should be the great fear of every true believer.

Jesus walked the life of perfect obedience to the will of His Father:

> *"The Father has not left Me alone, for I always do those things that please Him" John 8:29.*

Jesus always submitted Himself to the will of His Father, even when it meant enduring the extreme pain of being separated from Him:

"Father, if it is Your will, take this cup away from Me; nevertheless not My will, but Yours, be done" Luke 22:42.

Paul uses two other analogies to explain this principle to Timothy, his son in the faith:

"No one engaged in warfare entangles himself with the affairs of this life, that he may please him who enlisted him as a soldier. And also if anyone competes in athletics, he is not crowned unless he competes according to the rules" 2 Timothy 2:4-5.

What is the path of God's law for us today? In His 'Sermon on the Mount' Jesus clearly lays out the path we, as Christians, are required to walk. The New Testament writers teach the principles Jesus taught. There are tremendous blessings associated with obedience to the law of Christ, and severe chastening promised to those who 'neglect so great a salvation' (Hebrews 2:3). God is faithful in the chastening of His children who live with unconfessed sin in their lives.

Do you need to turn and commit yourself to follow His statutes? May we, each one, examine our walk with the Lord, and, if we need to turn, may we do it without procrastination.

"I will hurry, without lingering, to obey your commands" Psalm 119:60.

Puritan Quote:

"If you believe that rest grows in the furrows of the field, and happiness is found in the gold mine, and that earthly treasures can produce happiness, listen to the preacher: 'Vanity of vanities! All is vanity' Eccl 1:2. The utmost of earthly pleasures fall short of satisfying" George Swinnock, 1627-1673.

UNASHAMED

Reading: Psalm 119:73-80
"That I may not be ashamed" Psalm 119:80

S in, in the life of a believer, is something we cannot deny or ignore. As much as we seek after perfection, we will never experience it during this lifetime. The "old man," the old nature, although fatally wounded by the death of Jesus, continues to influence us to one degree or another. This must never be used as an excuse to sin, for the bible tells us to "fight the good fight," to "run the race that is set before us," and to "work out our own salvation with fear and trembling."

It is not so much that we enjoy sin, but that we become frustrated that we continue to give in to it. It does not matter what it is, if we know the Holy Spirit is speaking to us about it, it causes us shame the next time we set aside time to pray and have communion with our Heavenly Father. Or am I alone in this? I do not think so. If I have knowingly sinned, whether intentionally or reactively, I cannot wait to tell God "I am sorry, please forgive me, and help me to refrain from this activity or behavior in the future." But then the devil whispers in my ear, "Don't you get tired of confessing the same old sin(s) to God?" "Don't you think He gets tired of you continually approaching Him and asking forgiveness for the same thing over and over again?" "Are you not embarrassed to admit to God that you have failed again?" "Yes! Yes! Yes!" I cry out. "You are correct. I feel ashamed, so ashamed!"

Fellow believer, do not feel alone. This is an old ploy of Satan. He will do everything in His power to keep you from communion with God, and ashamedness is one of his more effective tactics. He will tell you that God has His limits, and sooner or later, He will lose patience with you, and cast you aside as a worthless piece of clay. BUT SATAN IS A LIAR, A DECEIVER, AND THE ENEMY OF YOUR SOUL. The bible tells us:

"The LORD is longsuffering and abundant in mercy, forgiving iniquity and transgression" Numbers 14:18.

The Lord is longsuffering concerning His people. His patience does not bend nor break:

"As a father pities his children, so the LORD pities those who fear Him. For He knows our frame; He remembers that we are dust" Psalm 103:13-14.

Do you really believe the Holy Spirit thinks we are perfect when He invites us to "come boldly to the Throne of Grace?" Even though we so often fail, this invitation is still applicable. The reason for going boldly into God's presence is to "obtain mercy and find grace to help in the time of need." This invitation is made in the context of our sin:

"Seeing then that we have a great High Priest who has passed through the heavens, Jesus the Son of God, let us hold fast our confession. For we do not have a High Priest who cannot sympathize with our weaknesses, but was in all points tempted as we are, yet without sin. Let us therefore come boldly . . ." Hebrews 4:14-15.

The Psalmist knew exactly what we are speaking about. If he did not at times feel ashamed before God, he would never have written:

"Let my heart be blameless regarding Your statutes, that I may not be ashamed" Psalm 119:80.

In other words, "Lord, help me to live in accord with Your Word, so I may not be ashamed in Your presence." The more time we spend in God's Word, the more we will learn what He expects from us. The Holy Spirit will convict us of our sins by speaking to us from the Word of God. He is the Author of the scriptures, and will use them to speak to us. He who claims to be a believer, yet reads his bible but once a week, is placing himself in treacherous waters. Take time to read Psalm 119 again, and take note of the multitude of ways the Holy Spirit can use it (His Word) in your life:

"For the word of God is living and powerful, and sharper than any two-edged sword, piercing even to the division of soul and spirit,

and of joints and marrow, and is a Discerner of the thoughts and intents of the heart" Hebrews 4:12.
"If we confess our sins, He is faithful and just to forgive us our sins and to cleanse us from all unrighteousness. If we say that we have not sinned, we make Him a liar, and His word is not in us" 1 John 1:9-10.

I have found that God is forever merciful and longsuffering. He has never told me, "I have forgiven you one time too many. Do not ask again!" He knows our weaknesses and will always forgive if we confess to Him. Remember, it is He who is faithful to forgive and cleanse. I have also discovered that the more communion I have with Him in prayer and meditation in His Word, the less power my sins have over me:

"So you see how it is: my new life tells me to do right, but the old nature that is still inside me loves to sin. Oh, what a terrible predicament I'm in! Who will free me from my slavery to this deadly lower nature? Thank God! It has been done by Jesus Christ our Lord. He has set me free" Romans 7:23, The Living Bible.

Puritan Quote:
"I am tempted to think that I am now an established Christian,—that I have overcome this or that lust so long,—that I have got into the habit of the opposite grace,—so that there is no fear; I may venture very near the temptation—nearer than other men. This is a lie of Satan. One might as well speak of gunpowder getting by habit of resisting fire, so as not to catch spark. As long as powder is wet, it resists the spark; but when it becomes dry, it is ready to explode at the first touch. As long as the Spirit dwells in my heart, He deadens me to sin, so that, if lawfully called through temptation, I may reckon upon God carrying me through. But when the Spirit leaves me, I am like dry gunpowder. Oh for a sense of this!" Robert M. M'Cheyne, 1813-1843.

COMFORT

Reading: Psalm 119:49-56
"This is my comfort in my affliction, for Your word has given me life"
Psalm 119:50

There is not one person who can honestly say they have not experienced affliction in one way or another. Affliction is a part of life, although its causes vary. The question is not whether or not we have affliction, for that is a given, but how do we respond when it comes knocking on our door?

The times in which we live are such that millions of people are facing afflictions in a manner they never thought would come their way. More people are unemployed than ever before in history, causing them to face problems they never thought would be their experience. Millions have lost their homes or are facing foreclosure because they cannot make their mortgage payments. Many of those same people are sick and have lost their health insurance. Numerous other ways, by which people can be considered "afflicted," can be named, but again, the question has to be, "How do we respond to it?"

"The worldling clutches his money bag and says, 'this is my comfort'; the spendthrift points to his gaiety, shouts, 'this is my comfort'; the drunkard lifts his glass, and sings, 'this is my comfort'; but the man whose hope comes from God feels the giving power of the word of the Lord, and he testifies, 'this is my fort'" C.H. Spurgeon.

Is there any connection to the reality that crime runs rampant in our cities and suicides, especially among our young people, have risen to new heights? Some are fortunate enough to find help and comfort in their family and/or friends, but many find themselves with nowhere to turn. However, the one who knows and loves God can look to their Savior's promise:

"I will not leave you comfortless: I will come to you" John 14:18 (KJV).

169

I know it is a lot easier said than done, and hindsight has perfect vision, but the testimonies of God's people are many. God's Word has been, and continues to be, the source of comfort and strength to those whose response is to turn to it:

"My soul melts from heaviness; strengthen me according to Your word"
"Let, I pray, Your merciful kindness be for my comfort, according to Your word to Your servant" Psalm 119:28, 76.

God has never promised that His children will be exempt from affliction, but can be comforted and strengthened in it. The same Word that brought us life maintains and sustains it. James wrote: "Of His own will He brought us forth by the word of truth" (James 1:18), and Peter, "Having been born again, not of corruptible seed but incorruptible, through the word of God which lives and abides forever" (1 Peter 1:23). The Word of God, be it spoken or written, is powerful, and, when used by the Almighty hand of our Creator, is used to bring life out of corruption, and comfort in the time of affliction. We are robbing ourselves of God's comfort when we ignore His Word or use it casually. David was comforted by God's Word because he also testified, "I delight in Your law" (Psalm 119:70, 174). It is like suffering with an illness and not taking the medication your doctor has prescribed:

"For whatever things were written before were written for our learning, that we through the patience and comfort of the Scriptures might have hope" Romans 15:4.

We must always remember that we are not alone in our affliction; that circumstance, which now tempts me to fall into depression or to question and criticize God, is not mine alone. Others have, and probably are, facing the same ordeal. Remember the words of Paul:

"No temptation has overtaken you except such as is common to man; but God is faithful, who will not allow you to be tempted beyond what you are able, but with the temptation will also make the way of escape, that you may be able to bear it" 1 Corinthians 10:13.

Your circumstance is "common to man." That in itself may not be of any comfort to you, for your affliction is personal, but remember, "God is faithful" and has provided a "way of escape." That escape is His Word.

This is the testimony of many that they have found comfort in God's Word. Unfortunately, we worry and stress out before we turn to the scriptures. I was speaking with a Christian brother recently who has been experiencing numerous afflictions, and who sought comfort from friends, pastors, and even psychiatric counselors. He found no help, until one morning he picked up his Bible, and just let it flop open, not looking for any particular passage. The first words he read were, "For You are my rock and my fortress; therefore, for Your name's sake, lead me and guide me. Pull me out of the net which they have secretly laid for me, for You are my strength. Into Your hand I commit my spirit; You have redeemed me, O LORD God of truth" (Psalm 31:3-5). The Holy Spirit, the Great Comforter, immediately took these words and brought an unbelievable peace and strength to his heart. If only we would consult God's Word immediately and constantly rather than look to others who are susceptible to the same afflictions.

Puritan Quote:

"He that attends to the Word of God, not only knows the words (which are but the shell) but he knows the things. He has spiritual light to know what faith and repentance are. Therefore must men judge of their profiting by the Word, not by carrying it in their memories, but by being made able by it to bear crosses and to resist temptations" Richard Sibbes, 1577-1635.

COUNSELORS

Reading: Psalm 119:17-24
"Your testimonies also are my delight and my counselors" Psalm 119:24

One of the benefits David found in the Word of God was that of counseling. Hundreds of thousands of regular folks today are in counseling of one form or another. Much of the time it is because they find it difficult to handle the stress(es) that life has thrown their way. There are multitudes of causes, including the breakup of a marriage, the loss of employment, or even personal characteristics including uncontrollable anger and addictions.

Webster defines "counselor" as "one who gives advice." The definition of the word translated "counselor" in our text, does not differ from this although it implies "One who gives advice, particularly in the form of a constructive plan."

In the previous verse, David speaks of the greatness of his trial: "princes also sit and speak against me." It was not just the gossiping of the man on the street, but princes, the elders and rulers of Israel, those whose selection he would have had a part. They were his counselors, he went to them for advice. The Hebrew word carries the meaning, "the men of my counsel," but, obviously, he could not go to them for advice and help. His counselors sat in special meetings discussing ways to unseat him, to oppose him, especially his commitment to Jehovah and His commandments. But David had his own remedy: "But Your servant meditates on Your statutes."

"Now he shows the double benefit which he had by the Word of God, not only wisdom how to carry himself during that trouble, but also comfort; comfort in trouble, and counsel in duty; it seasoned his affliction, and guided his business and affairs" Thomas Manton.

Almost every business and organization has developed a book of instructions and advice on how to handle the various situations that may present themselves in the course of running the business. During World

War II, the Pentagon issued a book titled, "Know the Enemy." It detailed responses to the enemy's actions—what to do, and what not to do.

God has written a book for His people, a book of comfort, advice, guidance, the devices and tricks of the enemy, and guarantees victory. The Word of God is quite simple really as it is based on the principle "If you will, then I shall":

"If you will indeed obey My voice and keep My covenant, then you shall be a special treasure to Me above all people; for all the earth is Mine. And you shall be to Me a kingdom of priests and a holy nation' Exodus 19:5-6.

For guidance, David meditated on God's Word, it was his delight. The wisdom of his counselors fell far short when compared to that which he received from Jehovah.

An important lesson for us here is that the counsel we receive from God's Word is sufficient for His children. I am sure many therapists mean well, but as David said, "Your word is a lamp to my feet and a light to my path" (Psalm 119:105). The light a therapist can shine on our path is but a shadowy glimmer when compared to that provided by God in His Word. How is this possible? The born again child of God has the Holy Spirit dwelling within him. It is He that takes dead words and makes them live in the believer's heart.

The Word of God is a living oracle to the believer. It shows us how to live in a world opposed to God, a world that hates the very name of Jesus and, as the princes to which David refers, sit and think of ways to abolish the name of Jesus from public forums. They may ban teachers from using the name Jesus in the classroom, they may abolish it from our court system, and change the name of Christmas, but they cannot remove it from the heart of those who know Him as their personal Savior.

When we are faced with making a decision, we have the opportunity to ask God for His direction:

"Commit your way to the LORD, trust also in Him, and He shall bring it to pass" Psalm 37:5.

"Commit your works to the LORD, and your thoughts will be established" Proverbs 16:3.

When David needed direction, he "inquired of the LORD, saying, 'Shall I go up to any of the cities of Judah?' And the LORD said to him, 'Go up.' David said, 'Where shall I go up?' And He said, 'To Hebron.' So David went up there" (2 Samuel 2:1-2).

When Israel lost their leader, they asked God for His advice: "Now after the death of Joshua it came to pass, that the children of Israel asked the LORD, saying, 'Who shall go up for us against the Canaanites first, to fight against them?' And the LORD said, 'Judah shall go up'" Judges 1:1-2.

To ask God for His guidance and counsel is one of the benefits and joys of being a child of God. Remember, however, when we ask His counsel, to look for His answer in His Word:

"Cause me to know the way in which I should walk, for I lift up my soul to You" Psalm 143:8.

Puritan quote:
"Oh! when a man goes every morning to God, and desires the direction of His Spirit, and professeth to God in the poverty of his own spirit, that he knows not how to guide his feet for that day, then God will teach him the way he shall walk" Thomas Manton, 1620-1677.

MOTIVATION

Reading: Psalm 119:129-136
"Your testimonies are wonderful; therefore my soul keeps them"
Psalm 119:129

Why do some men, even some theologians, spend their time examining the Word of God with the intent of disproving it, or casting doubt on its legitimacy? Perhaps it is so they feel they have a legitimate reason for not obeying its commands. Why should they when the Word cannot be trusted? But, to those who approach the Word of God for what it is, the revelation of a wonderful God to His children, everything it contains is wonderful.

The Word of God is the revelation of His wisdom. Who is man to challenge the wisdom of God? Even the angels revel in the wisdom of their Creator:

"To the intent that now the manifold wisdom of God might be made known by the church to the principalities and powers in the Heavenly places" Ephesians 3:10.

To those whose eyes have been opened to spiritual things, the testimonies of God are truly wonderful.

"Shall we doubt of that to be true which droppeth from God's own mouth, because it exceedeth our weak understanding?" Thomas Manton.

It is a trick of Satan that we look upon God's testimonies as burdensome. How many consider they will be punished by God should they fail to observe just one of His laws? David had a different reason for keeping God's testimonies: "Your testimonies are wonderful," not burdensome, not cumbersome, not to be feared, but because they are wonderful.

Each one of us should ask ourselves, "Do I reverence God's Word?" If I reverence God Himself, then surely the obvious thing is to reverence that which He says: *"So to God, reverence is the mother of obedience"* Thomas Manton.

"How sweet are Your words to my taste, sweeter than honey to my mouth!" Psalm 119:103.

Really, it is simple. No complicated debate or tension driven articles or denominational divisions are required to give us a reason to keep the commandments of your Lord. Keep them because they are wonderful! For years I lived under the concept that I would try to obey the Word of the Lord because He had commanded me to do so. Oh, but I found it so difficult, and suffered great distress when I failed. So often it seemed as if I was running round and round on a wheel like a Gerbil until I fell off exhausted and frustrated. I treated the commandments of my Savior as if they were the commands of God accompanied by thunder and fire.

How gracious you are, dear Lord, to give me a new reason for obeying your commandments—"Keep my commandments because you love them." That is what You ask of me.

If we love His Word, surely we love Him personally:

"If you love me, love my commandments. He who has My commandments and keeps them, it is he who loves Me" John 14:15 & 21.

Your Word, dear Savior, is not meant to be a hammer (however, there are times when this is necessary) to be used by You on those who love You, but rather the path that leads me into a more intimate relationship with Yourself, therefore keeping Your commandments will result in a life of joy and satisfaction.

What motivates us to keep God's Word as it is revealed to us? If you love Him and His Word, do you not want to please Him in everything you think and do? Paul's prayer for the Colossian believers was that:

"You may be filled with the knowledge of His will in all wisdom and spiritual understanding; that you may walk worthy of the Lord,

fully pleasing Him, being fruitful in every good work and increasing in the knowledge of God" Colossians 1:9-10.

Each time we sin we hinder this process of "walking worthy of the Lord." A true penitent heart will be quick to recognize his sin, confess it, and know that his loving Father has forgiven it. Only in this manner can his walk of worthiness be continued. Unrepented sin will always block the progress of our walk with Christ.

"Dear Master, help me to stay focused on Your Word, for the more I know it the more I will love it. As Your Word enters my soul, so does Your marvelous light, which, in turn, reveals You more intimately to me as it discards the clouds that hide You from the unsanctified heart."

Puritan Quote:

"We have not a true sight and sense of the word, if we admire it not. There is such transcendent love, admirable depths of wisdom, unsearchable treasures of happiness, raised strains of purity, a harmonious coincidence of all parts. What would we admire, but that which is great and excellent" Thomas Manton, 1620-1677.

ONE HUNDRED PERCENT

Reading: Psalm 119:65-72
"I will keep Your precepts with my whole heart" Psalm 119:69

As we have discovered, Psalm 119 speaks to us of God's Word, and both how God is faithful to His promises revealed in it, and how He requires His people to acknowledge and revere it. Neither Moses, nor the tribal leaders, gathered the manna for the people, they had to do it themselves. If they relied on someone else to gather manna, they went hungry. So it is with the Word of God. Sadly, most Christians have come to rely on their pastors and teachers to delve into the Word of God, while they idly sit in the pews, Sunday after Sunday, hoping to be fed. What happened to our personal responsibility to "Search the scriptures?"

The words *"with my whole heart"* are mentioned six times in Psalm 119, and only three more times in the entire Book of Psalms. The call is for God's people to seek and serve Him with everything they have. The word translated "heart" refers to one's inner person—mind, understanding, and underlying attitude. It is the seat of a person's inner being that guides their motivation or moral conscience:

> *"Blessed are those who keep His testimonies, who seek Him with the whole heart!" Psalm 119:2.*

The reward, if you will, for those who "seek Him with the whole heart" is that they will be blessed. There are integral blessings to all of God's people, but some blessings are reserved only for those whose entire being is controlled and governed by His Word:

> *"With my whole heart I have sought You; Oh, let me not wander from Your commandments!" Psalm 119:10.*

The sincere prayer of those whose heart is set on following their Master, is "keep me from straying from Your commandments." Keep me from sinning against You; keep me from violating Your Holiness. The more we dedicate our lives to Him, the more sensitive we become to sin. That which we once considered acceptable, has now become sin. If we have any paranoia, it should be to keep from offending God's Holiness:

"Give me understanding, and I shall keep Your law; indeed, I shall observe it with my whole heart" Psalm 119:34.

This request of a heart in total submission to God is the natural continuation of verse 10. Without the ministry of the Holy Spirit's conviction in our lives, there is no way for us to know everything contained in God's law. It was the prayer of Paul for the Ephesian believers that "the God of our Lord Jesus Christ, the Father of glory, may give to you the spirit of wisdom and revelation in the knowledge of Him, the eyes of your understanding being enlightened . . ." Ephesians 1:17-18:

"I entreated Your favor with my whole heart; be merciful to me according to Your word" Psalm 119:58.

The rightful expectation of every believer who seeks God's favor with their whole heart, is that God will fulfill the promises He has given us in His Word. It is either the height of audacity, or ignorance, to expect His mercy if we are less than one hundred percent committed to Him:

"The proud have forged a lie against me, but I will keep Your precepts with my whole heart" Psalm 119:69.

Who has not been the recipient of hurtful gossip propagated by others? Tragically, it is not only from those who hate God, and therefore those who do not claim Him as their Savior and Lord, but from fellow believers. The hate that spews from the mouths of some who say they are Christians, is the most hurtful of all. But, the Psalmist says, no matter what others may say against me, I will not depart from Your precepts, but will continue to abide by them with my whole heart:

"I cry out with my whole heart; hear me, O LORD!" Psalm 119:145.

The promise of God to His people is that His ear is open to their cry. Have we ever cried out to God and wondered if He has heard us? Whether or not we feel any different or cannot see an immediate answer, by faith we can be sure that He hears us. Implicit in the word "hear" is the thought that He will answer. Of course, God hears the cry of every person, but the promise that He will answer is for those who seek and serve Him with their entire being.

One thing we should understand—God requires one hundred percent of our lives, our love, our motivation, and our desires. Those who say, "I am 150% committed to this cause, are saying something they are unable to do. We know what they mean, but all God requires from us is 100%:

"You shall love the LORD your God with all your heart, with all your soul, and with all your mind" Matthew 22:37.

This is what God requires of His people—nothing more and nothing less. What a challenge! God will reward such devotion, but we cannot expect Him to bless us to the fullest if we are not willing to give Him the utmost of who we are.

"Trust in the LORD with all your heart, and lean not on your own understanding; in all your ways acknowledge Him, and He shall direct your paths" Proverbs 3:5-6.

Puritan Quote:
"Half heartedness seldom finds anything worth having. Half heartedness shows contempt for God. God will not reveal himself to half heartedness. It would be putting the highest premium possible upon indifference" F.G. Marchant, (1800's)

BOTTLE IN THE SMOKE

Reading: Psalm 119:81-88
"I have become like a wineskin in smoke, yet I do not forget Your statutes"
Psalm 119:83

These words are a perfect example of the importance of context. The previous verse (82) shows us that David was seeking deliverance from and comfort in his affliction. In those days, wine was fermented in bottles made from goat skins. They are the same type of bottles to which Jesus referred in Matthew 9:17: "Nor do they put new wine into old wineskins, or else the wineskins break, the wine is spilled, and the wineskins are ruined. But they put new wine into new wineskins, and both are preserved."

Once used, the bottles become dry and fragile, and would crack if new wine was placed in them. Old bottles would not survive the fermentation. This is a similitude of the believer—the flesh may crack and waste away like an old bottle, but not his new life in Christ. The new wine is not marred in the old bottle, just as the faith of a godly man is not marred under trials and afflictions.

Wineskins (bottles) hung in the chimney, would mellow the wine by the process of moderate heat and smoke, bringing the wine to an early perfection. Wine fermented much faster this way than if stored in a warehouse. David is saying that he keeps his eyes on God, not on the afflictions.

Along with David, we must recognize that God has a purpose for our afflictions, and that is to bring our personal character into the perfect image of His Son. We must understand that God has a purpose for hanging us in the chimney:

"It is good for me that I have been afflicted, that I may learn Your statutes" Psalm 119:71.

Can you even begin to understand the trial Abraham endured when, for three days, he travelled to Mount Mariah where he was to bind his son to the altar and offer him as a sacrifice? His response: "God will provide Himself a lamb."

How different from the trials of God's people in the wilderness; there they murmured and complained, and perished in the wilderness. The purpose of this trial is explained by Moses:

"And you shall remember that the LORD your God led you all the way these forty years in the wilderness, to humble you and test you, to know what was in your heart, whether you would keep His commandments or not" Deuteronomy 8:2.

There is a connection between our trial and our obedience of faith:

"In this you greatly rejoice, though now for a little while, if need be, you have been grieved by various trials, that the genuineness of your faith, being much more precious than gold that perishes, though it is tested by fire, may be found to praise, honor, and glory at the revelation of Jesus Christ, whom having not seen you love" 1 Peter 1:6-8.

When the grapes are crushed, the juice is separated from the dregs and poured into another vessel. Our sanctification is similar, it is the process of separation, separation from the world, ungodly desires, and selfish interests. The process of making wine is an analogy of our sanctification. The bottle in the smoke is the final stage of the process. The bottle outwardly deteriorates, but the wine is perfected. That in which God is interested is the inward beauty of the heart:

"Do not let your adornment be merely outward—arranging the hair, wearing gold, or putting on fine apparel—rather let it be the hidden person of the heart, with the incorruptible beauty of a gentle and quiet spirit, which is very precious in the sight of God" 1 Peter 3:3-4.

When prophesying of our Savior, Isaiah wrote, "He has no form or comeliness; and when we see Him, there is no beauty that we should desire Him" Isaiah 53:2.

When the Lord sent Samuel to find the next king of Israel from the sons of Jesse, he was looking for a man who, in his eyes, would qualify: "But the LORD said to Samuel, 'Do not look at his appearance or at his physical stature, because I have refused him. For the LORD does not see as man sees; for man looks at the outward appearance, but the LORD looks at the heart" 1 Samuel 16:7.

Trials and afflictions are an instrument in God's hands to bring about that purging process to a believer's soul:

"Therefore we do not lose heart. Even though our outward man is perishing, yet the inward man is being renewed day by day. For our light affliction, which is but for a moment, is working for us a far more exceeding and eternal weight of glory, while we do not look at the things which are seen, but at the things which are not seen. For the things which are seen are temporary, but the things which are not seen are eternal" 2 Corinthians 4:16-18.

Puritan Quote:

"The secret formula of the saints: When I am in the cellar of affliction, I look for the Lord's choicest wines" Samuel Rutherford, 1600-1661.

MERCY

Reading: Psalm 119:57-64
"The earth, O LORD, is full of Your mercy; teach me Your statutes"
Psalm 119:64.

The definition of mercy is "not receiving that which we deserve." Every believer's escape from the judgment of God is due to His immutable mercy. When we try to get a prospective on the meaning of the word mercy, we must first get a grasp on the word judgment. Until we understand the depths of what the Lord could rightly pass judgment on us, we will never understand, to any degree, the depths of the mercy He has poured out on His children.

The Lord could justly have condemned us all in our sins, and condemned us to hell, and, if there, no injustice would have been done. Anything this side of hell is mercy.

Why is mercy spoken of in conjunction with judgment?

1) Because mercy is the only means by which we can escape God's righteous judgment

2) Because, as God's children, we must always show mercy to others, rather than judgment.

Consider for a moment Paul's words:

"Therefore you are inexcusable, O man, whoever you are who judge, for in whatever you judge another you condemn yourself; for you who judge practice the same things. But we know that the judgment of God is according to truth against those who practice such things. And do you think this, O man, you who judge those practicing such things, and doing the same, that you will escape the judgment of God? Or do you despise the riches of His goodness, forbearance, and longsuffering, not knowing that the goodness of God leads you to repentance?" Romans 2:1-5.

This reminds me of the story of the woman caught in adultery (John 8:1-12). She had committed a capital crime, a crime punishable by stoning. This act is still considered a capital crime in some countries. Jesus, knowing the hearts of all men, challenged them, and said, "He who is without sin among you, let him throw a stone at her first" (John 8:7). Pharisees, such as Paul before his conversion, claimed to be blameless regarding the law (Philippians 3:6), yet not one of them threw a stone, but slinked off into the crowd. They had no mercy—they refused to see the corruption in their own hearts until Jesus forced them to look closer.

When we begin to understand the corruption in our own heart, only then will we begin to understand the magnitude of God's mercy to us.

"The earth is full of Your mercy." Every breath we breathe, every drop of water we drink, and every minute we live, is only because of God's mercy. This is true both for the believer and nonbeliever. The world exists today because of God's mercy:

"He makes His sun rise on the evil and on the good, and sends rain on the just and on the unjust" Matthew 5:45.

However, the day is coming when this will no longer be true. The heavens and earth will come to an end under the judgment of God, and will be destroyed. Only God's people will escape this judgment. They will be lifted up by the power of the Almighty out of this corruption while it is destroyed. God will create a new heaven and earth, and, along with Jesus as their Ruler and King, the redeemed will live forever on the new earth—there will be no corruption, and therefore will not require God's judgment.

Our eternal welfare is the result of God's mercy. Think of it—new earth, no sin, no corruption, no death, no judgment.

This does not mean God does not judge sin today. Sin has its consequences for both the believer and the nonbeliever. To the believer it comes as chastisement, not judgment. Jesus has already borne God's judgment for our sin, and there is no such thing as double jeopardy with God.

Even if your neighbor commits a capital crime, if you start throwing stones in his direction, you immediately despise the riches of His goodness, forbearance, and longsuffering—Romans 2:4.

If you know even the slightest condition of your own heart, you will know the seeds of that same corruption are there:

"Oh, the depth of the riches both of the wisdom and knowledge of God! How unsearchable are His judgments and His ways past finding out!" Romans 11:33.

Puritan Quotes:

"That which a man spits against heaven, shall fall back on his own face" Thomas Adams, 1583-1652.

"Nothing humbles and breaks the heart of a sinner like mercy and love. Souls that converse much with sin and wrath, may be much terrified; but souls that converse much with grace and mercy, will be much humbled" Thomas Brooks, 1608-1680.

I AM YOUR SERVANT

Reading: Psalm 119:121-128
"I am Your servant; give me understanding," Psalm 119:125

This stanza of Psalm 119 speaks of our relationship with Jehovah, not as children but as servants; "Be surety for Your servant for good" (Psalm 119:122). Master, I am Your servant, and happily so. As much as I want to serve You without error, I do make mistakes, but they are not intentional. It is my desire to serve you, please "deal with Your servant according to Your mercy" (vs 124).

Our failures do not disqualify us from being God's servant, instead, we may take comfort in it. We have never known God to break His promises or to dismiss from His household any who have failed Him. We can look back at His promises and take comfort in them. We read the document He gave us and claim the promises found there.

Seventeen times the Bible assigns the title of "servant" to Moses:

"These Moses the servant of the LORD and the children of Israel had conquered; and Moses the servant of the LORD had given it as a possession to the Reubenites, the Gadites, and half the tribe of Manasseh" Joshua 12:6.

This description is also ascribed to Joshua and David, and others—Paul, Epaphras, James, Peter and Jude, all are said to be bondservants of God and the Lord Jesus Christ. It was their honor to serve their Master, Jesus Christ.

This designation is not reserved only for those well known in God's work, but to everyone who knows Him as their Lord and Master. As believers, we belong to Him by means of covenant:

"Yes, I swore an oath to you and entered into a covenant with you, and you became Mine," says the Lord GOD" Ezekiel 16:8.

187

Jesus told the story of a nobleman who left on a long journey, and told his servants, "Do business till I come" (Luke 19:13). This is the core message to every servant of Jesus Christ. It does not matter what He has called us to do, do it constantly and faithfully, not for the rewards, but because of our desire to please Him.

I remember visiting a small church in the Faroe Islands with a congregation of no more than twelve people. After speaking to this small group, I was introduced to each of them personally. I asked each one how long they had been a Christian? Two of the twelve told me they had given their hearts to the Lord within the past nine months. I asked a pastor of a 400 member congregation here in the States how many souls he had seen saved over the past twelve months, and he said, "None, that I know of, but one man was saved seven years ago." My point is, it does not matter the size of your calling as long as you are faithful to it.

When the nobleman left to go on his journey, he gave his servants money and told them to invest it while he was gone. When he returned, he asked each one the results of their investment? One said tenfold, another fivefold, to whom he said, "Well done," but the one said, "none, but here is your money back—I did not lose it!" The master did not want his money back, he wanted to know how his servant had invested it and what were the returns? God expects us, His servants, to invest in His service the gifts He has given us, no matter what they are.

It is always an encouragement to know what the returns are with our investment, but it should not be necessary. As long as we invest in God's service we must trust Him to bring about a profit:

"Who then is Paul, and who is Apollos, but ministers [servants] through whom you believed, as the Lord gave to each one? I planted, Apollos watered, but God gave the increase. So then neither he who plants is anything, nor he who waters, but God who gives the increase. Now he who plants and he who waters are one, and each one will receive his own reward according to his own labor" 1 Corinthians 3:5-8.

Yes, I often fail, but dear Lord, deal with me according to Your mercy. "I am Your servant; give me understanding, that I may know Your testimonies"

(Psalm 119:125). I do not know what sin is until I learn from God's Word. Teach me from Your Word so I will know how to properly please You. His Word tells me:

> *"When you turn to the LORD your God and obey His voice (for the LORD your God is a merciful God), He will not forsake you nor destroy you, nor forget the covenant of your fathers which He swore to them"* **Deuteronomy 4:30-31.**

> *"Through the LORD's mercies we are not consumed, because His compassions fail not. They are new every morning; great is Your faithfulness"* **Lamentations 3:22-23.**

May we always remember that the Lord's mercy is greater that our failure. When the desire of our heart is to please Him, He is there to forgive, comfort and encourage us as only He can do.

Puritan Quote:

"*It speaketh comfort; for God will provide for his family, and will give maintenance, protection, direction, help, and finally wages, where he requireth and expecteth service : for the present, necessaries by the way; for the future, a blessed reward*" *Thomas Manton, 1620-1677.*

DIRECT MY STEPS

Reading: Psalm 119:129-136

"Direct my steps by Your word, and let no iniquity have dominion over me"
Psalm 119:133

T he believer soon realizes that he does not have the ability to live the life his new Master requires of him. Some give up without trying, some try but fail, while others pray the prayer of David, "Direct my steps by Your word."

These words contain three parts: 1) The prayer: "Direct my steps," 2) The means: "by Your word," 3) The purpose: "Let no iniquity have dominion over me."

First of all, the prayer. The Hebrew word 'kuwn' means to 'stand erect,' perpendicular, upright, and various versions translate it "Direct," "Establish," "Guide," and "Keep steady," each carrying a similar meaning. Whichever you are comfortable using, the thought is an acknowledgment that we need help.

Prayer is the believer's privilege and prerogative. Prayer must not be looked upon as an ask-once-and-never-again option. This is a prayer we should pray every day for our temptations are continuously before us. The most Godly men and women need this prayer to be on their lips continuously.

Paul writes:

"Walk worthy of the calling with which you were called" Ephesians 4:1
"Walk worthy of the Lord, fully pleasing Him" Colossians 1:10
"Walk worthy of God who calls you into His own kingdom and glory" 1 Thessalonians 2:12.

How many of us have cried to the Lord, "Father, I keep trying, but keep failing?" Paul had the same problem:

"For what I am doing, I do not understand. For what I will to do, that I do not practice; but what I hate, that I do" Romans 7:15.

Yes, Paul, I know what you are talking about. The Christian life can be very frustrating when attempted in our own wisdom. David, who had his own ups-and-downs, gives us the answer, "By Your word." God's word is our Operations Manual. Everything we need to know about "walking worthy" is to be found there—It is written by the Holy Spirit, interpreted by the Holy Spirit, and applied by the Holy Spirit.

The Prophet confesses that it is to no purpose for him to read or hear the law of God, unless his life is regulated by the secret influence of the Holy Spirit, that he may thus be enabled to walk in that righteousness which the law enjoins" John Calvin.

Many times God uses us in the answer to our own prayer. He does in this instance—the Holy Spirit says, "Read the Operations Manual." This is God's means to help us—read it, and do so with an open heart, a willingness to be directed by God.

How many church-goers pick up their Bible when they go to church, and never read it between Sundays? That person will always fail, if indeed he truly wants to have a successful Christian life. Prayer and the Bible are the Christian's most valuable assets. I would vouch to say that the Christian who does not read his Bible prays very little.

The reason for this prayer is that "no iniquity [should] have dominion over me." David does not ask for freedom from temptation, or even from sin itself. The key word here is "dominion." The more we sin any particular sin, the easier it is to commit it again. When that happens, that sin has dominion over us. It controls us, and we have no power over it.

David prayed in another place:

"Keep back Your servant also from presumptuous sins; let them not have dominion over me" Psalm19:13.

Paul addressed the same subject to the Believers in Rome:

"Therefore do not let sin reign in your mortal body, that you should obey it in its lusts. And do not present your members as instruments of unrighteousness to sin, but present yourselves to God as being alive from the dead, and your members as instruments of righteousness to God. For sin shall not have dominion over you, for you are not under law but under grace" Romans 6:12-14.

Sin, when allowed to continue unabated, is progressive. One things leads to another, and, before we know it, sin does have dominion over us. The more strength we allow it to have, the more we are under its control:

"But each one is tempted when he is drawn away by his own desires and enticed. Then, when desire has conceived, it gives birth to sin; and sin, when it is full-grown, brings forth death" (James 1:14-15). "For the flesh lusts against the Spirit, and the Spirit against the flesh; and these are contrary to one another, so that you do not do the things that you wish. But if you are led by the Spirit, you are not under the law" Galatians 5:17-18.

The Spirit of God leads, directs, guides, and helps us "walk upright" by opening our eyes to the instructions found in God's word.

Puritan Quote:

"I had rather be a prisoner to man all my life than be a bondage to sin one day. He says not, Let not this and the other man rule over me; but "let not sin have dominion over me." Well said! There is hope in such a man's condition as long as it is so" Michael Bruce, 1600s.

MORE THEN FINE GOLD

Reading: Psalm 119:121-128
"Therefore I love Your commandments more than gold, yes,
than fine gold!" Psalm 119:127

These words of the Psalmist are a statement of fact—he loves God's commandments more than gold. This is quite an acknowledgment, especially when spoken to God. God knows our heart and when we are speaking the truth. Can we honestly say, not to ourselves or to our friends, but to God, "I love Your commandments more than gold?" Gold is a very precious commodity, and it is but a small percentage of people that own it.

This statement does not merely say that David loves God's Word, but he compares that love to a very valuable commodity. The challenge to each of us is, How much do I love God's Word? Do I love it enough to read it every day? Do I love it enough to believe it? Do I love it enough to obey it? Do I hunger and thirst for it if I do not read it daily?

As David looked around him, he saw the Word of God being slighted, mocked, and neglected, but, as this was taking place, his love for it deepened. It is no different today—teachers in our schools are banned from quoting scripture or from mentioning the name Jesus. The Ten Commandments cannot be posted in government buildings and there are those who try to ban the nativity scene from the public arena, and so on. However, to those of us that love the Lord, His Word is precious. To Job, the words of God were more precious than food:

"I have not departed from the commandment of His lips; I have treasured the words of His mouth more than my necessary food" ***Job 23:12.***

Jeremiah, the weeping prophet, who was thrown into a muddy dungeon, said:

"Your words were found, and I ate them, and Your word was to me the joy and rejoicing of my heart" Jeremiah 15:16.

Earlier in this Psalm, David wrote:

"How sweet are Your words to my taste, sweeter than honey to my mouth!" Psalm 119:103.

To David, the value of silver and gold shrank in comparison to the Word of God. Here, he does not say he always keeps them, but that he loves the law of God. It is true, the more we read the Word the more we understand it, and the more we understand it the more we will love it, and the more we love it the more precious it becomes. This process will always result in God's Word becoming the most important and valuable commodity in our life:

"Receive, please, instruction from His mouth, and lay up His words in your heart. If you return to the Almighty, you will be built up; you will remove iniquity far from your tents. Then you will lay your gold in the dust, and the gold of Ophir among the stones of the brooks. Yes, the Almighty will be your gold and your precious silver; For then you will have your delight in the Almighty, and lift up your face to God" Job 22:22-26.

Of course it is necessary that we work for money—that is not the point. It is a matter of priorities. The important word is **"more."** "I love Your commandments *more* than gold;" "I have treasured the words of His mouth *more* than my necessary food." What holds the highest priority in our life—gold, food, or God's Word?

Peter, known for his brash statements, had told Jesus, "Even if all are made to stumble because of You, I will never be made to stumble" (Matthew 26:33). So, after he had denied Him, Jesus asked Peter, "Do you love Me *more* than these?" (John 21:15). Some commentators suggest Jesus is speaking of Peter's possessions, his boat, fishing equipment, or business, while others think He is referring to the other disciples. No matter the inference, the question remains, "Do you love me *more* than these?"

It does not matter what or who it is, is there anything in your life you consider more precious than God's Word. If you answer "Yes," Jesus is more precious, then you must remember that Jesus is the Word, for "the Word became flesh and dwelt among us" (John 1:14).

David continues with his thought by saying:

"Therefore all Your precepts concerning all things I consider to be right; I hate every false way" Psalm 119:128

Here the important word is "all"—"*all* Your precepts," and "*all* things" and "*every* false way"—there is no room for exceptions. How important these small words are.

Puritan Quote:

"Oh, Christians! how much more is your portion to you than the miser's treasure! Hide it; watch it; retain it. You need not be afraid of covetousness in spiritual things: rather "covet earnestly" to increase your store; and by living upon it and living in it, it will grow richer in extent, and more precious in value" Charles Bridges, 1794-1869.

UNFOLDING GOD'S WORD

Reading: Psalm 119:129-136
"The entrance of Your words gives light;
it gives understanding to the simple" Psalm 119:130

As we travel through this Psalm it becomes obvious that God's Word and light are closely associated. The words of our text give us another analogy. Books, in their current format of sheets of paper stitched and bound, gradually replaced the traditional scroll. Christianity is credited with this development in the 4th-5th centuries in their desire to make the Bible easier to read. But, that's another story.

When a scroll was opened, it was said to be "unfolded," and that is exactly the meaning of the Hebrew word 'pethach'—"entrance." Some newer versions read, "The unfolding of Your words gives light" NAS, NIV, RSV, AMP. The picture is of a scroll containing the Torah being opened or unfolded by the priest. The truth of God is contained in the scroll, and when unfolded, shines forth like a light. Of course, the same thing applies to the Bible no matter which format it is in. We have it in book form which we open, not unfold.

Luther translates this verse, "When thy word is revealed, so it delivers us, and makes the simple wise." The point is, the scroll has to be unfolded in order for the truth of God to be revealed. The Bible does us no good if it sits on a bookshelf gathering dust.

This word is also used to describe a gate (Joshua 20:4; Judges 9:35), and then a door, as of a tent or the temple (Genesis 18:1; 1 Kings 6:8), or the gate of a city (Isaiah 3:26). That is exactly what the Word of God is—a door into the mind and heart of God.

It is only to a true believer, one who is born again by the Spirit of God, that the contents of the Bible are a light—to all others they are merely words—their eyes being blinded to the truth:

"But their minds were blinded. For until this day the same veil remains unlifted in the reading of the Old Testament, because the veil is taken away in Christ. But even to this day, when Moses is read, a veil lies on their heart. Nevertheless when one turns to the Lord, the veil is taken away" 2 Corinthians 3:14-16.

For one who loves God's Word, it is like opening the door of a beautiful mansion, and walking into a room filled with furniture made of the finest quality materials, and beautifully crafted bookshelves containing exquisite sculptures made of gold and precious stones. You remove your shoes for fear of polluting the floor with dirt brought in from outside. The more you gaze at the scene before you, the more amazed you become with the quality and value of the items. A staircase leads to an upper floor where a man clothed in beautiful garments smiles, and says, "Welcome to my home."

This is what awaits those who know Jesus Christ as their Savior. That dust covered book becomes the most valuable of his possessions. How foolish it would be to place the book on a table, draw up a chair, and sit and stare at it without opening it. To such a person it will remain just as it appears to be—a book. Open it and read it, and God's light will begin to permeate the darkness of your soul. It will bring comfort to the sorrowful, strength to the weak, understanding to the simple, joy to a saddened heart, and, yes, excitement as the Holy Spirit reveals the truth of who God is, His attributes and principles, what He has done, is doing, and will do. You revel in God's promises as you begin to realize they are personal, they are given to you. Unlike many promises made by others, these you can trust. No value can be placed on God's Word, for the more you "unfold" it, the more precious it becomes.

Is this living in a world of fantasy? It may seem so to some, but I can guarantee there are some reading these words who are responding with a hearty "Amen!" I have shared with some of you personally how my heart reacted when I opened my Bible after twenty-three years of rebellion against God—without reading a word, the sight of my open Bible brought me to tears. I sobbed for three hours straight. I had lived in spiritual poverty for all those years, but now, before me, was the most precious item I possessed, the Word of God.

Most of us have heard the story of the man who lived in extreme poverty for his entire life. He lived in a shack on wilderness property handed down to him by his father. After he died, the new owners of his land discovered that beneath its surface were millions of barrels of oil. They drilled, and today that land has become one of the largest oil producing reserves in the country. Such is the Word of God to those who do not drill, or who fail to "unfold the scroll" that contains more value than can be conceived—its value remains hidden.

I once met an elderly Christian lady in the Lake District in England who loved the Word of God dearly. She was poor in the eyes of the world because she had very few possessions, and, in their eyes she was ignorant because she had no learning other than what 92 years of living had taught her. She knew nothing of the arts, technology, or of those things designated by the world as important. However, she could hold her own when it came to understanding God; His loveliness, power and glory.

One of the highlights of my life was when I listened as she recited the 23rd Psalm. With her eyes closed and her hands folded in her lap, her face literally glowed as she spoke the words. By the time she finished the six verses, her face was wet with tears of joy, as were mine. I have heard many preachers quote these words, including myself, but none impressed me that they truly understood their meaning like this simple woman. Oh to have my eyes opened to the beauty of God's Word as were hers. I visited her home many times, and one thing never changed—her Bible was always open on the small, scratched table next to her chair. She knew the meaning of Psalm 119:30.

"Open my eyes, that I may see wondrous things from Your law"
Psalm 119:18.

Puritan Quote:
"This is one great characteristic of the word of God,—however incomprehensible to the carnal mind, it is adapted to every grade of enlightened intelligence" W. Wilson, 17th century.

EXCELLENCY OF GOD'S WORD

Reading: Psalm 119:137-144

"Your word is very pure; therefore Your servant loves it" Psalm 119:140

Most of God's children are familiar with the concept of being tried by Him in order that we might learn what is right and wrong in His eyes. The work of the Holy Spirit is to make us more like Jesus:

> *"But we all, with unveiled face, beholding as in a mirror the glory of the Lord, are being transformed into the same image from glory to glory, just as by the Spirit of the Lord" 2 Corinthians 3:18.*

It is the purpose of God to "purify for Himself His own special people" (Titus 2:14). The analogy used in scripture is that of raw metal being purged by fire until all impurities have been removed:

> *"He will sit as a refiner and a purifier of silver; He will purify the sons of Levi, and purge them as gold and silver, that they may offer to the LORD an offering in righteousness" Malachi 3:3.*

The same word (*tsaraph*) is applied to the Word of God, "Your word is very pure (tried and well refined)" (Amplified Bible). The Psalmist is saying that he has proved God's Word to be perfect; whenever he has had to rely on it, it has not failed him. David used this word eight times in the Psalms, which goes to show how much he turned to it as his source of guidance, encouragement, and support:

> *"As for God, His way is perfect; the word of the LORD is proven; He is a shield to all who trust in Him" Psalm 18:30.*

Solomon, David's son, said the same thing: "Every word of God is pure; He is a shield to those who put their trust in Him" (Proverbs 30:5). When gold is subjected to such heat, it suffers no loss, for the impurities have been removed. This is the Word of God—it is pure, it has no impurities, it can be trusted—there is no defect in the word of God:

"The words of the LORD are pure words, like silver tried in a furnace of earth, purified seven times. You shall keep them, O LORD" Psalm 12:6-7.

To be sure every impurity was removed the metal was refined seven times. It is possible to have gold that is not pure. If you are fortunate enough to own gold coins, look at them carefully. Imprinted on one side will be .999 or .9999, the difference is the purity of the gold. The value of a .999 coin is less than a .9999 coin. Seven times purified, or the furnace was heated seven times its norm to make sure the gold or silver contained no impurities. There is no impurity in God's Word for it was inspired by God Himself (2 Timothy 3:16-17), and God cannot lie (Titus 1:2). Such is the foundation upon which we can build our trust in the Word of God. We could rightly be called foolish if we chose something that was unstable upon which to build our faith:

"Therefore whoever hears these sayings of Mine, and does them, I will liken him to a wise man who built his house on the rock: and the rain descended, the floods came, and the winds blew and beat on that house; and it did not fall, for it was founded on the rock. But everyone who hears these sayings of Mine, and does not do them, will be like a foolish man who built his house on the sand: and the rain descended, the floods came, and the winds blew and beat on that house; and it fell. And great was its fall" Matthew 7:24-27.

This analogy speaks to the infallibility of God's Word. It is the pastime of some to search the scriptures to find inconsistencies, and they conclude they have found some, and proudly publish their findings. But they are fools on a fool's errand, for I would rather believe the word of my infallible God than that of a man who figures he can outwit Him. The Bible is God's revelation to His creation as to who He is, His plan of redemption, and the glorious future that awaits those who trust Him.

The promises of God have been proven time and time again—they have been tried in the refiner's fire. Saints throughout the ages have sought comfort, strength, and encouragement in the Word of God. The last request of my grandmother as she lay on her deathbed was to have her daughter read the 23rd Psalm to her.

My mother could no longer read her Bible because her sight was failing, so she asked for a large print version. My uncle, who carried a small New Testament in his pocket during his military service in Word War II, read it whenever he could as he and his buddies hid in the trenches. Such is the value Christians place on God's Word. We believe it is infallible, therefore trust it:

"All Scripture is given by inspiration of God, and is profitable for doctrine, for reproof, for correction, for instruction in righteousness, that the man of God may be complete, thoroughly equipped for every good work" 2 Timothy 3:16.

Puritan Quote:

"It is true, indeed, despisers will esteem both God and his word as trifling; but oh, what an unknown treasure doth the word, the promises, the covenant relation of the divine things of Jesus contain! They are more to be desired than gold, yea, than pure gold; sweeter also than honey and the honeycomb" Robert Hawker, 1753-1827.

GREAT PEACE

Reading: Psalm 119:161-168
"Great peace have those who love Your law,
and nothing causes them to stumble"
Psalm 119:165

It does not take long before a new Christian realizes that he is involved in warfare. It is the conviction of his sins that drove him to Jesus Christ, yet he quickly discovers he is still plagued by them. When he reads God's Word he discovers:

> *"We do not wrestle against flesh and blood, but against principalities, against powers, against the rulers of the darkness of this age, against spiritual hosts of wickedness in the Heavenly places" Ephesians 6:12.*

He then reads that he is not alone, for even the great apostle Paul admitted that "What I am doing, I do not understand. For what I will to do, that I do not practice; but what I hate, that I do" (Romans 7:15). But God, in His love and grace, leads him to passages that give him hope, hope that puts a smile on his face:

> *"Be anxious for nothing, but in everything by prayer and supplication, with thanksgiving, let your requests be made known to God; and the peace of God, which surpasses all understanding, will guard your hearts and minds through Christ Jesus" Philippians 4:6-7.*

He reads our text: "Great peace have those who love Your law, and nothing causes them to stumble" (Psalm 119:165). Peace—here is something he did not know before he was saved. In the middle of all this warfare he can have peace. The Bible not only tells him peace is available, but what he must do to obtain it—"pray about everything. Tell God what you need, and thank

202

him for all he has done" (NLT); "Great peace," not just ordinary peace, but "abundant" peace (for that is the meaning of this word), comes to those who love God's Word. There are things he must do, but they are things a Christian should want to do.

This is true—most believers will tell you so because they have proven it. It continually amazes me that when trials and temptations come my way, I have a peace, a peace that I know comes from outside of myself. My natural tendency is to worry or, as the Bible puts it, be "anxious," but, as we grow in Christ, His peace overrides our anxieties. This is one of the great values in reading and loving His Word.

I note with sadness the methods and means of those outside of Christ as they seek for some degree of peace when trials come their way. The believer is not always protected from the onslaughts of the devil, but he does have a personal relationship with the Prince of Peace:

"The work of righteousness will be peace, and the effect of righteousness, quietness and assurance forever" Isaiah 32:17.

One of the glorious miracles God performs in the life of every one He saves is that He gives them the righteousness of His Son. Righteousness is like tree that bears fruit, and the fruit is peace, quietness, and assurance. Our righteousness is Christ's righteousness, and he gives us His fruit. As Christians we have peace with God (Romans 5:1) and the peace of God (Philippians 4:7).

The requirement for peace is not that we keep God's Word, but love it. The more we read it and meditate in it, the more we will love it. Are you not constantly amazed and in awe as the Holy Spirit opens up truths in His Word? The result of this is "nothing causes them to stumble." Fill your heart with the Word of God and see for yourself that these words are true:

"Oh, that you had heeded My commandments! Then your peace would have been like a river" Isaiah 48:18.
"The LORD will give strength to His people; the LORD will bless His people with peace" Psalm 29:11.

"Now may the Lord of peace Himself give you peace always in every way" 2 Thessalonians 3:16.

Puritan Quotes:

"The godly, it is true, are also tormented or distressed, but this inward consolation wipes away all their sorrow, or, raising them up, enables them to surmount all stumbling-blocks, or so relieves them, that they faint not" John Calvin (1509-1564).

"Amidst the storms and tempests of the world, there is a perfect calm in the breasts of those, who not only do the will of God, but "love" to do it . . . No external troubles can rob them of this "great peace, "no "offences" or stumbling blocks, which are thrown in their way by persecution, or temptation, by the malice of enemies, or by the apostasy of friends, by anything which they see, hear of, or feel, can detain, or divert them from their course. Heavenly love surmounts every obstacle, and runs with delight the way of God's commandments" George Horne, 1730-1792.

AWE OF GOD'S WORD

Reading: Psalm 119:161-168
"My heart stands in awe of Your word" Psalm 119:161

If any reader of this Psalm has any doubt as to how David felt about God's Word, a reading of this stanza will erase those doubts. He sums it all up with the first words of the stanza, "My heart stands in awe of Your word." A man of such a standing might have little that causes him to stand in awe. He is the King of Israel, possesses more riches and material wealth than any other in the entire nation, has the love of the most beautiful women in the kingdom, and servants that obey his every command. Yet he stands in awe of God's word.

Throughout the next seven verses, David tells what effect God's Word has had on his life. If we do indeed stand in awe of His Word, it will affect our life. It becomes more than a book we enjoy reading and meditating on. David says, "I rejoice at Your Word (vs 162). It makes him happy; it makes him sing and dance. Tears wet his face when he plays his harp, and the crescendo causes him to shout out in praise to his God.

More than anything else, he says, "I love Your law" (vs 163). I want it before me at all times. I meditate on it day and night. I never let it out of my sight or out of my mind. When I am disheartened I read it for strength; when my enemies come against me I read it for wisdom; when I am sorrowful I read it for comfort, and when I do not know which step to take next, I read it for guidance. My soul overflows with praise—"Seven times a day I praise You."

Because he loves God's Word, he says, "I do Your commandments" (vs 166). He considers what God commands of him a privilege and an honor to obey. God's commands are not a millstone around his neck, not a hindrance to happiness, but a doorway into a closer relationship with his Creator.

Because he loves God's Word, he says, "My soul keeps Your testimonies" (vs 167). There is a big difference between obeying God's Word out of a sense of duty than obeying it because you love it. The one is obeying it with the approval of your head, and the other is obeying it because it is in your heart. You obey it because you love it, not because you have to.

No matter what it is, Lord, "I keep Your precepts and Your testimonies" (vs 168). I keep both the practical and doctrinal parts of God's Word:

"It is a blessed thing to see the two forms of the divine word, equally known, equally valued, equally confessed: there should be no picking and choosing as to the mind of God" C.H. Spurgeon.

So often Christians hold so dogmatically to the doctrines of the faith, yet live loosely when it come to the practical life commanded by God, and vise-versa. Is it not enough that God sees and knows all we say and do? "All my ways are before You," nothing is hid from Your eyes.

When God took Ezekiel into the temple, He showed him what the elders of the city were doing:

"Son of man, have you seen what the elders of the house of Israel do in the dark, every man in the room of his idols? For they say,'The LORD does not see us'" Ezekiel 8:12.

It does not matter whether others know of our sins, for God does. Nothing is hidden from His eyes—we cannot fool Him. Besides, this will not be a problem if we can honestly say with David, "I love Your Word." True love of God will always equal obedience to what He commands of us.

Will we ever fail Him? Of course we will, the "old man" may have received a death blow by Jesus' death and shed blood, but he is still alive and has an influence in our lives. Praise God there is action we can take when we do fail Him:

"If we confess our sins, He is faithful and just to forgive us our sins and to cleanse us from all unrighteousness. If we say that we have not sinned, we make Him a liar, and His word is not in us" 1 John 1:9-10.

It is the heart that God works on our heart, and the heart is the seat of affection. If we do not love God's Word with our heart, but with our head only, all outward affection is nothing but pretense and hypocrisy:

"Inasmuch as these people draw near with their mouths and honor Me with their lips, but have removed their hearts far from Me, and their fear toward Me is taught by the commandment of men" Isaiah 29:13.

Herein lies the difference—one is taught by the Holy Spirit, while the other lives by the letter of the law, believing only what their own carnal heart wants to believe:

"LORD, You have searched me and known me. You know my sitting down and my rising up; You understand my thought afar off. You comprehend my path and my lying down, and are acquainted with all my ways. For there is not a word on my tongue, but behold, O LORD, You know it altogether" Psalm139:1-4.

We stand in awe of God's Word because it *is* the Word of God and carries His omniscient authority. "Where the word of a king is, there is power [authority]" (Ecclesiastes 8:4). How much more then the Word of the King of Kings?

Puritan Quote:
"We are not likely to be disheartened by persecution, or driven by it into sin, if the word of God continually has supreme power over our minds" Charles H. Spurgeon.

DAVID'S HEART CRY

Reading: Psalm 119:169-176
"Let my cry come before You, O LORD" Psalm 119:169

If ever there was a passage of scripture where one of God's children poured out his heart to God, it is these eight verses. Seven times David pleads with God from the depths of his heart. This was no soul repeating the Lord's Prayer out of mere habit with little or no feeling. This was his heart cry; a cry to his Lord from a desperate heart.

David had learned many lessons about God, but he knew there was much more. His heart ached because the Spirit of God continually convicted him of his sins; he wanted to know God in a more personal way. As much as he loved God, he was not satisfied. Read his petitions again:

Let my cry come before You, O LORD (169)
Let my supplication come before You (170)
Deliver me according to Your word (170)
Let Your hand become my help (173)
Let my soul live (175)
Let Your judgments help me (175)
Seek Your servant (176)

Although our English translations use the word "Let" or "May" five times, in the Hebrew language the author uses five different words, although with similar meanings.

"Let my cry come before You, O LORD." The word 'qarab' is a frequently used word that is translated several ways: 'draw near,' 'come,' 'bring,' and in Leviticus is often translated as 'offer,' as in to offer a sacrifice. To better understand its meaning here, we must consider the conclusion of the sentence; "give me understanding according to Your word."

One of the places where 'qarab' is used, is in the following:

"Then Moses spoke to Aaron, 'Say to all the congregation of the children of Israel, 'Come near (qarab) before the LORD, for He has heard your complaints'" Exodus 16:9.

David also had his complaint to the Lord where his prayer is similar to our text:

"Give ear to my prayer, O God, and do not hide Yourself from my supplication. Attend to me, and hear me; I am restless in my complaint, and moan noisily, because of the voice of the enemy" Psalm 55:1-3.

Often we face circumstances we do not understand, and the cry on our lips is "Why Lord, I do not understand?" David continued his cry, "give me understanding according to Your word." How do we listen for God's answer? Are we much in God's Word? We should be, for He often answers our prayer while we are meditating in it.

"Let my supplication come before You; deliver me according to Your word" (vs 170). David reminds God of His promises: "Lord, in Your Word You promised to deliver me if I love You and faithfully keep Your commandments." God has made many promises to His people, and there is nothing irreverent about repeating them to Him in your prayers.

As God's children we have choices to make. Do we heed the Word of God or do we choose to walk a different path? If we knowingly walk a different path we cannot expect the Lord to honor our prayers. David, however, chose God's way:

"I have chosen Your precepts. I long for Your salvation, O LORD, and Your law is my delight" (vss 173-174).

David could have confidence when he prayed because he chose the right path. If it seems that God's ears are closed to our supplications, we should first examine ourselves to see if indeed we are in compliance to what the Holy Spirit is telling us. If we are holding on to anything He has told us to give up, then you have found the reason for God's silence. David knew this and acknowledged it: "I have gone astray like a lost sheep," he confesses.

A sheep does not get lost by lifting its head and deciding the grass is greener on the other hill. No, he keeps his nose to the ground, nibbling to his hearts content. Little by little, his nibbling leads him into strange pastures, so, when he does decide to look up, he does not know where he is. The message to us is to feast on the Bread of Life, but with our eyes wide open to those little things that cause us to wander from our Provider.

"Seek Your servant," David prays. "Come and find me." "Put me on Your shoulders and bring me back to Your fold." That is where we need to be at all times. "Oh God, I have strayed away, I have heard your voice but chose another path. I am sorry. Forgive me. Come to me. Lift me up and hold me in Your arms. 'My lips shall utter praise . . . My tongue shall speak of Your word.'

Samson had prayed, "Let me die" (Judges 16:30), but David wanted to live: "Let my soul live, and it will praise You" (vs 175). Praise should continually be on our lips:

> *"Though like a sheep estranged I stray,*
> *Yet have I not renounced thy way.*
> *Thine hand extend; thine own reclaim;*
> *Grant me to live, and praise thy name."*
> *Richard Mant—1776-1848.*

Puritan Quote:

"If David prays for life, it is not that he may live, but "live and praise God" *William Gurnall, 1617-1679.*

CREATOR/CREATURE

Reading: Genesis 1:26
"So God created man in His own image" Genesis 1:27

Genesis is the book of beginnings: the beginning of the world, man, human history, sin, death, and indeed of the Scriptures themselves. The word itself (Genesis) is 'bereeshiyt,' and is taken from the first word in the Bible, "in the beginning."

Because this is the creation of man, it might well be said that it is also the beginning of God's relationship with man. On one hand, this is true, for how can one have a relationship with an entity that does not exist? On the other hand, man has been in the mind of God from eternity past:

"Then the word of the LORD came to me, saying: 'Before I formed you in the womb I knew you; before you were born I sanctified you; I ordained you a prophet to the nations'" Jeremiah 1:5.

These words to the Prophet Jeremiah speak to the reality that the Eternal God both knew him, and planned his life for him, before he was even conceived. This does not mean God and Jeremiah had a relationship prior to his conception, for he was non-existent other than in the mind and plan of God. In this way, God *"knew"* him. Paul touches on this subject in his letter to the assembly in Ephesus, when he wrote:

"Just as He chose us in Him before the foundation of the world"
Ephesians 1:4.

In the counsels of eternity, God did not suddenly decide it would be a good idea to create a likeness of Himself, a being with which He could have a relationship.

The only part of God's creation that doubts, questions, and disobeys His voice, is man. It did not take long for the greatest of all His creation to disobey Him. "Let us make man in our own image," God said. Let us create someone with whom we can communicate and enjoy fellowship, someone who, of his own free-will will love us, and upon whom we will shower every blessing: Forever in the plan of God, yet so soon separated from Him.

Sin, the destroyer of relationships, could not destroy the Creator/Creature bond, but certainly was the cause of the break-up of fellowship.

The restoration of fellowship and communion between God and His creation could not be restored until God, once again, created something new. This new creation, although it involves the soul and body, does not happen at one time. When a man is born again by the Spirit of God, his soul is once more capable of communication with its Creator. The banishment from the presence of God is lifted, and the sword bearing Cherubim are nowhere to be seen:

"So He drove out the man; and He placed cherubim at the east of the garden of Eden, and a flaming sword which turned every way, to guard the way to the tree of life" Genesis 3:24.

The new birth is referred to as a "new creation," the emphasis is on the word new, not revamped, refurbished, or remodeled, but new:

"Therefore, if anyone is in Christ, he is a new creation; old things have passed away; behold, all things have become new" 2 Corinthians 5:17.

The new creation of our body is guaranteed, but is delayed for a specific time in the future:

"As was the man of dust, so also are those who are made of dust; and as is the Heavenly Man, so also are those who are Heavenly. And as we have borne the image of the man of dust, we shall also bear the image of the Heavenly Man" 1 Corinthians 15:48-49.

The following quote from Bishop N.T. Wright's book "Surprised By Hope" both enlightened and encouraged me. He is writing in the context of Philippians 3: 20-21:

"For our citizenship is in heaven, from which we also eagerly wait for the Savior, the Lord Jesus Christ, who will transform our lowly body that it may be conformed to His glorious body."

"When Paul says, 'We are citizens of heaven,' he doesn't at all mean that when we are done with this life we'll be going off to live in heaven. What he means is that the Savior, the Lord, Jesus the King—all of those were of course imperial titles—will come from heaven to earth to change the present situation and state of His people. The key word here is transform: He will 'transform our present humble bodies to be like His glorious body.' Jesus will not declare that present physicality is redundant and can be scrapped. Not that He will simply improve it, perhaps by speeding up its evolutionary cycle. In a great act of power—the same great power that accomplished Jesus' own resurrection, as Paul says in Ephesians 1:19-20—He will change the present body into the one that corresponds in kind to His own as part of His work in bringing all things into subjection to Himself. In Philippians 3, though it is primarily speaking of human resurrection, indicates that this will take place within the context of God's victorious transformation of the entire cosmos."

So, that which sin destroyed is created anew through the transaction of the new birth. The same power of the Almighty that spoke *"and it was so,"* is at work in the salvation of His people—a new creation, new heavens and a new earth, a new Jerusalem, a new song—Paul sums it all up with the words, "behold, all things have become new."

Puritan Quote:

"Regeneration . . . is produced by a creating act of the power of God, and it is applied into the essential faculties of our soul. This new creation does not consist in just a new course of action, but in renewed faculties" John Owen, 1616-1683.

CREATOR/FRIEND

Reading: John 15:9-7
"This is my beloved, and this is my friend" Song of Songs 5:16

To be a friend of God is one of those spiritual realities beyond my comprehension. If Jesus Himself had not designated me as such, I would fear I was regarding my relationship with Him frivolously. To have a personal relationship with the Almighty, Omniscient Creator, before whom the hosts of heaven bow in continuous worship, is in itself gloriously remarkable, but to know He considers me a friend is . . . beyond words.

From the very beginning, God and Adam were friends—they enjoyed each other's company as they walked together in the coolness of the evening—the words imply this was a regular feature of their day. Sin ruined this very special friendship, and God drove Adam and Eve from the garden and blocked their return by appointing sword baring angels at the garden's gate.

Only two men in the Old Testament, Abraham and Moses, are spoken of as being a friend of God (Exodus 33:12; 2 Chronicles 20:7), and God never referred to anyone as His friend until Jesus when He called Lazarus "our friend" (John 11:11). Then to His disciples He said:

"You are My friends if you do whatever I command you" John 15:14.

First of all, this was a remarkable revelation that God, in the Person of Jesus Christ, would consent to call His disciples "friends." Man, in his fallen state, God considered to be His "enemy" (Romans 5:10; 8:7), and how can enemies be friends? There is only one way—they must be reconciled. This is the wonderful thing Jesus accomplished by His death on the cross:

"For if when we were enemies we were reconciled to God through the death of His Son, much more, having been reconciled, we shall

be saved by His life. And not only that, but we also rejoice in God through our Lord Jesus Christ, through whom we have now received the reconciliation" Romans 5:10-11.

This is how God can once again be friends with His creation. This friendship, however, has conditions:

"You are My friends if you do whatever I command you" John 15:14.

What sort of friendship is this if we have to obey Jesus implicitly? That describes a servant, not a friend. Jesus goes on to describe the grounds for this friendship by saying, "You did not choose Me, but I chose you" (vs 16). Out of the many fishermen of Galilee Jesus chose two pair of brothers—Peter and Andrew and James and John. He also chose Matthew, a very unpopular man, a tax collector. Jesus chose His friends—they did not seek His friendship. Jesus took the initiative, and established the ground upon which that friendship was to be based.

Obedience was not something the disciples originally agreed to, but it became proof of their friendship. Jesus chose wisely, for when He called them, "they immediately left their nets and followed Him." Their immediate response was obedience. Had they dithered or made excuses, they would not have become His chosen ones.

While this statement of Jesus can be applied generally, it is also specific in that He is referring to the commandment He has just mentioned:

"This is My commandment, that you love one another as I have loved you" John 15:12.

The love for our neighbor is the second most important commandment:

"The second is like it: 'You shall love your neighbor as yourself" Matthew 22:39.

It is, therefore, very important to Jesus that His children love each other:

"A new commandment I give to you, that you love one another; as I have loved you, that you also love one another. By this all will know that you are My disciples, if you have love for one another." John 13:34-35.

If we say we are friends with Jesus yet do not love our brother and sister—all of them—then our friendship with God is a fantasy, for it is a necessary requirement. It is only as the love of God flows through us that this is possible. To love the unlovely is an attribute of God, not of man, even a Christian:

"Everyone who believes that Jesus is the Christ is a child of God. And everyone who loves the Father loves his children, too. We know we love God's children if we love God and obey his commandments" 1 John 5:1-2, NLT.

Puritan Quote:
"'You are my friends'—He does not mean that we obtain so great an honor by our own merit, but only reminds them of the condition on which he receives us into favor, and deigns to reckon us among his friends; as he said a little before, 'If you keep my commandments, you will abide in my love'" John Calvin, 1509-1564.

REDEEMER/PURCHASED

Reading: Luke 2:36-38
"She gave thanks to the Lord, and spoke of Him to all those who looked for redemption in Jerusalem" Luke 2:38.

The old woman, Anna, a widow and a prophetess, has three verses dedicated to her memory. She was a faithful servant of God who fasted and prayed in the temple "night and day." Her message to those who would listen was about one thing—she "spoke of Him to all those who looked for redemption in Jerusalem."

Knowing what we know today, wouldn't it have been wonderful to listen as she expounded on the many Old Testament scriptures that speak of the "Redeemer of Israel"? When she opened the scroll and read, "For the redemption of their souls is costly" (Psalm 49:8), I wonder if she had any idea how costly, and with what the price would be paid?

Anna "looked for Redemption in Jerusalem" based on scriptures like:

"'Fear not, you worm Jacob, you men of Israel! I will help you,' says the LORD and your Redeemer, the Holy one of Israel" Isaiah 41:14.
"'When the enemy comes in like a flood, the Spirit of the LORD will lift up a standard against him. The Redeemer will come to Zion, and to those who turn from transgression in Jacob,' says the LORD" Isaiah 59:19-20.

The Jews were in bondage to Rome—they were the "enemy" that came in like a flood. Anna believed with all her heart that the Lord's promise of a Redeemer was near at hand. However, the redemption God had in mind was different than the redemptive concept of the Old Testament. There, it was more to do with buying back land, but New Testament redemption has more to do with deliverance.

The Greek word *'apolutrosis'* occurs ten times with the primary meaning "redemption" in the sense of "deliverance." The Bible is clear as to whom the Redeemer is, whom He redeemed, and the price He paid to secure the redemption of His people:

"Jesus Christ . . . In Him we have redemption through his blood"
Ephesians 1:5, 7, see also Colossians 1:14.

Jesus Christ is the Redeemer, the redeemed are those He came to save, and the price He paid was His blood. Jesus willingly gave His life and suffered the extreme physical and spiritual agony of His soul. Jesus came to establish His kingdom, and this is how He is populating it.

The question is frequently asked, "To whom was the price paid?" Before we were saved we "were in bondage under the elements of the world" (Galatians 4:3), and the "bondage of corruption" (Romans 8:21); and we all know who the prince of the world is—the devil. But the devil was not paid for the release of our souls—God forbid.

When Adam sinned, mankind came under bondage to sin—he violated the holiness of God. The Bible tells us "all have sinned" and "the wages of sin is death." Unless the demands of God's holiness are met, every man and woman will stand before Him at the Great White Throne of judgment.

The sacrifice of thousands of bulls, rams and doves, could only temporarily delay God's judgment; they were but a type of the Son of God who shed His blood, and procured eternal salvation and deliverance from God's wrath for all who come to Christ in repentance, and surrender their lives to Him:

"For it is not possible that the blood of bulls and goats could take away sins" Hebrews 10:4.

Not only could bloody sacrifices not obtain redemption for us, but silver and gold was also worthless in this cause:

"You were not redeemed with corruptible things, like silver or gold . . . but with the precious blood of Christ" 1 Peter 1:18-19.

So far ranging is the redemption acquired by Jesus that a new song broke out in heaven in acknowledgment of His sacrifice: "You were slain, and have redeemed us to God by Your blood out of every tribe and tongue and people and nation, and have made us kings and priests to our God" Revelation 5:9-10.

What does it mean to be redeemed by Jesus Christ?

"These were redeemed from among men, being firstfruits to God and to the Lamb. And in their mouth was found no deceit, for they are without fault before the throne of God" Revelation 14:4-5.

Whereas once we were guilty in the tribunal of God, by the act of redemption we are now "without fault" in the eyes of Him who sees all and knows all. This Jesus, our Savior and Redeemer, is worthy of all praise and worship, and we will, throughout eternity, stand in awe of Him.

Puritan Quote:

"Whatever difficulties lay in the way of Christ, as unto the accomplishment and perfection of the work of our redemption, he would not decline them, nor desist from his undertaking, whatever it cost him" John Owen. 1616-1683.

FATHER/SON

Reading: Matthew 6:1-8

"Let your light so shine before men, that they may see your good works
and glorify your Father in heaven" Matthew 5:16

I have chosen Matthew 5:16 as our text because it is the first mention of
God as our Heavenly Father in the New Testament. Jesus brought a new
message to God's people—that of God as "our Father."

Throughout the Old Testament, God was seen more as a Judge than a
Father. He was the Lawgiver, and exercised severe judgment on unrepentant
lawbreakers. In Matthew alone, Jesus spoke of God as "your Father" 18 times,
as "My Father" 16 times, and "our Father" once. Jesus wanted to present the
reality of God as the Heavenly Father as an important foundation of His
message under the New Covenant.

This is a concept that Paul appeared to revel in, for his epistles begin
with the greeting:

**"Grace to you and peace from God our Father and the Lord Jesus
Christ."**

Obviously, before we can have sons we must have a father, and fathers
come in all shapes and sizes, with as many varying personalities; good
fathers and bad fathers, some are loved and some hated, some we love to
go home and visit while others are left behind as their children mature into
adulthood, and leave home at the earliest possible moment with no intention
of ever returning. I thank God constantly for my father and mother who
were of the good kind, and whom I loved dearly.

I remember with joy the words of my father when he said to me, "I am
very proud of you." I therefore have an advantage, I believe, over those who
have never enjoyed a close relationship with their father, for I can readily
understand some of the qualities of a good father in my Heavenly Father.
Not that He reflects the attributes of my earthly father, but vice versa—he

was a born again believer. When God says, 'I love you with an everlasting love,' I have some basis upon which to understand what He means.

On the other hand, those whose relationship with their earthly father is strained or almost non-existent, take great comfort in the fact that their Heavenly Father provides with abundance those elements of a good father that is/was missing from their earthly relationship. So, the Fatherhood of God to His children is, or should be, a matter of great significance to them.

Unfortunately, this filial relationship between God and His children is often relegated to the repetition of the Lord's Prayer on Sunday mornings. The issue is not so much that their relationship with their earthly father was bad, but that their understanding of their Heavenly Father is lacking.

Generally speaking, our experience with our Heavenly Father is willfully lacking. Yes, Jesus is the one who introduces us to His Father, and He constantly points us toward Him. Jesus is the Son of God, the Son of the Father, The only way of really getting to know a person is not only to read about them or read their autobiography, but to spend time with them.

Just before going to bed one evening in early November 1999, a verse of Scripture came into my mind. Looking back, I thought that the Scripture seemed strange. It was Isaiah 6:1: "In the year that King Uzziah died, I saw the Lord . . . ." I read no further. I could not. I started to cry. My body shook as my crying turned to sobbing. "Oh, God, this is what I need. This is what I have to have in my life. I need to see You."

Obviously, I knew I could never actually see God in this lifetime and, as time passed, the real meaning of my prayer became a reality; my heart was crying out with the same desire as Paul when he said, "That I may know Him" (Philippians 3:10), only for me it was more specifically God the Father.

This may sound sacrilegious to some, but try to understand from where I was coming. Throughout my Christian walk from age 14 to 27, all of my studies and preaching had to do with Jesus Christ, the Father's Beloved Son, much to the exclusion of the Father Himself. I prayed to Jesus, sang about Jesus, studied about Jesus, and preached about Jesus, yet it was against the Father that I was angry and blamed Him for everything that had gone drastically wrong. I was not upset with Jesus, because as I often sang as a child, "Jesus loves me, this I know, for the Bible tells me so. Little ones to

Him belong, they are weak but He is strong." After all, the Father was the Father, so He got all the blame.

God used these words from Isaiah 6:1 like a sledge hammer. I saw myself as a large stone—hard, stubborn and unbreakable, but after three days and nights of being hammered on the stone, I lay crushed before the powerful hand of God. Yes, He could have accomplished His plan for me in one moment—I believe now that He swung His hammer on me for three days so I would never again forget His mighty work in my heart:

"Is not My word like a fire?" says the LORD, "and like a hammer that breaks the rock in pieces?" Jeremiah 23:29.

As sons and daughters of our Heavenly Father, the Holy Spirit within us instills the desire to get to know Him better; to understand His principles, His attributes, and purpose. There is no limit to the desire of God's children, for with each insight the desire is strengthened and the child's capacity is deepened. God's revelation of Himself can be likened to a slide show where He does not move on to the next picture until we grasp a level of understanding of the current one.

Puritan Quote:
"If God be my Father, He loves me. And oh. how He loves me . . . When He is a Father, He is the best of fathers' C.H. Spurgeon (1834-1892).

FATHER/SON (CONT'D)

Reading: Matthew 6:1-8
"He who loves Me will be loved of My Father" John 14:21,
"The Father Himself loves you" John 16:27

O ur previous thought closed with the words of Charles H. Spurgeon, *"If God be my Father, He loves me. And oh. how He loves me . . . When He is a Father, He is the best of fathers."*

Our Heavenly Father loves His children. He has not adopted us into His family so He can rule over us with an iron rod, but so He can shower us with "every spiritual blessing in Christ Jesus (Ephesians 1:3):

"Behold what manner of love the Father has bestowed on us, that we should be called children of God!" 1 John 3:1.

We also noted that Jesus' declaration of God as the personal Father of those who love Him, and not only their Judge, was a new revelation.

The fact that "God so loved the world" was another eye opener to the early followers of Jesus. Jehovah was the God of Israel, their Master and Lord. People of other nations could become citizens of Israel through special dispensation, but Jehovah remained exclusively the God of Israel. Now, Jesus reveals that God loves the world; not only Israel but peoples of every nation, including those detested gentiles.

Another of Jesus' announcements was "He who loves Me will be loved of My Father" (John 14:21), "The Father Himself loves you" (John 16:27). This was astounding news. Tragically, we Christians in the 21st century, take it rather for granted. It is not news to us that we are loved by the Father; some of us were raised with this knowledge, and, while we are extremely thankful to be so loved, it often takes many years before we gain a greater appreciation for what this means.

I remember standing on a mountain in one of our National Parks and looking over valleys and mountains, streams and forests, a slightly clouded sky, and two Bald Eagles gliding on an air current, when the immensity and greatness of God's creation swept over me more than ever before. I remembered that this magnificent, omnipotent Creator is my Heavenly Father, and, more than that, He loves me, and I have permission to communicate with Him on any day, at any hour, anytime, anywhere.

I thought of the Cherubim that guarded the entrance to the Garden of Eden where Adam walked with God—now there are no Cherubim blocking my entrance into the presence of God Almighty, for, in His love for me, He has opened the gate to His throne room, and all the angels have been told to step aside when I approach. I am welcome to commune with my Heavenly Father whenever I wish, because He loves me. I am His son, and He is my Father. Amazing love! My soul cannot begin to lay hold of such love, but He is teaching me more every day. Oh, if only I could praise Him adequately for His love:

"The LORD your God in your midst, the Mighty one, will save; He will rejoice over you with gladness, He will quiet you with His love, He will rejoice over you with singing" Zephaniah 3:17.

One of the greatest, if not the greatest, blessings we have as those loved by our Father, is the permission to have communion with Him. Would we not be extremely grateful to simply be a citizen of His kingdom? We could bow before Him as He passes by in His royal chariot. He could wave to us and smile as He graciously acknowledges our loyalty to Him. He is our King and He deigns to wave and smile—what a wonderful King He is.

What if God was just our Master and we His servants—what a privilege that would be. We have heard of Masters who treat their servants badly, and even abuse them, but our Master is kind and gentle, even providing us with benefits we do not really deserve. He constantly reminds us that "My door is always open." We are so fortunate to have such a Master as this.

How happy we are to have the Great Jehovah as our Shepherd; after all, we are but sheep grazing all day long with our noses in the grass. He is such a conscientious Shepherd that He watches over us 24 hours a day. Occasionally we stray a little because, after all, we just nibble the grass, not watching where we are going. I remember once when I strayed from the flock so far that I was lost before I realized it. I looked up from my nibbling, and my Shepherd was nowhere to be found. I panicked because I had heard tell of wolves in the area, but I had always had my Shepherd to protect me. I will never forget the day when I thought I heard His voice calling my name. I listened harder and, yes, it was He. He had left the flock and came to search for me. He could easily have let me go, for, after all, what is one sheep to Him?

Would we not be satisfied if all this were true? But there is more—much more.

Let us face reality; we are all criminals in God's estimation. He is the "Judge of all the earth" and what He says goes. He has the authority to place us on probation, put us in prison for as long He deems fit, or even send us to the executioner. But no, He looks at us, sees His Son in us and declares:

"There is therefore now no condemnation to those who are in Christ Jesus" Romans 8:1.

What! No condemnation! Can it be true? A Judge with a heart; a Judge who believes in and practices justice; a King who invites us to have audience with Him anytime—how fortunate for us that we are His sons and daughters.

Puritan Quote:
"I speak not now of temporal blessings, but of everlasting love, and all the fruits of it, that here it hangs. Now, I say, you are built in a rock higher than all powers of darkness; now a key is put into thy hand to unlock all God's treasure; now thou art in the very lap of love, wrapped up in it, when here thy heart rests; and therefore, if this be thus, see it, and wonder his name has moved him to love me" Thomas Shepard (1605-1649.)

FATHER/SON (CONT'D)

Reading: Luke 15:11-24

"This my son was dead and is alive again; he was lost and is found" Luke 15:24.

I cannot move on to another relationship between God and His people without considering the passage of scripture that is the dearest to my heart. The parable of the Prodigal Son can be interpreted in several ways, each of which has an element of truth, however, as many of you know, these words of Jesus are a perfect depiction of my testimony.

There are no words to adequately express what my Heavenly Father accomplished in my heart on that November day in 1999. After twenty-three years of anger and rebellion against God, He placed such restlessness and anxiety in my mind until I cried along with the prodigal son:

"Father, I have sinned against heaven and before you, and I am no longer worthy to be called your son" Luke 15:18-19.

When the prodigal was met by his father, he was received, not with rebuke and rejection, but with compassion—open arms, rejoicing, and a kiss:

"And he arose and came to his father. But when he was still a great way off, his father saw him and had compassion, and ran and fell on his neck and kissed him" Luke 15:20.

The compassion of our Heavenly Father for a repentant backslidden son is something incomprehensible to any who have never experienced it. That welcoming embrace is an experience that never diminishes no matter how long ago it happened. The returning son, having wasted his inheritance, rightfully expecting reprimand and admonition, finds himself embraced in his Father's arms.

The embrace is more than that; he is squeezed, hugged, held tightly (whatever adjective you can think of). I do not mean to be irreverent, but your Heavenly Father's embrace holds you so close that you feel His heartbeat.

When God told Jacob to return to his home, his brother

"Esau ran to meet him, and embraced him, and fell on his neck and kissed him, and they wept" Genesis 33:4.

I know there are some reading these words who find themselves struggling apart from God. He has been speaking to your heart to repent and return to Him. The message on my heart today is simply this—repent of that which drove you away, return to your Heavenly Father, and receive His compassionate embrace. You have no need to be afraid of how He will receive you.

When the Shepherd found the lost sheep, "He lays it on his shoulders, rejoicing. And when he comes home, he calls together his friends and neighbors, saying to them, 'Rejoice with me, for I have found my sheep which was lost'" Luke 15:5-6.

When the widow found her lost coin, "She calls her friends and neighbors together, saying, 'Rejoice with me, for I have found the piece which I lost'" Luke 15:9.

So, when the prodigal returned home:

"The father said to his servants, 'Bring out the best robe and put it on him, and put a ring on his hand and sandals on his feet. And bring the fatted calf here and kill it, and let us eat and be merry; for this my son was dead and is alive again; he was lost and is found.' And they began to be merry'" Luke 15:22-24.

In each parable, Jesus emphasized the fact that the reunion of that which was lost is a time of rejoicing and merriment, not one of rebuke, reprimand, or chastisement.

I need to constantly remind myself of this truth, for there are times when Satan lays a heavy feeling of remorse on my heart; remorse for having wasted so many years apart from Him who never stopped loving me. Believe me, such remorse can be devastating if you allow it to take hold of your mind.

When I shared with a friend that God had restored me to Himself, and the terrible remorse I felt, he pointed me to the words in Joel:

> *"I will restore to you the years that the locust hath eaten . . . And ye shall eat in plenty, and be satisfied, and praise the name of the LORD your God, that hath dealt wondrously with you: and my people shall never be ashamed" Joel 2:25-26, KJV.*

Remember also, whether you have been living in a backslidden condition for one day or twenty-three years, God's compassion is the same, for "with the Lord one day is as a thousand years, and a thousand years as one day" 2 Peter 3:8.

Puritan Quote:

"Though Christians be not kept altogether from falling, yet they are kept from falling altogether" William Secker (d. 1681?)

HEAD/BODY

Reading: Colossians 1:15-18
"And He is the head of the body, the church" Colossians 1:18

Paul is explaining to the Colossian believers their relationship with Jesus Christ in His kingdom that was given to Him by His Father for completing the work He had sent Him to do. As far as believers are concerned, he says, You have been delivered from the power of darkness, and conveyed into the kingdom of the Son of His love.

Jesus is the "image of the invisible God, [and] the firstborn over all creation . . . All things were created [by Him] that are in heaven and that are on earth, visible and invisible, whether thrones or dominions or principalities or powers. All things were created through Him and for Him." Therefore, He is "before" all things. The word *'pro'* is translated "before" 44 times, "above" 3 times, and "ever" twice.

Jesus confirms this when He said, "I am the Alpha and the Omega, the Beginning and the End," and "the First and the Last" (Revelation 1:8, 11). No one or no thing is before or over Him. It is this fact that fallen man refuses to accept, yet will, unless delivered from the power of darkness and redeemed by His blood, one day be forced to acknowledge—Philippians 2:9-11.

In the light of this revelation, Paul concludes that Jesus is "the head of the body, the church." That which He is committed to build, (Matthew 16:16) is likened to a body, an allegory Paul used to explain the functioning relationship of Jesus and His redeemed people.

It is interesting to note there is both unity and diversity in this allegory. The unity lies in the fact that the head and the members are one body. The head, arms, feet, etc. do not act independently of the head. The diversity is noted in that the head is not an arm, neither does the arm have the same function as the leg:

"For as the body is one and has many members, but all the members of that one body, being many, are one body, so also is Christ. If the foot should say, 'Because I am not a hand, I am not of the body,' is it therefore not of the body? And if the ear should say, 'Because I am not an eye, I am not of the body,' is it therefore not of the body? If the whole body were an eye, where would be the hearing? If the whole were hearing, where would be the smelling? But now God has set the members, each one of them, in the body just as He pleased. And if they were all one member, where would the body be?" 1 Corinthians 12:14-19.

As members of His body, Jesus uses believers to act in His name as His representatives. His last words to the disciples were, "You shall be witnesses to Me in Jerusalem, and in all Judea and Samaria, and to the end of the earth" (Acts 1:8). He has given the responsibility of spreading the gospel to His followers—some are called to function as His legs and feet, some His arms and hands, etc.

Not all are called to the same activity, He "gave some to be apostles, some prophets, some evangelists, and some pastors and teachers" (Ephesians 4:11), some plant the seed while others water the ground (1 Corinthians 3:6). No matter the work God calls us to, "we are God's fellow workers" 1 Corinthians 3:9.

Another thought for us to contemplate is: What can any part of the body feel that the head would be unconscious of, and not participate in?

"For we do not have a High Priest who cannot sympathize with our weaknesses, but was in all points tempted as we are, yet without sin" Hebrews 4:15.

So close is the relationship between Christ the Head, and His church, the members, that He is aware of every trial and temptation we suffer, and everything of which we have need. The writer to the Hebrews immediately follows with:

"Let us therefore come boldly to the throne of grace, that we may obtain mercy and find grace to help in time of need" Hebrews 4:16.

Jesus, as our Head, is not only our Support and Strength in the time of trial, but the Supplier of those things of which we are in need. What comfort this is if we would only keep this wonderful truth in the forefront of our mind.

Paul concludes our reading with the overall purpose of this relationship. It is not that He is our Strength and Support, but "that in all things He may have the preeminence" Colossians 1:18.

When we experience the faithfulness of our Savior, be it in the small everyday things He provides for us, or in definite miraculous answers to prayer, it is not only our duty, but hopefully our immediate response, to give Him the praise and glory He rightfully deserves. Our lives should reflect that in all things, and on every occasion, we give Him preeminence.

Puritan Quote:

"*What can any part of the body feel which the head would be unconscious of, and not participate in? It will equally delight you to remember that all the needs of the body must be known and felt by the glorious head, and be by him supplied*" *Robert Hawker (1753-1827).*

CHIEF CORNERSTONE/LIVING STONES

Reading: Ephesians 2:14-22
"Jesus Christ Himself being the chief cornerstone" Ephesians 2:20.

As a young man in England, I would enjoy visiting the magnificent old churches and cathedrals such as St. Paul's in London and the Cathedral in the city of York. One of the objects I would always look for was the cornerstone. Often distinguished by its color (a light sandstone), it would have engraved on it the date it was placed, and other interesting information such as the name of the architect and builder. Although each structure is different in regards to its size and design, they all had this one thing in common—a cornerstone, sometimes referred to as the foundation stone.

The purpose for the cornerstone was not for the information it contained, but for its importance to the structure itself. Wikopedia says: "The cornerstone is important because all other stones will be set in reference to this stone, thus determining the position of the entire structure."

Jesus' project until He returns is to build His church (Matthew 16:18), a structure, not made of brick and mortar, but of "Living stones," a "spiritual house":

> *"Coming to Him as to a living stone, rejected indeed by men, but chosen by God and precious, you also, as living stones, are being built up a spiritual house" 1 Peter 2:4-5.*

The concept of Jesus as the Cornerstone comes from Psalm 118:22: "The stone which the builders rejected has become the chief cornerstone." This verse is quoted six times in the New Testament, including 1 Peter 2:7.

The significance of Jesus as the Cornerstone depends on our relationship with Him:

"To you who believe, He is precious; but to those who are disobedient, 'The stone which the builders rejected has become the chief cornerstone,' and 'A stone of stumbling and a rock of offense'" 1 Peter 2:7-8.

One Cornerstone and two relationships: "To those who believe, He is precious," but to those who do not believe, He is "a stone of stumbling and a rock of offense." It all depends on our relationship with Jesus Christ.

"To you who believe, He is precious." One who has walked with Christ for many years can look back and acknowledge with joy and thanksgiving that this is true. In times of tragedy when we so desperately needed strength, Jesus was precious; when sorrow seemed to overwhelm us and we needed comfort, Jesus was precious; when the roar of the devil drowned out everything else and we began to doubt, Jesus was precious as He quietly gave us the assurance we needed; when we were awed by the beauty of His creation, Jesus was precious as He listened to and accepted our adoration; when a loved one or a best friend died, Jesus was precious as He proved to be our dearest friend, and when He sought His wayward sheep and laid him on His shoulders rejoicing, oh, how precious was He then?

Three reasons (among many) why our Chief Cornerstone is precious:

Jesus is given by His Father as the Foundation upon which His church is being built: "Behold, I lay in Zion a stone for a foundation, a tried stone, a precious cornerstone, a sure foundation" (Isaiah 28:16). There is no other foundation, and no other is needed. He is the "Sure Foundation." For this reason He is precious.

Jesus is chosen by God: "rejected indeed by men, but chosen by God" (1 Peter 2:4). God did not choose an Archangel to be our Savior, He chose His only Son to be sin for us, that by His shed blood we might be reconciled to Himself, adopted as sons and daughters into the family of God, and given the assurance of everlasting life with Him. For this reason He is precious.

Jesus is the Cornerstone of our faith and of the "Spiritual House" He is building, the house in which He resides. This guarantees those "who believe" will enjoy for ever the presence of their Savior. There is no worry this building will collapse, for Jesus is the Architect, Builder, and Cornerstone of it. For this reason He is precious.

Puritan Quote:

"Jesus is precious, says the Word,
What comfort does this truth afford!
And those who in His name believe,
With joy this precious truth receive.

To them He is more precious far,
Than life and all its comforts are;
More precious than their daily food,
More precious than their vital blood.

Not health, nor wealth, nor sounding fame,
Nor earth's deceitful empty name,
With all its pomp and all its glare,
Can with a precious Christ compare.

In every office He sustains,
In every victory He gains,
In every council of His will,
He's precious to His people still.

As they draw near their journey's end,
How precious is their Heavenly Friend!
And, when in death they bow their head,
He's precious on a dying bed"
   James Smith, 1802-1862.

MASTER/SERVANT

Reading: 1 Corinthians 7:20-24
"He who is called while free is Christ's slave" 1 Corinthians 7:22.

"*A friend of God is high; a son of God is higher; but the servant, or, in the above sense, the slave of God is higher than all;—in a word, he is a person who feels he has no property in himself, and that God is all and in all*" (*Adam Clarke's Commentary*).

In today's world, the word 'slave' conjures up a negative concept of brutality, disdain, and worthlessness. The physical role of servility compared to that of freedom is, of course, not one usually chosen, but forced upon.

The Bible speaks of mankind apart from Christ, as being slaves to sin (Romans 6:6), and slaves to corruption (2 Peter 2:19). Sin was our master before our salvation. This was not a matter of choice; it was a matter of fact. All have sinned (Romans 3:23), therefore:

> *"Do you not know that to whom you present yourselves slaves to obey, you are that one's slaves whom you obey"* *Romans 6:16.*

There are two procedures whereby one can be released from servitude: 1) Manumission—an owner can grant his slave freedom, or 2) another person can pay the asking price and thereby purchase him or her—the slave remains a slave, but has a new owner.

Manumission requires a legal document signed by the slave owner and approved by a judge, while the transference of ownership requires a price to be paid. Those "called in the Lord" (1 Corinthians 7:22) are "bought at a price" (vs 23):

> *"You were not redeemed with corruptible things, like silver or gold, from your aimless conduct received by tradition from your fathers, but with the precious blood of Christ, as of a lamb without blemish and without spot"* *1 Peter 1:18-19.*

"The precious blood of Christ" was the price paid for our release from the power of sin. The price, however, was not paid to the master of sin, but to God who has therefore freed us from His anger, punishment, and condemnation. The song of the saints was to Him who was "slain, and have redeemed us to God by Your blood" (Revelation 5:9). We have been redeemed "to God" by the "precious blood of Christ."

Humanly speaking, to be a slave means that he/she is the property of another. He is owned and is classified as chattel, property, just as any other item such as oxen and household furniture.

To be purchased to God by the blood of Christ still means that we are not our own, but belong to God: We are His property, we belong to Almighty God. However, the born again Christian counts it an honor and privilege to have Jesus Christ as His Master.

Paul opened several of his letters with this acclamation: "Paul, a bondservant of Jesus Christ" (Romans 1:1; Galatians 1:10; Philippinas 1:1; Titus 1:1), also did James and Jude. Paul, who told the chief captain, "I was free-born" (Acts 22:28), now declares with honor "I am a servant of Jesus Christ."

Along with this honor comes a responsibility. Every master establishes rules and regulations for his household—God is no different. While we have liberty in Christ (Galatians 5:1, 13), we are exhorted not to use it as an excuse to sin:

> *"For this is the will of God, that by doing good you may put to silence the ignorance of foolish men—as free, yet not using liberty as a cloak for vice, but as Bondservants of God" 1 Peter 2:15-16.*

The doctrine that mistakenly says you can sin any way you wish because you can always pray for forgiveness and receive it, is dishonoring to God and offensive to His Holiness. The truly born again believer has a desire to please God and live in accordance with His will, not offend Him.

The Holy Spirit, who indwells every believer, will convict the child of God of sin. As the Christian grows in the knowledge and understanding of Jesus Christ, he will become more sensitive to those things that displease God, and will do everything he can to avoid them.

God had a message for His people through Malachi:

"'A son honors his father, and a servant his master. If then I am the Father, where is My honor? And if I am a Master, where is My reverence?' says the LORD of hosts" Malachi 1:6.

If we sin because we know God will forgive us, He asks, "If I am your Master, where is My reverence?" Some versions translate the word reverence as fear, and others respect. Our Master is not cruel, He does not mistreat us. The reverse is true, He is loving and kind, faithful to His promises, and can be trusted to have our best interest at heart. Why is it then that we would not serve Him with great reverence and respect? If we truly love Him, we will.

Puritan Quote:

"Jesus Christ is our Master and Lord; , , , He is our Master, didaskalos—our teacher and instructor in all necessary truths and rules, as a prophet revealing to us the will of God. He is our Lord, kyrios—our ruler and owner, that has authority over us and propriety in us" Matthew Henry's Commentary.

SHEPHERD/SHEEP

Reading: John 10:11-16
"I am the good shepherd" John 10:11

If ever there was a meaningful and comforting relationship between Jesus and His church, it is that of the Shepherd and His sheep. To him that has backslidden, Jesus is the Shepherd who seeks him out, rescues him, and carries him on His shoulders, rejoicing, as He returns him to the fold (Luke 15:4-6).

To him who is facing danger, Jesus goes to battle to protect His sheep, as did David when he slew the lions and bears that would kill his sheep:

"But David said to Saul, 'Your servant used to keep his father's sheep, and when a lion or a bear came and took a lamb out of the flock, I went out after it and struck it, and delivered the lamb from its mouth; and when it arose against me, I caught it by its beard, and struck and killed it'" 1 Samuel 17:34-35.

To him who is in need, the sheep can say with confidence, "The Lord is my Shepherd, I shall not want" Psalm 23:1.

To the one who is "dead in his trespasses and sins," Jesus offers him "life, and that . . . more abundantly" John 10:10.

Jesus' sheep are followers, disciples; they follow in His steps, joyously keeping His commandments, willing to follow Him, even if it means for the moment walking through the swamps of life:

"Yea, though I walk through the valley of the shadow of death, I will fear no evil; for You are with me; Your rod and Your staff, they comfort me" Psalm 23:4.

His sheep hear the voice of their Shepherd as He says, "This is the way, walk in it" Isaiah 30:21.

The sheep, belonging to Jesus, take comfort and strength in His promises, "I give them eternal life, and they shall never perish; neither shall anyone snatch them out of My hand" John 10:28.

At the end of the day, after feeding His flock, and protecting them from every "lion" that would endanger them, His sheep can testify:

"He makes me to lie down in green pastures; He leads me beside the still waters. He restores my soul; He leads me in the paths of righteousness for His name's sake" Psalm 23:2-3.

Yes, Jesus is the **Good Shepherd**, the Protector and Provider of His sheep.

Jesus is also the **Chief Shepherd**, the Leader of all whom He has selected as pastors to His flock. Those to whom He has given the gift of pastor, for the building up of His flock (Ephesians 4:11-12), are under-shepherds, appointed by Him to follow His example. The modern-day pastors that assign to themselves the title of "Head Pastor" are taking to themselves the title that belongs only to Jesus Christ, the "Chief Shepherd" of His sheep. Jesus is known as "the Shepherd and Overseer of your souls" (1 Peter 2:25), a title only He is qualified to carry. All others are equally sheep of His flock. Beware, pastors, that you do not seek to elevate your position in the flock of Christ to that which is rightfully His. Satan once tried to elevate himself to be equal with God.

Jesus is that "**Great Shepherd** of the sheep" (Hebrews 13:20), the One who gave His blood as the sacrifice to God for our sins. The word translated "great" is "*megas*," from which we derive our word "mega," a word that has become popular in describing churches with large congregations. This is the word chosen by the Holy Spirit to describe Jesus: He is the "Mega Shepherd" of His flock; a designation given only to Him, and none other.

Micaiah, the prophet, said "I saw all Israel scattered on the mountains, as sheep that have no shepherd" (1 Kings 22:17), but this can never be said of the church of Jesus Christ, for He is their Good Shepherd that protects, guides, and leads His sheep; He is their Chief Shepherd, who is unequalled in title, position, and ability, and from whom rewards will be received; and

He is their Great Shepherd, Mega in who He is, Mega in what He has and is yet to accomplish, and Mega in His mercy, grace and love for His sheep.

Puritan Quote:

"God, in the Scripture, frequently takes to himself the name, and puts on the character of a shepherd, and this is no mean token of his tender love towards us. As this is a lowly and homely manner of speaking, He who does not disdain to stoop so low for our sake, must bear a singularly strong affection towards us. It is therefore wonderful, that when he invites us to himself with such gentleness and familiarity, we are not drawn or allured to him, that we may rest in safety and peace under his guardianship" John Calvin, 1509-1564.

VINE/BRANCHES

Reading: John 15:1-8
"I am the vine, you are the branches" John 15:5

I am fortunate enough to live in orchard country. Everywhere I go there are orchards stretching out across the landscape—apples, pears, cherries, and grapes. The trees are known not only by the fruit they bear, but by the shape of the tree, the shape of the leaves, and the blossom.

There are however, branches that blend in with all the others—there is little difference in the way they look. However, when the fruit begins to develop, it is judged to be inferior, and cannot be mixed with the quality fruit.

As I read the parable in John 15:1-17, I am impressed that the key word is not "vine", "branches", or even "fruit", but "abide". The other words are vitally important, but are to no avail unless there is an abiding.

The word *'meno'* is used 120 times in the New Testament and is used to describe one who lives or dwells in a house (John 1:39—"dwelt" and "abode"). It is also translated as "continue" (2 Tim 3:14), and "remain" (Acts 27:41). In 1 John 1:24 it is translated by three different words:

"Let that therefore abide in you, which ye have heard from the beginning. If that which ye have heard from the beginning shall remain in you, ye also shall continue in the Son, and in the Father" *(KJV).*

Jesus speaks of a mutual abiding:

"Abide in Me, and I in you. As the branch cannot bear fruit of itself, unless it abides in the vine, neither can you, unless you abide in Me" *John 15:4*
"He who abides in Me, and I in him, bears much fruit; for without Me you can do nothing" John 15:5, see also vs 7.

The spiritual union between Jesus and His disciples is vital if they are to produce quality fruit. A branch cannot bear acceptable fruit unless it is securely a part of the tree. Every true believer, whether Jew or Gentile, is grafted into the Vine (Romans 11:16-24). The conclusion is that "without [Jesus] you can do nothing."

Another result of this mutual abiding is, "you will ask what you desire, and it shall be done for you" (John 15:7). Answered prayer is the privilege and expectation of the one that continues or remains in Christ. The truth, and the freedom it brings, is revealed to those who enjoy this mutual abiding (John 8:31-32).

Jesus used a different analogy when He said, "He who eats My flesh and drinks My blood abides in Me, and I in him" (John 6:56). He who eats the "Living Bread" (John 6:51) and drinks the "Water of Life" (Revelation 21:6), the "Living Water" (John 4:10-14), shall have "everlasting life."

Jesus uses His relationship with His Father as an example of abiding:

"As the Father loved Me, I also have loved you; abide in My love"
John 15:9.
"If you keep My commandments, you will abide in My love, just as I have kept My Father's commandments and abide in His love"
John 15:10.

Study these two things if you wish to understand what it means to have a mutual abiding with Jesus. Study how Jesus was loved by His Father, and how Jesus kept the will of His Father: "Nevertheless not My will, but Yours, be done" Luke 22:42.

The result of Non-abiding:

"Every branch in Me that does not bear fruit He takes away; and every branch that bears fruit He prunes, that it may bear more fruit" John 15:2.

It is not the fruit that is removed, but the branch. If it is a non-fruit-bearing branch, what was it doing in the vine in the first place? This parable is a direct teaching to the Jews who thought they were exclusively God's people. The gospel changed all that: "if you are Christ's, then you are Abraham's seed, and heirs according to the promise" (Galatians 3:29). Under the New Covenant God's people are known by their union with Jesus Christ—both Jew and Gentile. The unbelieving Jew is "cast out as a branch and is withered; and they gather them and throw them into the fire, and they are burned" (John 15:6), and the believing Gentile is grafted into the Vine and enjoys that mutual abiding with Jesus Christ.

Conclusion

"He who says he abides in Him ought himself also to walk just as He walked" 1 John 2:6.
"Whoever transgresses and does not abide in the doctrine of Christ does not have God. He who abides in the doctrine of Christ has both the Father and the Son" 2 John 9.
"But you, beloved, building yourselves up on your most holy faith, praying in the Holy Spirit, keep yourselves in the love of God, looking for the mercy of our Lord Jesus Christ unto eternal life" Jude 20-21.

Puritan Quote:
"'That my joy may abide in you.' By the word abide [Jesus] means, that it is not a fleeting or temporary joy of which he speaks, but a joy which never fails or passes away. Let us therefore learn that we ought to seek in the doctrine of Christ the assurance of salvation, which retains its vigor both in life and in death" John Calvin, 1509-1564.

BRIDEGROOM/BRIDE

Reading: Revelation 19:1-9
"As the bridegroom rejoices over the bride,
so shall your God rejoice over you" Isaiah 62:5

One of the most beautiful relationships between Jesus and His people is that of Bridegroom and Bride. There are few relationships that present such love and closeness: "Therefore a man shall leave his father and mother and be joined to his wife, and they shall become one flesh" Genesis 2:24.

When a Jewish man and woman fell in love, there were four characteristics of their marriage:

First, that of betrothal or espousal. The closest we have to this in our culture is engagement, although an engagement does not carry the same level of commitment. This was the relationship Joseph and Mary had when she became pregnant by the Holy Spirit (Matthew 1:18). Although not married, the man was referred to as the husband. It was a serious commitment which required a legal divorce if the couple wanted to separate. This is what is meant by Joseph wanting to "put her away privately" vs 19.

When we are saved by the grace of God, we are said to be espoused to Jesus Christ:

"I have betrothed you to one husband, that I may present you as a chaste virgin to Christ" 2 Corinthians 11:2.

When we are saved, a union takes place—we become one with Jesus—we are betrothed to Him.

Second, there is an interim period. This is when the man makes arrangements for his betrothed. He secures a home, furnishes it, and makes it ready for his bride.

This is what Jesus is engaged in presently:

"In My Father's house are many mansions; if it were not so, I would have told you. I go to prepare a place for you" John 14:2.

Jesus is preparing a place for His bride. But the Bible also tells us that the bride must prepare herself for Him. "It has not yet been revealed what we shall be, but we know that when He is revealed [comes for His bride], we shall be like Him, for we shall see Him as He is. And everyone who has this hope in Him purifies himself, just as He is pure" 1 John 3:2-3.

When speaking of the marriage supper, the Bible says, "His wife has made herself ready" (Revelation 19:7). This must be the focus of every one who professes to love Jesus Christ, to be as pure as possible, to cast aside and avoid everything that displeases Him:

"And to her it was granted to be arrayed in fine linen, clean and bright, for the fine linen is the righteous acts of the saints" Revelation 19:8.

The bride's dress is made of "fine linen, clean and bright," not just any linen cloth, but the very best. There is no stain or blemish of any kind, for it represents the righteousness of Jesus Himself, with which we have been clothed (Isaiah 61:10).

Third, the procession. When all the preparations are complete, the Bridegroom goes with his friends to get his bride, and escort her to the marriage feast:

"And if I go and prepare a place for you, I will come again and receive you to Myself; that where I am, there you may be also" John 14:3.

There are many scriptures that speak of Jesus coming with His "holy angels" and "with all His saints" Mark 8:38; 1 Thessalonians 3:13:

"When the Son of Man comes in His glory, and all the holy angels with Him, then He will sit on the throne of His glory" Matthew 25:31.

Fourth, there is the marriage feast. This is the culmination of the wedding functions. What a joyous occasion this will be:

"And I heard, as it were, the voice of a great multitude, as the sound of many waters and as the sound of mighty thunderings, saying, "Alleluia! For the Lord God Omnipotent reigns! Let us be glad and rejoice and give Him glory, for the marriage of the Lamb has come, and His wife has made herself ready" Revelation 19:6-7.

The rejoicing will sound like the roar of Niagara Falls, like the crashing of great thunder. "Hallelujah!" Praise the Lord! Our "Lord God Omnipotent" has taken His bride, and they will live together for ever.

Oh, what a Savior that He would enter into such a relationship with those He came to save. What a joy to be His bride. May He find us ready when He comes to accompany us to the wedding feast and to the place He has prepared for us.

Puritan Quote:

"O sirs, here is a cord of love let down, and the upper end of it is fastened to Christ's heart, and the lower end of it hanging down the length of your hearts. And, O! shall not Christ's heart and yours be knit together this day. Here is a cord to bind His heart to your heart, and your heart to His heart" Ralph Erskine, 1685-1752.

PROPHET/SCRIBE

Reading: Acts 3:11-26

"I will raise up for them a Prophet like you from among their brethren, and will put My words in His mouth, and He shall speak all that I command Him" Deuteronomy 18:18

Among the many titles applied to Jesus Christ, one that is seldom considered is that of "Prophet." Through Moses, God promised to raise up a Prophet for the Israelites, one through whom He would speak, one who would speak His words as He was commanded; implicit obedience to God—one who would neither add to them nor change them in any way.

This Prophet would be raised from among their number, not a foreigner who suddenly appeared on the scene from nowhere, but one raised in their culture, who spoke their language, and understood their hopes and expectations.

When Jesus rode into Jerusalem on the back of a donkey, the people sang His praises, and shouted, "This is Jesus, the prophet from Nazareth of Galilee" (Matthew 21:11). Whether they associated Him as the Prophet promised by God through Moses is debatable, yet they spoke the truth.

On the road to Emmaus, when Jesus asked what they were talking about, they answered, "The things concerning Jesus of Nazareth, who was a Prophet mighty in deed and word before God and all the people" Luke 24:19.

But Jesus was more than a Prophet, He is The Prophet, the fulfillment of God's promise. He was the last of the Old Testament Prophets:

"Do not think that I came to destroy the Law or the Prophets. I did not come to destroy but to fulfill" Matthew 5:17.

That of which the ceremonies spoke, and the sacrifices and offerings, the extensive Law under which Israel struggled, Jesus is the Great Fulfillment.

But what is a prophet without a scribe? The prophet was the spokesperson of the Word of God, but his scribe read the Law and wrote down the words of the prophet. The great example is the relationship between Jeremiah and his scribe, Baruch. Baruch is mentioned 24 times in the Book of Jeremiah, yet he remains in the shadow of the prophet. Jeremiah relied on him to a great extent, and it is a very worthwhile study to examine the passages where he is mentioned, and then apply his ministry to that which we, as the scribes of Jesus, are called to do.

But, you may ask, "How are we the scribes of Jesus?" An important scripture comes to mind, when David said:

"My tongue is the pen of a ready writer" Psalm 45:1.

Jesus placed great emphasis on speaking. The primary mission of His disciples was to preach the gospel, to "go into all the world and preach," use your tongue as a scribe uses his pen—write with words that God has laid on your heart. Was there a greater scribe than Paul? Everywhere he went he preached the gospel of Jesus Christ. When he was imprisoned he wrote to the churches and to those who he called "sons in the faith," Timothy was an example (1 Timothy 1:2, 18; 2 Timothy 1:2, 2:1) and Titus (Titus 1:4), and Onesimus (Philemon vs 10).

Look back in Christian history to Polycarp (A.D. 69-155), who was among those martyred because they refused to stop preaching the gospel, and the puritans who were burned at the stake, who would rather give their bodies as fuel to the flames than still their tongues of the love of Christ. Even today, in many countries, our brothers and sisters in Christ are dying or languishing in prisons because they are faithful to their commission to preach the gospel.

How much more should we, who live in countries where we can still preach, read and write about the love and grace of Jesus Christ, use our God-given talents to be a scribe to the greatest of all Prophets. We have tongues—let us use them as the "pen of a ready writer." We have eyes—let us read the Word of God regularly and saturate ourselves in the truths of God. We can write—let us not be afraid to share the gospel with those to whom we write. With the benefits of today's technology we can send an email in a second with no cost of postage (at the moment).

Not everyone has been given the gift of writing books and articles, but those who have, let us use that gift to the glory of God. Tens of thousands of books are published every year—let us utilize this means as best we can as faithful scribes of Jesus Christ.

May what is said of Ezra be said of us:

"This Ezra came up from Babylon; and he was a skilled scribe in the Law of Moses, which the LORD God of Israel had given" Ezra 7:6.

To be a skilled scribe in the Gospel of Jesus Christ, which the Lord God of heaven and earth has given, is high calling indeed.

Puritan Quote:

"I think it is not very difficult to discern by the duties and converses of Christians, what frames their spirits are under. Take a Christian in a good frame, and how serious, Heavenly, and profitable, will his converses and duties be! What a lovely companion is he during the continuance of it!" John Flavel, 1627-1691.

KING/SUBJECT

Reading: Luke 19:28-38
"Blessed is the King who comes in the name of the LORD!" Luke 19:38.

The great hope and expectation of the Jews was the coming of a great King, one who would deliver them for ever from the tyranny of other nations. For centuries they had lived under the oppression of empires that had treated them as second class citizens. Was this Jesus of Nazareth the One? He was known for casting demons out of the possessed, healing the blind, deaf and dumb, and teaching of personal freedom and victory over the enemy. Now, in our text, He showed His authority over the animal kingdom by riding an unbroken, untrained ass.

Everything pointed to Jesus as the Messiah, the Deliverer of the Jews. While it is true a conquering King would be expected to ride into his city on a large white stallion, not a donkey, the scene unfolding before them was prophesied in great detail by Zechariah:

"Rejoice greatly, O daughter of Zion! Shout, O daughter of Jerusalem! Behold, your King is coming to you; He is just and having salvation, Lowly and riding on a donkey, a colt, the foal of a donkey" Zechariah 9:9.

A few days after this, Jesus was ridiculed by the people by dressing Him up in royal robes, and giving Him a reed for a scepter, and weaving a crown of thorns and pressing it upon His head. The people accused Jesus of blasphemy for saying He was King of the Jews, and when Pilate asked Him, "Are you King of the Jews?" He answered, "It is as you say" Mark 15:2.

Even after all of this had transpired, and Jesus was crucified for saying He was the King of the Jews, His disciples still wondered if He was the one of whom it was prophesied, "The King of Israel, the LORD, is in your midst" Zephaniah 3:15.

Their Master had conquered death, and now stood before them in Jerusalem. He told them to "wait for the promise of the Father," which prompted them to ask, "Lord, will You at this time restore the kingdom to Israel?" Acts 1:6.

Today, in hindsight, we know that Jesus is not only the King of the Jews, but the "King of the saints" and the "King of kings" Revelation 15:3; 17:14; 19:16.

When Jesus returned victorious to His Father, He was given a kingdom:

"Then to Him was given dominion and glory and a kingdom, that all peoples, nations, and languages should serve Him. His dominion is an everlasting dominion, which shall not pass away, and His kingdom the one which shall not be destroyed" Daniel 7:14.

All who know Him as their Lord and Savior, also acknowledge Jesus as their King. They are His subjects, citizens of His everlasting kingdom. They willingly live under His authority, obey His laws, and bow in adoration to none other.

When writing to Timothy, Paul spoke of Jesus as:

"The blessed and only Potentate, the King of kings and Lord of lords, who alone has immortality, dwelling in unapproachable light, whom no man has seen or can see, to whom be honor and everlasting power" 1 Timothy 6:15-16.

The relationship we have with this "blessed and only Potentate" should be our motive to "pursue righteousness, godliness, faith, love, patience, gentleness" and to "fight the good fight of faith, lay[ing] hold on eternal life, to which you were also called" 1 Timothy 6:11-12.

As citizens of His kingdom and beneficiaries of all the benefits that entails, we have the responsibility to be faithful combatants in the face of His enemies. We ride into battle under His banner, identifying ourselves as His subjects.

We have the benefit of knowing our King is victorious and has never lost a battle. We ride knowing victory is assured. This knowledge spurs us on as we fight our individual battles. When our battles appear to be overwhelming, and we cry out, "Who will deliver me from this body of death?" the answer will always be, "I thank God—through Jesus Christ our Lord!" Romans 7:24-25.

Earthly potentates live in castles and palaces, and are separated from their subjects by large gates, high walls, and personal guards, but the King of kings invites His citizens to "come boldly to the throne of grace, that we may obtain mercy and find grace to help in time of need" Hebrews 4:16:

"Oh, clap your hands, all you peoples! Shout to God with the voice of triumph! For the LORD Most High is awesome; He is a great King over all the earth" Psalm 47:1-2.

Puritan Quote:

"The church celebrates the ascension of Christ, because then he was "highly exalted; "then he became terrible to his enemies, all power in heaven and earth being committed to him; and then he began to display the excellent majesty of his universal kingdom, to which he was then inaugurated, being crowned "King of kings, and Lord of lords" George Horne, 1730-1792.

HIGH PRIEST/PRIESTS

Reading: Acts 3:11-26
"We have a Great High Priest!" Hebrews 5:5.

These words are both a statement and an announcement, written to men and women who were Jews by nationality and Christians by faith. The High Priest, an office ordained by God, was vital to the spiritual welfare of His chosen people. He was the Head Priest in a "kingdom of priests" (Exodus 19:6), and was separated from them by his clothing, the duties he performed, and the specific requirements placed on him as the spiritual head of the people.

The writer of the Book of Hebrews made the High Priesthood of Jesus the central theme of his writing. As in all things prophetic and typified in the Old Testament, Jesus is set forth as the Christians High Priest. He is not simply our High Priest, but our "great High Priest" (Hebrews 4:14). The word translated "great" is "*megas*", a word (mega) that has been popularized in today's economy.

The Book of Hebrews presents Jesus in both a negative and positive way:

"Seeing then that we have a great High Priest who has passed through the heavens, Jesus the Son of God, let us hold fast our confession. For we do not have a High Priest who cannot sympathize with our weaknesses, but was in all points tempted as we are, yet without sin" Hebrews 4:14-15.

Our great High Priest has "passed through the heavens" and "is seated at the right hand of the throne of the Majesty in the heavens" (Hebrews 8:1)—something no other has accomplished. The reality of this should be our motivation to "hold fast our confession" or to "cling to him and never stop trusting him" (NLT).

Jesus was "appointed" by God, and was born a man, to fulfill the office of High Priest in His eternal kingdom:

> *"Therefore, in all things He had to be made like His brethren, that He might be a merciful and faithful High Priest in things pertaining to God, to make propitiation for the sins of the people" Hebrews 2:17.*

While separate from and distinct in His office from "His brethren," it is important that He had to be made like them in His nature. The bottom line is that Jesus became the Great High Priest for us. He is our Representative "in things pertaining to God."

To turn the "do not have" into a "we have" is to say that our High Priest can "sympathize with our weaknesses" because "in all points [He was] tempted as we are, yet without sin." How can we be encouraged by one who does not know what he is talking about?

A unique relationship exists between our Great High Priest and His people. Just as the nation of Israel was to be a "kingdom of priests" to God, so Christians are being "built up a spiritual house, a holy priesthood" to Him:

> *"To Him who loved us and washed us from our sins in His own blood, and has made us kings and priests to His God and Father, to Him be glory and dominion forever and ever. Amen" Revelation 1:5-6.*

As with every relationship with Jesus Christ there comes responsibility: We are to "offer up spiritual sacrifices acceptable to God through Jesus Christ" (1 Peter 2:5). Just as priests under the old covenant, Christians are to offer up sacrifices. There are, however, two qualifying aspects: 1) They are to be "spiritual" sacrifices and 2) They are to be "acceptable to God."

The blood of bulls. lambs, and goats, are no longer acceptable. They were a type of the sacrifice Jesus made on the cross. He is the fulfillment of them, and never again will they be required by God. Once a "type" has been fulfilled there is no further need for it.

What is a spiritual sacrifice? David wrote: "Sacrifice and offering You did not desire . . . Burnt offering and sin offering You did not require. Then I said, 'Behold, I come; In the scroll of the book it is written of me. I delight to do Your will, O my God, and Your law is within my heart" (Psalm 40:6-8). The bottom line is that *"when you do the will of God from your heart, when you studiously strive to find out what God's will is, and then conscientiously endeavor to attend to it, you are as priests offering spiritual sacrifices acceptable to God by Jesus Christ"* C.H. Spurgeon.

We are to present ourselves body, soul, and spirit, as a sacrifice to God (Romans 12:1-2); we are to "offer the sacrifice of praise continually . . . for with such sacrifices God is well pleased" (Hebrews 13:15-16); we are to separate ourselves from the world, and have our minds transformed by the work of the Holy Spirit—all these things are expressed in the words, "I delight to do Your will, O my God."

The priests of God are known by their holiness, by their walk with God, not by their flowing robes and white collars. God does not look on the outside, but on the inside.

Every born again person, no matter their station in life, is a priest unto God. They have been chosen and ordained by God as such, and it is our joy and honor to be known as "priests unto our God" Revelation 1:6.

Puritan Quote:

"It is only as we are seen in union with the apostle and high priest of our profession, that the Father allows us to serve him as priests, and accepts the sacrifices which we present" C.H. Spurgeon, 1834-1892.

LEADER/FOLLOWER

Reading: John 14:1-6
"As for me, being on the way, the LORD led me" Genesis 24:27

From time immemorial it has been important for travelers to know the proper way to their destination. We can ask directions from total strangers, consult a map, or, in modern days, we can use the GPS system. Sometimes we have a choice, but the important thing is that we arrive at our intended destination. Some ways are better than others—we may choose a certain way because of the scenery, or because the roads are better and we want to reach our destination as quickly as possible. We may have the choice as to how we get there; by car, train or plane.

As born-again believers our destination was changed when we were saved. Because we were born in sin, our destination was judgment at the Great White Throne of God, and from there—hell. Heaven is now our destination.

A popular concept today is that there are many ways to reach heaven. As long as we live a good moral life, helping others whenever we can, and attending church, temple, or synagogue, we will reach our intended destination safely. But Jesus disagrees with that. He said:

"I am the Way, the Truth, and the life. No one comes to the Father except through me" John 14:6.

In the 45th chapter of Isaiah God says, "I am God, and there is no other" (vss 5,6,14,18, 21,22).

Every believer is on a journey. Every day decisions have to be made—some easy and some difficult. The good news is that Jesus is not only The Way, but our Leader, and our Guide. He will guide us into making the correct decisions. David prayed, "Direct my steps by Your word" (Psalm 119:133). This prayer should be on our heart every morning, afternoon, and night.

Kings of old are remembered by the decisions they made. The memorial to Ahaz is that "he walked in the way of the kings of Israel" (2 Kings 16:3). This meant that "he did not do what was right in the sight of the LORD his God" (vs 2). This was a term of condemnation. Ahaz was compared to his father David in the words, "he did not do what was right in the sight of the LORD his God, as his father David had done."

In the Book of Hebrews Jesus is spoken of as "the Captain of their [our] salvation" (2:10). The word translated here as "Captain" is *"archegos"* which means "chief leader." It is used in only three other places where it is translated as "prince" (Acts 3:15 and 5:31) and "author" (Hebrews 12:2).

All four references speak of Jesus in a leading capacity. He is every believer's Leader: He is the Captain of our salvation, the Prince who protects His people, and the Author of our faith. He is the Compiler of the map of life, and knows every curve in the road, and how to traverse every valley and mountain. But He is more than that, He not only knows the way, He is the Way.

Nothing takes Him by surprise for He has traversed the road before us. He knows every temptation we face, and every obstacle in our way. He is our Shepherd, and, as His sheep, we must follow Him.

The very word "disciple" (*mathetes*) refers to one who follows, or more specifically a learner or pupil. When Jesus called His disciples He said, "Follow Me," not advise Me, show Me, or lead Me.

The proof we are disciples of Jesus is:

"If you abide in My word [hold fast to My teachings and live in accordance with them], you are truly My disciples" John 8:31, AMP;
And again:
"By this all will know that you are My disciples, if you have love for one another" John 13:35;
And again:
"By this My Father is glorified, that you bear much fruit; so you will be My disciples" John 15:8.

True followers of Jesus will be known by the life they live. Unlike many of the kings, it will be said of them, "They walked in the way of the King of Kings."

Early Christians were spoken of as "People of The Way" (Acts 9:2; 19:9,23; 22:4; 24:14,22). Before his conversion, Saul's mission was to persecute those "who were of the Way" (Acts 9:2). It was not so much their verbal testimony, but the manner in which they lived. Jesus said:

"Let your light so shine before men, that they may see your good works and glorify your Father in heaven" (Matthew 5:16).

This was how Saul identified the disciples of Jesus—by the way they lived. This is the challenge to every Christian, "How are we identified as followers of Jesus Christ?" Is it because we attend church regularly? Is it because we talk the talk, or is it because we walk the walk?

"The way of the LORD is strength for the upright" Proverbs 10:29.

"Behold, I set before you the way of life and the way of death" (Jeremiah 21:8). May we always seek the face of God to seek strength from His promise: "I will instruct you and teach you in the way you should go; I will guide you with My eye" Psalm 32:8.

Puritan Quote:

"Consider how weak you are in yourselves, and how great a need to watch, lest you disobey your Heavenly pilot before you are even aware of it. It is a lazy heart that would loiter when it should follow" Richard Baxter, 1615-1691.

PATTERN/DESIGN

Reading: Philippians 3:17:21
"... the Lord Jesus Christ, who will transform our lowly body that it may
be conformed to His glorious body" Philippians 3:20-21

I was very fortunate as a child to have my Grandmother and aunt living in
the house next to where I was raised. When my aunt was three years old
she suffered from Polio, and her left leg shrank so her foot hung level to her
right knee. She had to use crutches for the rest of her life. She made a living
as a seamstress, and I remember going to her room and seeing several bolts
of fabric stored on a shelf. I used to watch as she went to work with a pair
of scissors, cutting out various shapes from a pattern. With those pieces
of fabric she sewed a beautiful dress for a customer. I remember when she
made the wedding dress for a Duchess and dresses for her bridesmaids.

When a person is born-again, they are made a new creation by the
Spirit of God, "old things have passed away; behold, all things have become
new" 2 Corinthians 5:17. Then begins a process we call sanctification:

*"But we all, with unveiled face, beholding as in a mirror the glory of
the Lord, are being transformed into the same image from glory to
glory, just as by the Spirit of the Lord" 2 Corinthians 3:18.*

Every one who has a personal relationship with Jesus Christ is being
transformed into the same image—the image of their Savior. Jesus is the
Pattern and the Holy Spirit is the "Dressmaker."

Not only is our heart being changed, but our bodies will be also:

*"... Jesus Christ, who will transform our lowly body that it may be
conformed to His glorious body" Philippians 3:20-21.*

No matter what our body is like at the present time, God's promise is
that one day it will be changed.

259

"It refers to the body as it is in its present state, as subject to infirmities, disease, and death. It is different far from what it was when man was created, and from what it will be in the future world. Paul says that it is one of the objects of the Christian hope and expectation, that this body, so subject to infirmities and sicknesses, will be changed" (from Barnes' Notes).

Jesus is our "Forerunner" with His resurrection body, the one that ascended into heaven and today represents us at His Father's right hand. When Jesus returns for His people, we shall be changed into His likeness. His glorious body is the pattern to which ours is likened:

"Beloved, now we are children of God; and it has not yet been revealed what we shall be, but we know that when He is revealed, we shall be like Him, for we shall see Him as He is" 1 John 3:2.

"I take it that, while it will consist in our sharing in the Redeemer's power, the Redeemer's joy, and the Redeemer's honour, yet, from the connection of the text, it lies mainly in our being spiritually and morally like him, being purified, even as he is pure" C.H. Spurgeon.

We have been changed, for we have been made "new creatures" in Jesus Christ; we are being changed into His likeness, as the Holy Spirit removes that which is ungodly in our life into that which reflects His godliness, and our bodies will be changed from that which is currently subject to weakness, disease, and death, into that which is like that of our Savior's resurrected body, where it will be free of all the effects of sin, including pain, suffering, sorrow, and death:

"Behold, the tabernacle of God is with men, and He will dwell with them, and they shall be His people. God Himself will be with them and be their God. And God will wipe away every tear from their eyes; there shall be no more death, nor sorrow, nor crying. There shall be no more pain, for the former things have passed away" Revelation 21:3-4.

This hope and expectation we as Christians enjoy, should be our motivation and desire to live everyday as much like Jesus as possible: "And everyone who has this hope in Him purifies himself, just as He is pure" 1 John 3:3.

Paul wrote:

"Therefore [because we are being transformed], . . . we do not lose heart. But we have renounced the hidden things of shame, not walking in craftiness nor handling the word of God deceitfully, but by manifestation of the truth commending ourselves to every man's conscience in the sight of God" 2 Corinthians 4:1-2 (parenthesis added).

If, as children of God, we want to know what the future holds, we need only to look at Jesus, for He is the Pattern into which our final design is framed.

Puritan Quote:

"We expect to be like Christ, the Beloved of God, because we also are beloved of God. It is according to the nature and purpose of the love of God to make its object like God. We therefore expect that divine love will work with divine light and divine purity and make us into light and purity too . . . There our hope begins, and there our hope ends. Thou, O Christ, art all our confidence! We know of none beside. This, then, is the believer's hope; a hope to be made like Christ, a hope based upon Christ" C.H. Spurgeon, 1834-1892.

PRIEST/CONFESSOR

Reading: 1 John 1:1-10
"If we confess our sins, He is faithful and just to forgive us our sins and to cleanse us from all unrighteousness" 1 John 1:9.

While, in the strictest sense, God is not presented here as a Priest who hears the confessions of His people, it is implied. For many centuries, much of Christendom has incorrectly taught and practiced that, in order to be forgiven, Christians must confess their sins to a priest. Within protestant ranks, a confessor is one who confesses their sins to God, not one who hears and forgives sins—our "Father Confessor" is God, not a priest who himself needs forgiveness of his sins.

To be able to confess our sins to God is one of the most blessed of mercies the believer has received from the hand of God. To know that God, the One who sees all and knows all, hears every sincere confession of His children, and forgives them, is priceless beyond measure.

We have a Priest who is "Faithful and True" (Revelation 3:14), One who can be trusted to do that which is right. He is "just," which means He will do that which He has promised. Never can He be accused of changing His mind, or going back on His promises.

Along with God's promises is His ability to keep them. When God promised Abraham the impossible:

> *"He did not waver at the promise of God through unbelief, but was strengthened in faith, giving glory to God, and being fully convinced that what He had promised He was also able to perform" Romans 4:20-21.*

What confidence and encouragement can we have if it is a sinful man that forgives us our sins? When a sinner is told to pay penance for his sin, it is an affront to the mercy and grace of God. Jesus suffered and died for our sins—is that not sufficient?

When we sin, the door to forgiveness and cleansing is wide open. Jesus said, "I am the Door" (John 10:7-9), and "I am the Way" (John 14:6), and this is appropriate when it comes to our forgiveness and cleansing.

It is true that when we are born-again, we are fully and completely justified in God's eyes. Jesus paid the price in full to satisfy the justice of God against sin. This, however, does not give a believer liberty to continue in sin.

A person's life, including his attitude toward God and sin, is changed when he is saved. As we grow in Christ Jesus, we become more sensitive to that which displeases God—and sin displeases God. A Christian will sin, for we have an enemy who "walks about like a roaring lion, seeking whom he may devour" (1 Peter 5:8), and who is relentless in his pursuit:

"If we say that we have no sin, we deceive ourselves, and the truth is not in us . . . If we say that we have not sinned, we make Him a liar, and His word is not in us" 1 John 1:8-10.

Confession is the means by which we can walk with a clear conscience with God. The Christian wants nothing to stand between God and himself. Sin interferes with our prayer life, our walk with God, and our testimony before others. Sin is like a splinter in our eye:

"Why do you stare from without at the very small particle that is in your brother's eye but do not become aware of and consider the beam of timber that is in your own eye? Or how can you say to your brother, Let me get the tiny particle out of your eye, when there is the beam of timber in your own eye? You hypocrite, first get the beam of timber out of your own eye, and then you will see clearly to take the tiny particle out of your brother's eye" Matthew 7:3-5, AMP.

When we confess our sin, there is an implied agreement that we will forsake, or work toward not committing that sin again. "Work" is not a dirty word for a Christian. We are told to "work out your own salvation with fear and trembling; for it is God who works in you both to will and to do for His good pleasure" Philippians 2:12-13.

The two operative words in our text are "forgive" and "cleanse." *"Forgiveness is absolution from sin's punishment, and cleansing is absolution from sin's pollution" Wycliffe Bible Commentary.*

The faithfulness of God must never be questioned, however, for it to be experienced in the context of forgiveness and cleansing, it requires our acknowledgement and penitence. An unrepentant believer will experience God's faithfulness, however, it will be in the form of discipline—still within the expression of God's love (Hebrews 12:6):

"I acknowledged my sin to You, and my iniquity I have not hidden. I said, 'I will confess my transgressions to the LORD,' and You forgave the iniquity of my sin" Psalm 32:5

Puritan Quote:

"It is the birthright of every child of God to be cleansed from all sin, to keep himself unspotted from the world, and so to live as never more to offend his Maker. All things are possible to him that believeth; because all things are possible to the infinitely meritorious blood and energetic Spirit of the Lord Jesus" Adam Clarke (1760-1832).

POTTER/CLAY

Reading: Isaiah 64:1-8
"We are the clay, and You our potter" Isaiah 64:8

The analogy of the potter and clay to describe this particular relationship between God and His people is found in both testaments. Both Isaiah and Jeremiah use it to describe the relationship between God and His special people Israel.

Israel (the ten Northern tribes) had rejected God and was about to face His judgment for their persistent sin (Isaiah 64), and 150 years later, Judah followed (Jeremiah 18). Israel was to be scattered throughout the world, never to be reunited as a nation, whereas Judah's judgment came in five ways—the sword, famine, wild beasts, pestilence, and captivity (Ezekiel 14:21-22).

The conclusion in both cases was that God does with His people what the potter does with the clay. If ever an analogy speaks of the sovereignty of God it is this:

"Then the word of the LORD came to me, saying: 'O house of Israel, can I not do with you as this potter?' says the LORD. 'Look, as the clay is in the potter's hand, so are you in My hand, O house of Israel'" Jeremiah 18:5-6.

This is a stark reminder that God is supreme, and His counsel and decisions are final.

"The mystery of God's providence is a most sublime consideration. It is easy to let our reason run away with itself. It is at a loss when it attempts to search into the eternal decrees of election or the entangled mazes and labyrinths in which the divine providence walks" Ezekiel Hopkins, 1634-1690.

One of man's greatest fallacies is when he tries, at all costs, to search into the unsearchable in order to know the unknowable:

"Oh, the depth of the riches both of the wisdom and knowledge of God! How unsearchable are His judgments and His ways past finding out! For who has known the mind of the LORD? Or who has become His counselor? Or who has first given to Him and it shall be repaid to him? For of Him and through Him and to Him are all things, to whom be glory forever. Amen" Romans 11:33-36.

Recently, I heard a woman who had lost her teenage son to the recklessness of a drunk driver, say, "So much of God is a mystery, and we must learn to live within that mystery." She had been asked, "Do you ever ask God "Why?" "Oh yes," she replied, "but God has given me great peace in this tragedy."

Our incessant pursuit of delving into the mysteries of God has divided the church into countless sects and denominations, and brought about rifts among those who are commanded to "love one another."

The sovereignty of God is much maligned among Christians because we are unwilling to bow down before Him and accept without question His will and providence. "Thy will be done" is frequently repeated when we say the Lord's Prayer, but when the rubber meets the road, how many of us really mean it?

Paul asked the all important question when he wrote:

"O man, who are you to reply against God? Will the thing formed say to him who formed it, 'Why have you made me like this?' Does not the potter have power over the clay, from the same lump to make one vessel for honor and another for dishonor?" Romans 9:20-21.

Thomas Watson wrote: "*God always knows what is best for us, and how to best comfort us. He keeps His medicine handy for our fainting (2 Cor 7:6). He knows when affliction is best, and when it is best to give a bitter potion (1 Peter 1:6). The Father knows when to make evil things work for good to His children (Rom 8:28), and He can make a sovereign antidote for poison.*"

Do we trust God sufficiently to accept our condition or position in this life as that which He deems best for us? It is easy to look at someone else and say, "if only . . . ." If we are honest, we may know why our health is the way it is, or why brother Jim has more money in the bank, or sister Suzy lives in a nicer home.

God knows our heart better than we know it ourselves. We should accept our trials and afflictions in the light of God's sovereignty, and in the light of what He has acquired and guaranteed for our eternity. It is not always easy. May God answer our prayer as we pray, "Lord, increase my faith."

Puritan Quote:

"*Even to discuss the authority of Almighty God seems a bit meaningless, and to question it would be absurd. Can we imagine the Lord God of Hosts having to request permission of anyone or to apply for anything to a higher power? To whom would God go for permission? Who is higher than the Highest? Who is mightier than the Almighty? Whose position antedates that of the Eternal? At whose throne would God kneel? Where is the greater one to whom He must appeal?*" A.W. Tozer, 1897-1963.

CONQUEROR/CONQUERORS

Reading: John 16:25-33
"In the world you will have tribulation; but be of good cheer, I have
overcome the world" John 16:33.

Of the many accomplishments of Jesus for which we admire and praise
Him, it is that He has "overcome the world." Included in His conquest
is His victory over Satan, for Jesus called him the "ruler of this world (John
12:31; 14:30; 16:11). Before we were saved the devil was our father, and we
were under his control (John 8:44).

The word translated "overcome" is *'nikao'* which means to subdue, as in
to conquer, prevail, and get the victory. Jesus said, "Be of good cheer, I have
conquered the world," (which includes the devil)—everything that stands
in opposition to God and the gospel has been conquered. Yes, there is still
much rebellion in the world, as there is when any kingdom is conquered.
Nevertheless, the fatal blow has been struck, and skirmishes are constantly
being won, until finally, the day when the King of kings, the mighty
Conqueror, will enjoy complete and total dominance.

If we are Christ's, we are a conquered people. We, who were once at
enmity against Him, are now subjects of His kingdom:

*"And I looked, and behold, a white horse. He who sat on it had a
bow; and a crown was given to him, and he went out conquering and
to conquer" Revelation 6:2.*

We, as loyal subjects of Christ's kingdom, are daily faced with opposition.
Paul confidently declares:

*"Who shall separate us from the love of Christ? Shall tribulation,
or distress, or persecution, or famine, or nakedness, or peril, or
sword? . . . Yet in all these things we are more than conquerors
through Him who loved us. For I am persuaded that neither death*

nor life, nor angels nor principalities nor powers, nor things present nor things to come, nor height nor depth, nor any other created thing, shall be able to separate us from the love of God which is in Christ Jesus our Lord" Romans 8:35-39.

We are counted as one in Christ; we are all sons of God, made one with Him. His victory is our victory. When Jesus conquered the world, the flesh, and the devil, He did so for every member of His kingdom. In Him we are "more than conquerors."

We face battles every day, and we all know what it is like to be defeated. The important thing is that we learn from these defeats. It is when we try to defeat the enemy in our own strength—that is when we fail.

Jesus said, "without Me you can do nothing" (John 15:5): this is a lesson we all need to learn. Paul did: "I can do all things through Christ who strengthens me" (Philippians 4:13). His exhortation to the Ephesian Christians was: "Be strong in the Lord and in the power of His might" (Ephesians 6:10). The power of God is the fuel we need in order to be victorious. This is the same power that raised Jesus from the dead (Ephesians 1:19-20); and that created the heavens and earth.

One of the first demonstrations of God's power was when He said, "'Let there be light,' and there was light" (Genesis 1:3). God's power has not changed or deteriorated over the centuries; it this very same power that is available to us in our daily confrontation with sin and temptation. When we fail to utilize God's power, it is like pushing our car when it runs out of gasoline, and there is a can of gas in the trunk.

When Jesus promised wonderful things to the churches, He did so to those "who overcome" (Revelation 2:2,7,11,17,26; 3:5,12,21). This is the same word (*nikao*) that is translated "conquers."

As strong as our opposition is, there is no reason why we should live in constant defeat. Using the strength and power of God is a learning process. Paul speaks of the "excellence of the power" of God, and says:

"But we have this treasure in earthen vessels, that the excellence of the power may be of God and not of us. We are hard-pressed on every side, yet not crushed; we are perplexed, but not in despair;

persecuted, but not forsaken; struck down, but not destroyed" 2
Corinthians 4:7-9.

Defeat is not in the temptation or trial, but in how we confront it.

When Moses addressed the Israelites, he warned them of the enemies
they would confront. The promise he gave them is applicable to us today:

*"When the LORD your God delivers them over to you, you shall
conquer them and utterly destroy them"* Deuteronomy 7:2.

The condition, however, was that they "love Him and keep His
commandments" (vs 9). Failure is assured if we walk according to our own
ways and not according to His commands. Our own strength is inadequate,
but God's is always victorious:

"Now thanks be to God who always leads us in triumph in Christ"
2 Corinthians 2:14.

Puritan Quote:

*"Our great Pattern hath showed us what our deportment ought to be in all
suggestions and temptations. When the devil showed Him "all the kingdoms of
the world and the glory of them," He did not stand and look upon them, viewing
their glory, and pondering their empire . . . . but instantly, without stay, He cries,
"Get thee hence, Satan." Meet thy temptation in its entrance with thoughts of
faith concerning Christ on the cross; this will make it sink before thee. Entertain
no parley, no dispute with it, if thou wouldst not enter into it" John Owen,
1616-1683.*

WISDOM IN PRAYER

Reading: Psalm 119:65-72
"Teach me good judgment and knowledge, for I believe Your commandments" Psalm 119:66

It seems to me, that one of the most important and difficult things for a believer to learn, is how to pray. The very fact that Satan seeks to interrupt and interfere when we seek to draw near to God, indicates that prayer is very important in our spiritual growth and walk with our Heavenly Father. How often, when we pray, does our mind wander into paths of little consequence, or our eyes become heavy and we find ourselves drifting into sleep?

When we do pray, how flippantly we often approach the throne of grace. We ask God to give us this and that, wondering, without any confidence, whether or not He will grant us that for which we are asking.

In this section of Psalm 119, the Holy Spirit, through His servant David, grants us insight on how to pray:

"You have dealt well with Your servant, O Lord, according to Your word" vs 65.

In other words, we should remind God of the many ways He has blessed us in the past. Of course, God does not need reminding, but in so doing, we ourselves remember the many benefits we have received from His hand—our salvation, our protection, those occasions when the Spirit of God has opened up His Word to us in a very wonderful way, etc. In my personal experience I frequently remember in great detail when my Heavenly Father restored me to Himself, and welcomed me back into His arms. Instead of reprimanding me for twenty-three years of anger and resentment against Him, He threw His arms around me, and kissed me, as portrayed in the parable of the Prodigal Son. I also remember when it was time to pay our property taxes and we did not have the money, and a check arrived in the mail for the exact amount from a totally unexpected source.

Remembering God's blessings to us will give us confidence that He will continue to bless us. Such memories will enforce our trust in Him that He will always do that which is for the good of His children.

"*O Lord, thou hast dealt graciously with thy servant.*" David does not imply that his past blessings brings to a close the benefits he will receive from God, rather that God is unchangeable and will continue to deal with him favorably, but only in accordance with His will—His judgments and commandments as revealed in His Word. God's grace is never lessened, but He will always increase it.

Remembering such occurrences fills my heart with praise and thanksgiving—is there any better way to approach the Throne of Grace than with a rejoicing heart?

The next verse contains a very important, yet often neglected, part of prayer:

> *"Teach me good judgment and knowledge, for I believe Your commandments" vs 66.*

The previous verse ends with the words, "according to Your word." God never deals with His children outside the promises and regulations of His Word. It is, therefore, extremely important that we have an understanding of what those regulations are. If, in our prayer, we ask God to grant us that which violates His Law or Word, we cannot expect Him to grant it:

> *"Now this is the confidence that we have in Him, that if we ask anything according to His will, He hears us. And if we know that He hears us, whatever we ask, we know that we have the petitions that we have asked of Him" 1 John 5:14-15.*

> *"Whatever you ask in My name, that I will do, that the Father may be glorified in the Son. If you ask anything in My name, I will do it" John 14:13-14.*

Jesus did not promise to give us anything just because we asked for it—he laid down conditions, so it is imperative that we know what those conditions are. The only way to learn what is "according to His will" is to read and study the document where His will is explicitly laid out. Time spent in His Word is never wasted.

God's Word is a well that can never be drawn dry:

"The law of Your mouth is better to me than thousands of coins of gold and silver" Psalm 119:72.

Puritan Quote:

"For David demandeth of God none other thing but to know the contents of the law, and the doctrine thereof, that he might be ruled thereby, and his whole life framed thereafter" John Calvin, 1509-1564.

"IN THIS MANNER"

Reading: Matthew 6:5-15
"In this manner, therefore pray" Matthew 6:9

In these marvelous words, Jesus introduced something new—something that would change forever the way God's people considered their relationship with Him. This prayer is sometimes called the Lord's Prayer, or the Disciple's Prayer, or the Perfect Prayer, while actually it is none of these. It is more a pattern than a prayer—a pattern as to how we should pray.

It is common among many professing Christians to repeat these words, and, in so doing, feel they have satisfied their need for prayer. I was raised in a church where "The Lord's Prayer" was dutifully repeated in parrot-like fashion in every service. Sometimes, the pastor would say it for us in a machine-gun-fashion: it sounded like he wanted to get it over with as quickly as possible.

In considering this "prayer," we must first take note that Jesus taught it to His disciples, not to the general populous, as in the Sermon on the Mount. "It is a prayer adapted only to those who are the possessors of grace, and are truly converted" C.H. Spurgeon. When Jesus spoke to the ungodly, He said, "You are of your father the devil, and the desires of your father you want to do" (John 8:44). Here, Jesus said, "In this manner, therefore, pray: Our Father in heaven."

> "A son honors his father, and a servant his master. If then I am the Father, where is My honor? And if I am a Master, where is My reverence? says the LORD of hosts" Malachi 1:6.

There is no honor in one who says, "Our Father" on Sunday mornings, then uses His name as a curse for the rest of the week. An unbeliever can call God many things, such as Creator and Judge, but never can he rightfully call Him "Father."

When Jesus spoke of God as "Our Father," it must have stirred something special in the hearts of His disciples. Until then, even God referred to Himself as "the Father" (Malachi 1:6). The gospel changed the relationship of God with His people from that of a Father to a nation, to a personal one, whereby we can now call on Him as "Abba, Father."

Yet another amazing revelation is that Jesus referred to God as "Our Father." While He had a special relationship with God as the "only begotten Son" (John 3:16), He now embraces His disciples as brothers, and He becomes known as the "first begotten" (Revelation 1:5). Every born-again Christian has been adopted into God's family, therefore we can call Him "Father."

"As God prescribed Moses a pattern of the tabernacle (Exodus 25:9), so Christ has here prescribed a pattern of prayer" Thomas Watson.

Jesus did not say, "In these words, therefore, pray" but "In this manner, therefore, pray." Our prayers and petitions should be consistent with the pattern presented by Jesus—all the way from acknowledging Him as to who He is, to crying out for forgiveness for our constant weaknesses and failures.

This prayer pattern includes six petitions: the first three relate to the glory of God, and the remaining three to that which relates to our salvation.

Once we recognize the amazing reality that we are sons of God, and own the joy and privilege of calling Him "Father," we must acknowledge His greatness, and His attributes, and honor His name, for that is the meaning of 'hallowed'; 'hagiazo' to make holy, i.e. (ceremonially) purify or consecrate; (mentally) to venerate. This word is used 29 times in the New Testament, and in all but three occasions is translated "sanctify."

"Inasmuch as there is none like You, O LORD (You are great, and Your name is great in might)" Jeremiah 10:6.

The words of Jesus assume that God's children pray. He said, "When you pray (Matthew 6:5), not "if you pray." Prayer is not automatically an easy practice for many Christians, which is why it is so easy to rely on the repetition of written prayers. When a child of God enters into prayer, the devil goes to work: he has distraction down to an art—the phone rings, UPS delivers a package, children need your attention, and, his greatest distraction of all—wandering thoughts.

The advice of Jesus concerning prayer contains three things:

1) Go into a private room
2) Do not use vain repetitions
3) In this manner, pray.

The promise of Jesus is: "Your Father who sees in secret will reward you openly." In these words we can be assured that our Father hears us and answers accordingly. The fact He will do it "openly" is secondary to the reality that He hears and answers, and is in comparison to the hypocrites who love to be seen praying, and whose reward is the admiration of those who see them.

Puritan Quote:

"It was not the intention of the Son of God, (as we have already said), to prescribe the words which we must use, so as not to leave us at liberty to depart from the form which he has dictated. His intention rather was, to guide and restrain our wishes, that they might not go beyond those limits and hence we infer, that the rule which he has given us for praying aright relates not to the words, but to the things themselves" John Calvin, 1509-1564.

"OUR FATHER"

Reading: Matthew 6:5-15
"Our Father in heaven" Matthew 6:9

What a wonderful thought the word "our" is here—wonderful and important. For Jesus to include His disciples as sons along with Himself is one of the most gracious thoughts in Christianity.

The Father of Jesus is our Father. He is your Father and my Father. Amazing grace. He is our Father by the new birth and by our adoption into His family. Throughout His ministry, Jesus refers to "My Father" and "His Father," but here it is "Our Father." We stand in union with Him—one with Him. What a blessed relationship.

When His disciples asked Jesus to teach them how to pray (Luke 11:1), He directed their thoughts first to His Father. This tells us that God must be the focus of our prayers.

Does this mean that we should not address our prayers to Jesus or the Holy Spirit? We must always remember that the Son of God and the Spirit of God subsist in one Godhead. They are God and cannot be separated by personalities. While each are subscribed different works they cannot be separated—they are one in nature. When we address the Father, we address the Son and Holy Spirit, therefore when we address the Son we address the Father and the Holy Spirit. The Father is not offended (to use a human term) if we address the Son . . . .

"The Father is mentioned because He is first in order; but the Son and Holy Ghost are included because they are the same in essence . . . though we name but one person, we must pray to all" Thomas Watson, 1620-1686.

Try as we might, the concept of the Trinity remains a mystery and transcends human comprehension.

The order of our prayer must begin by focusing on God. How often we begin by telling Him what we need. When we do this we are making ourselves the focus, not God.

Before our petitions are mentioned, Jesus shows us that His Father's name must be hallowed, or honored. Then He broadens the concept of God to speak of His kingdom. Our Father is a King also, for every kingdom by definition must have a king. Within this kingdom our Father rules, for the prayer is for "Your will to [be] done on earth as it is in heaven."

We honor our Father by reverencing His name. This is done when we strive to please Him in everything we do. When Joseph's wife sought to seduce him, he said:

"How then can I do this great wickedness, and sin against God?" Genesis 39:9.

"We show our honor to our Heavenly Father by doing all we can to exalt Him, and make His excellencies shine forth. Though we cannot lift Him up higher in heaven, yet we may lift Him up higher in our hearts" Thomas Watson.

The entire prayer depends upon the first two words. If God is not our Father, then the rest of the prayer is irrelevant. In fact, if He is not our Father, our entire faith and all the benefits of it, mean nothing.

Because God is our Father all the promises of scripture are ours. He has made us "heirs of promise" (Hebrews 6:17), whereas the ungodly are by default heirs of curses. Every person falls into one of these two categories, but those who have been adopted into God's family are recipients of His riches:

"If children, then heirs—heirs of God and joint heirs with Christ" Romans 8:17.

The Bible is filled with God's promises to His children. Included is the promise of pardon (Jeremiah 33:8); the promise of healing (Isaiah 57:19); the promise of salvation (Jeremiah 23:6), and the promise of His presence (1 Samuel 12:22; Hebrews 13:15).

John Chrysostom (349-407 A.D) compared God's promises to fruit trees in a garden (the scriptures). A child of God may go to any promise in the Bible, and pluck comfort and strength from it—he is an heir of the promise:

"Let my beloved come to his garden and eat its pleasant fruits" **Song of Solomon 4:16.**

The benefits of having God as our Father are innumerable, the greatest of all is that we are His children, therefore we can "come boldly to the throne of grace, that we may obtain mercy and find grace to help in time of need" Hebrews 4:16.

Puritan Quote:

"'Father!' It is the language of the believing heart. As the adoption of His people is the highest act of God's grace, so the filial response of His children to that adoption is the highest act of our faith. Could faith on its strongest pinion soar higher than the Fatherhood of God? Oh, it is a marvelous fact, a stupendous truth, that God should be our Father! Higher than this the soul cannot rise" Octavius Winslow, 1808-1878.

"HALLOWED BE YOUR NAME"

Reading: Matthew 6:5-15
"Hallowed be Your name" Matthew 6:9

In these days when the name of God is blasphemed without thought or concern, these words of Jesus at the beginning of His prayer carry great import.

The first of seven petitions in this prayer is for God's name to be hallowed. The word 'hagiazo' occurs 29 times in the New Testament, and all but twice is translated "sanctify(ied).

"Our Father who is in heaven, let Your name be venerated" Wuest's Expanded Translation. The NLT translates it as, "May your name be honored." The Septuagint says, "Sanctified be thy name."

The placement of this petition shows us that the honoring of God's name must come before all other things. We pray for our daily necessities to be provided—"Give us this day our daily bread"—but not before we honor the name of the Provider. How readily we neglect God's holy name, and begin our prayers with "Give us."

The hallowing of God's name was not a new concept to the disciples. Jesus reminded them of God's words to Moses:

"You shall not profane My holy name, but I will be hallowed among the children of Israel" Leviticus 22:32.

"As the vessels of the sanctuary were said to be hallowed, so, to hallow God's name, is to set it apart from all abuses, and to use it holily and reverently. In particular, hallowing God's name is to give Him honor and veneration, and render His name sacred" Thomas Watson.

To honor the name of God means to give to the Lord the glory due to His name. When David brought the Ark of the Covenant to Jerusalem, he unabashedly sang and danced before God and the people: "Give to the

LORD the glory due His name," he sang. In his heart and by his actions, he was honoring the name of God.

How do we hallow God's name? David continues in his song to show us:

"Bring an offering, and come before Him. Oh, worship the LORD in the beauty of holiness! Tremble before Him, all the earth" **1 Chronicles 16:29-30.**

Here are four ways of honoring the name of God: 1) Bring an offering, 2) Come before Him, 3) Worship the Lord, 4) Tremble before Him.

God no longer requires the offerings of bulls and sheep, but rather that of ourselves:

"I beseech you therefore, brethren, by the mercies of God, that you present your bodies a living sacrifice, holy, acceptable to God, which is your reasonable service. And do not be conformed to this world, but be transformed by the renewing of your mind, that you may prove what is that good and acceptable and perfect will of God" **Romans 12:1-2.**

We hallow God's name when we separate ourselves from the world both physically and mentally. Where do our desires lay? Whenever we choose God over the world, we honor His name. Every act of obedience to God's commandments hallows His name. Honor, respect, reverence, venerate, are all words to describe the hallowing of God's name.

When Ezekiel and John fell on their faces in awe and worship, they honored the name of God (Ezekiel 1:28; Revelation 1:17).

Again, David said, "For our heart shall rejoice in Him, because we have trusted in His holy name" (Psalm 33:21). Every time we trust God we honor His name. When God told Abraham he and Sarah would have a son in their old age,

"He did not waver at the promise of God through unbelief, but was strengthened in faith, giving glory to God, and being fully convinced that what He had promised He was also able to perform" **Romans 4:20-21.**

Abraham trusted God, and in so doing he gave "glory to God." Unbelief leads to disobedience, and disobedience is an affront to God. When we trust in God and His Word it brings glory to His name. "He who does not believe God has made Him a liar" (1 John 5:10)—strong words, indeed.

At Christ's birth, the angels sang: "Glory to God in the highest" (Luke 2:14)—may this be the desire and intent in each of our lives, for then we shall hallow God's glorious name.

Puritan Quote:

"*We hallow and sanctify God's name when we never make mention of it but with the highest reverence. His name is sacred, and it must not be spoken of but with veneration. To speak vainly or slightly of God is profaning His name, and is taking His name in vain*" *Thomas Watson, 1620-1686.*

"YOUR KINGDOM COME"

Reading: Matthew 6:5-15
"Your kingdom come" Matthew 6:10

When Pilate asked Jesus, "Are you the King of the Jews?" He answered, "My kingdom is not of this world" (John 18:36). In His response, Jesus acknowledged four things: 1) By implication there is another kingdom; 2) He has a kingdom; 3) He is a King; 4) His is not an earthly kingdom.

1) There is another kingdom. Paul refers to this other kingdom as "the power of darkness" (Colossians 1:13), and its ruler as the "prince of this world" (John 12:31, KJV), and the "god of this world" (2 Corinthians 4:4, KJV). This other kingdom is populated with those who serve the "prince of this world," and against whom Christ's servants are in constant warfare, against "principalities, against powers, against the rulers of the darkness of this age, against spiritual hosts of wickedness in the Heavenly places" (Ephesians 6:12-13).

2) Jesus has a kingdom. With the words "My kingdom," Jesus acknowledges personal ownership of His kingdom—it belongs to Him alone. It was given to Him by His Father in recognition of His "finished" work of Redemption (Daniel 7:13-14). The kingdom of God is populated with those who love and serve Him (Matthew 25:14).

3) Jesus is the King of His kingdom. By the nature of it, a kingdom must have a king. Without knowing the reality of his words, Pilate told the Jews, "Behold your King" (John 19:14).

As His subjects, it is always beneficial for us to behold our King. The world mocked Him by dressing Him in a purple robe, and pressing a crown of thorns on His head, but we see Him as the King of Kings:

"The LORD reigns, He is clothed with majesty; the LORD is clothed, He has girded Himself with strength" Psalm 93:1.

He is "clothed with power" (Psalm 65:6), and is "glorious in His apparel, traveling in the greatness of His strength" (Isaiah 63:1). The writer of Hebrews said, "But we see Jesus," (2:9), and when we do we cry out with the Psalmist:

"O LORD my God, You are very great: You are clothed with honor and majesty, Who cover Yourself with light as with a garment" Psalm 104:1-2.

4) His is not an earthly kingdom. Both the kingdom of Satan and the kingdom of God are spiritual kingdoms. Until the Day of Judgment, when the devil and his kingdom are "cast into the lake of fire and brimstone" (Revelation 20:10), the two are enemies and are engaged in perpetual battle.

When Jesus exhorted His disciples to pray "Your kingdom come," it was that we pray against Satan's Kingdom—that his kingdom may be demolished in this world. The kingdom of God is not something that will be established sometime in the future, it began when Jesus rose from the dead. He is the Forerunner of all who would be saved. He is building His church one stone at a time. Every time a man, woman, or child is born again, they are snatched away from Satan's kingdom into the Kingdom of God.

To pray "Your kingdom come" is an encouragement to every believer. It reminds us that our Ruler is a conquering King, and that He is building His church as He promised, and that the "gates of Hades shall not prevail against it" Matthew 16:18.

It reminds us of the victory Jesus gained on the cross, that Satan was dealt a fatal blow, that he is a defeated enemy, and has "no power against us" Revelation 20:6.

To pray "Your kingdom come," is to pray that God's righteousness will continue to gain hold in this world as souls are converted away from the kingdom of Satan:

"The kingdom of God is . . . righteousness and peace and joy in the Holy Spirit. For he who serves Christ in these things is acceptable to God and approved by men" Romans 14:17-18.

When the Pharisees asked Jesus when the kingdom of God would come, He said, "The kingdom of God does not come with observation; nor will they say, 'See here!' or 'See there!' For indeed, the kingdom of God is within you." (Luke 17:20-21). The kingdom of God is within us because the righteousness of Christ has been imputed to us (Romans 5:22-24).

The Jews, including the disciples, after all the teachings of Jesus on the Kingdom of God, were still looking for a physical kingdom to be restored to Israel (Acts 1:6), but Jesus said:

"It is not for you to know times or seasons which the Father has put in His own authority. But you shall receive power when the Holy Spirit has come upon you; and you shall be witnesses to Me in Jerusalem, and in all Judea and Samaria, and to the end of the earth" **Acts 1:7-8.**

In other words, you are the kingdom, and are made subjects when the Holy Spirit has come upon you. You will go into the world and be My witnesses, and so the kingdom of God will grow.

When we pray, "Your Kingdom come," we are praying for every ambassador of Jesus Christ who has gone into all the world preaching the kingdom of God. It is written that Paul "received all who came to him, preaching the kingdom of God and teaching the things which concern the Lord Jesus Christ" Acts 28:30-31.

Puritan Quote:

"In this petition the disciples were taught to pray for the success of the Gospel, both among Jews and Gentiles; for the conversion of God's elect, in which the kingdom of God would greatly appear, to the destruction of the kingdom of Satan" John Gill, 1697-1771.

"YOUR WILL BE DONE"

Reading: Matthew 6:5-15
"Your will be done on earth as it is in heaven" Matthew 6:10

The greatest obstacle that stands in the way of a believer doing the will of God is his own will. Throughout the life of every believer a battle rages—the battle of wills, ours and God's.

"The will here intended is mainly our active obedience to His revealed word" Thomas Manton.

When we pray, "Your will be done," we pray for God's will over ours. There is a sense where we pray for His will to be done in a broader sense as in the affairs of mankind, but God is Sovereign and we know that certain things will be done according to His predetermined plan no matter what man does. The return of Jesus and the judgment of mankind are examples of this.

Some things are clearly described in His Word. When a lawyer asked Jesus, "Teacher, which is the great commandment in the law?" he answered, "You shall love the LORD your God with all your heart, with all your soul, and with all your mind. This is the first and great commandment. And the second is like it: You shall love your neighbor as yourself" (Matthew 22:35-39).

Just before Jesus gave His disciples this pattern for prayer, He spoke on six different laws to be obeyed: "You have heard that it was said . . . But I say to you . . ." (Matthew 5:21-48). A believer is known by the way he lives—by the fruit evidenced in his life (Matthew 7:16). These things among others are the indisputable will of God.

Other things that are specific to the individual believer's life must be determined through prayer. The words of Paul should constantly be on our lips:

"Lord, what do You want me to do?" Acts 9:6.

In heaven, God's will is obeyed explicitly and without question. There, no angel or child of God violates God's will because the battle between the two wills is ended: So Father, may Your will be done in my life as it is in heaven—unequivocally and without question. May Your will be my greatest desire:

"Teach me to do Your will, for You are my God; Your Spirit is good. Lead me in the land of uprightness" Psalm 143:10,

and grant me the ability to carry it out:

"Now may the God of peace . . . make you complete in every good work to do His will, working in you what is well pleasing in His sight, through Jesus Christ, to whom be glory forever and ever. Amen" Hebrews 13:. 20-21.

The obvious consideration is that we must know God's will before we can do it, but to know God's will is not enough. Knowledge does not automatically mean we will obey. Obedience is the true essence of the Christian life. God's declaration has not changed:

"Obey My voice, and I will be your God, and you shall be My people. And walk in all the ways that I have commanded you, that it may be well with you" Jeremiah 7:23.

It is a simple directive, one that is repeated throughout the scriptures, "If you will, then I shall." For centuries, men have argued over "free will," well, here it is. From the moment of our new birth in Christ we have the option to obey God's laws and commandments or not. If we are truly "new creatures" in Christ, the Holy Spirit will continue His work of revealing God's will to us, and will nurture the desire of our heart to obey.

If we wish to comply with God's will we must learn self denial. Unless we deny our own will, we shall never do God's will. He wills one thing, we will another.

"He calls us to be crucified to the world, by nature we love the world; He calls us to forgive our enemies, by nature we bear malice in our hearts. His will and

ours are contrary, and until we can cross our own will, we shall never fulfill His"
Thomas Watson.

David prayed, "Teach me to do Your will" (Psalm 143:10) and "Teach me good judgment and knowledge, for I believe Your commandments" (Psalm 119:66). It is as if David prayed, "I do not need to be taught my will, for that I know only too well, but teach me Your will, for it is what I want to do."

If we wish to honor God and enjoy the benefits of the abundant life, we must heed the three-fold directive God gave to His people when they were about to enter the Promised Land: "Love the LORD your God . . . obey His voice . . . and cling to Him" Deuteronomy 30:20.

Willing obedience is a direct result of a sincere love for God. As a river is fed by many cascading waters from its mountain source, so obedience is the result of the many blessings we have from God—His love, His mercy, His grace, His providence, and many, many more. Our obedience to God is in direct proportion to our love for Him. A shallow love will never produce a deep and willing obedience.

By doing the will of God, we demonstrate the sincerity of our faith. As Jesus said, "If you love me, you will keep my commandments" (John 14:15, RSV). *"We do not honour the ruler if we hate his laws" Isidore, 560-636.*

We honor God by doing His will in the way He says to do it. The context of the Lord's Prayer is a good example: "When you pray, go into your room, and when you have shut your door, pray to your Father who is in the secret place . . . and when you pray, do not use vain repetitions as the heathen do" Matthew 6:6-7. Yet how many count their prayers offered among hundreds in a church building as their principle prayer life? To pray is God's will, but to pray in a manner opposite to His declared pattern cannot honor Him.

Puritan Quote:

"A Christian's soundness is not to be judged by his profession; but the estimate of a Christian is to be taken by his obediential acting, his doing the will of God. This is the best certificate and testimonial to show for heaven" Thomas Watson, 1620-1686.

"GIVE US THIS DAY OUR DAILY BREAD"

Reading: Matthew 6:5-15
"Give us this day our daily bread" Matthew 6:11

Augustine wrote: *"He loves Thee too little, who loves anything as well as Thee which he does not love for Thy sake."* This may sound awkward in today's language, but Augustine is challenging us to love God and His glory more than anything we possess.

In the Lord's Prayer, it is important to observe the order in which the petitions come. The honoring of God's name and His glory must always come first. This was so important to Jesus; He preferred His Father's glory more than His own:

"I honor My Father, and you dishonor Me. And I do not seek My own glory" John 8:49-50.

God shares much of Himself with His children—His blessings (Ephesians 1:3), His strength (Ephesians 6:10), His righteousness (Romans 4:6), but of His glory He said, "I am the LORD, that is My name; and My glory I will not give to another" Isaiah 42:8.

With the words, "Give us this day our daily bread" we can ask God to provide actual food for our table. Agur prayed, "Feed me with the food allotted to me" (Proverbs 30:8). He did not ask for an abundance of food, but for that which was necessary.

My first year of missionary training was spent in the boy's dorm (even though we were all in our twenties) along with 12 others. One evening we set the table including cups of water, but no food—we had none. We gave thanks for our water and for past blessings, and put our current need before the Lord.

No sooner had we said "Amen" when someone knocked on the door. It was a friend with whose elderly mother I held a weekly Bible Study. He told us that when he and his mother sat down for their evening meal, she told him to pack some food and take it to the boy's dorm.

"Can't we eat first?" he asked.

"No," she replied. "The Lord is telling me to do it now."

He stood at our door holding a picnic basket with enough food for several days.

That provision from God made a lasting impression on me of God's faithfulness and my friends obedience to the voice of God.

"Jehovah Jireh," said Abraham—"The Lord will provide" Genesis 22:14.

"Give us this day our daily bread" can also mean "provide those things that are necessary for me." Jesus said:

"If then God so clothes the grass, which today is in the field and tomorrow is thrown into the oven, how much more will He clothe you" Luke 12:28.

In these days of unparalleled unemployment, the petition for God to provide is on the lips of many of God's people. What a test of faith this is for those who have lost their jobs and have no other means of support. It is easy to pray "Give us this day our daily bread" when we have everything we need.

To those who have what they need the message is clear—do not take your provisions for granted. All we have comes from God's hand. God said, "Every beast of the forest is Mine, and the cattle on a thousand hills," and He has promised to provide for His children.

As a child is dependant on his parents to provide what he needs, so God's children are dependant on Him, and, as Paul wrote:

"My God shall supply all your need according to His riches in glory by Christ Jesus" Philippians 4:19.

God knows what we need and will provide accordingly. When I was a child during the Second World War, food was rationed. It was then my father taught me the difference between need and want. With what little money we had, along with the ration book stamps, my parents were able to provide what we needed—and we survived. Once in a while they would surprise me with a bar of chocolate, which we shared equally.

God promises to meet our needs, but His provisions are so often more than that. It does us well to take inventory of what God has provided for us, and surely, it will give way to praise as we see how He has met not only our needs, but some of our wants also.

God knows what is best for us. A smaller portion may be best for some than for others. Whatever our lot, let us say with Paul:

"Not that I speak in regard to need, for I have learned in whatever state I am, to be content: I know how to be abased, and I know how to abound. Everywhere and in all things I have learned both to be full and to be hungry, both to abound and to suffer need. I can do all things through Christ who strengthens me" Philippians 4:11-13.

Puritan Quote:
"He who prays as he ought will endeavor to live as he prays" John Owen, 1616-1683.

"FORGIVE US OUR DEBTS"

Reading: Matthew 6:5-15
"And forgive us our debts" Matthew 6:12

Surely, it is our unconfessed sins that hinder our communion with God. In the light of this reality it behooves every believer to ask for forgiveness, otherwise we cannot expect God to consider our requests.

> *"Your iniquities have separated you from your God; and your sins have hidden His face from you, so that He will not hear" Isaiah 59:2.*

Jeremiah wrote: "You have covered Yourself with a cloud, that prayer should not pass through" (Lamentations 3:44, compare Isaiah 44:22). How can we therefore ever expect God to hear, let alone answer, our prayer? John provides the answer:

> *"If we confess our sins, He is faithful and just to forgive us our sins and to cleanse us from all unrighteousness" 1 John 1:9.*

The sincere confession of our sins to God removes the cloud that hinders our prayers. If sin hinders God from hearing our prayers, why is this petition not the first in order?

Calvin suggests: *"Christ, in arranging the prayers of his people, did not consider which was first or second in order . . . We ought always, therefore, to begin with the forgiveness of sins: for the first hope of being heard by God beams upon us, when we obtain his favor; and there is no way in which he is "pacified toward us," (Ezekiel 16:63,) but by freely pardoning our sins."*

This must not be confused with the glorious doctrine of Justification whereby God pardons the sins of those who believe in Jesus for salvation. The sins of a believer will not shut heavens door to them, but it will effect both their fellowship with Him now, and their rewards that are to be distributed when they stand before the Judgment Seat of Christ (1 Corinthians 3:12-15, comp 2 Timothy 4:7).

Why is sin called a debt? A debt is an obligation, a responsibility, or not paying that which is due. We must always keep in mind that Jesus directed these words toward His disciples, and Jesus' disciples sin.

When we sin, no matter how large or small we deem it to be, we dishonor God. Sin in any form is an affront to His holiness—this is why the Holy Spirit convicts God's children of their sins. A believer should live a life that honors God; a true believer wants to honor God. Sin is an act of disrespect against Him who is holy; it is an act of disloyalty against the King to whom we have sworn allegiance, and against the Father who has adopted us into His family:

"'A son honors his father, and a servant his master. If then I am the Father, where is My honor? And if I am a Master, where is My reverence?' says the LORD of hosts" *Malachi 1:6.*

We have nothing with which to pay our debts—our spiritual account shows a zero balance. There is only one way by which our obligation can be met—ask God to forgive our debt.

God knows how spiritually bankrupt we are and is willing to forgive our debt. Jesus said, "Therefore, pray . . . Our Father in heaven . . . forgive us our debts."

We know this is in accord with God's will because Jesus would never tell His disciples to pray for that which is not His will:

"Now this is the confidence that we have in Him, that if we ask anything according to His will, He hears us" *1 John 5:14.*

The Psalmist wrote of a glorious truth:

"If You, LORD, should mark iniquities, O Lord, who could stand? But there is forgiveness with You, that You may be feared" *Psalm 130:3-4.*

In the context of these thoughts, how can we, as children of God, approach Him to worship or petition Him when the dark cloud of unconfessed sin hovers over us? The only petition He will hear is, "Father, forgive me my sins." These are the words He wants to hear, and we can be sure that "there is forgiveness with Him."

What was it moved the prodigal son to return home to his father? Was it the dire circumstance he found himself in, or was it the knowledge and memory that he had a loving father looking for him, a father whose heart he had broken? He was willing to return home as a servant instead of a son, but the only way in which he was received was that of a son (Luke 15:20-24).

When we approach our Heavenly Father and ask His forgiveness, no matter what our sin may be, He will always receive us with open arms, and we will hear His words, "I will, be thou clean" Luke 5:12-13.

"Puritan Quote:

"*Sin is the abominable thing that God hates, and the only thing that he does hate in the world. And hear, "Father, forgive them, forgive them!" Would you exchange it for this, Father, give them long life! Father, make them rich! Father, put their hands on the neck of their enemies"? O what possession conceivable to the human mind, what conception that the heart of man can entertain, is comparable to the richness of the forgiveness of God! Forgiveness!" B.H. Carrol, 1843-1914.*

"DO NOT LEAD US INTO TEMPTATION"

Reading: Matthew 6:5-15
"Do not lead us into temptation" Matthew 6:13

These words were a puzzle to me for a long time until I took time to look in to their true meaning. Surely our Heavenly Father does not "lead" His children into temptation? The Bible says: "Let no one say when he is tempted, 'I am tempted by God'; for God cannot be tempted by evil, nor does He Himself tempt anyone" (James 1:13). God does not lead anyone toward that which He is so adamantly opposed.

When the Bible says God tempted Abraham (Genesis 22:1 KJV), more recent translations are correct when they translate the word as "tested."

Temptation is the plague all believers are faced with, and will be as long as they remain in this world. We will never be free from temptation as long as Satan continues in his power. It is futile to pray for freedom from temptation, for nowhere in scripture is such a promise made. It is entering into temptation that we are to pray against.

When we enter into temptation, it does not mean we have been conquered by it, or that we are guilty of committing the sin into which the temptation is leading us.

Jesus entered into temptation, but was not conquered by it (Matthew 4:1-11). Paul likens "fall into temptation" to falling into a pit or deep place where there are traps or snares by which he may be entangled (1 Timothy 6:9).

The warning is clear: "Let him who thinks he stands take heed lest he fall" (1 Corinthians 10:12)—lest he become entangled and caught in the trap Satan has laid out for him, lest he falls into that pit from which he does not know how to escape.

"When sin knocks at the door, we are at liberty; but when a temptation comes in and we allow it to parlay with our heart, reason with our mind, entice and allure our affections, for a long or short time, sin subtly and almost imperceptibly

draws our soul to take particular notice of it, then we "enter into temptation"
John Owen.

We must always remember how weak are really are, and how readily we are in ourselves to yield to the enticements of the devil. Sometimes he lures us gently with appetizing things, and it is only when we bite that we become aware of the danger. The devil will dangle temptations before us like a worm on a hook dangles in front of a fish. It is only when the fish bites that it becomes aware of the hook that has pierced its mouth and taken control over its entire body.

At other times, Satan is pictured as a "roaring lion, seeking whom he may devour" (1 Peter 5:8). The devil is never dissuaded from his pursuit, no matter he is a defeated foe—his persistence is perpetual.

There is, however, good news. Peter, when speaking of the devil, tells us:

"Resist him, steadfast in the faith, knowing that the same sufferings are experienced by your brotherhood in the world" 1 Peter 5:9.

James tells us the same thing:

"Resist the devil and he will flee from you" James 4:7.

In ourselves we are unable to stand against the wiles of the devil" (Ephesians 6:11). How then can we keep from falling into Satan's snare? Paul says:

"Put on the whole armor of God, that you may be able to stand against the Wiles of the devil" Ephesians 6:11.

James says:

"Therefore submit to God. Resist the devil and he will flee from you. Draw near to God and He will draw near to you" James 4:7-8.

It is important to note the sequence of events James lays out: First, "submit to God." It is only as we submit to God and His ways that any resistance against the devil will be effective. The devil will flee from us only when he is challenged by the strength and power of Christ: "Be strong in the Lord, and in the power of His might" Ephesians 6:10.

When we fall into temptation our heart becomes infected. Therefore, James continues, "Cleanse your hands . . . purify your hearts . . . Humble yourselves in the sight of the Lord, and He will lift you up" James 4:8-10.

"Our Father in heaven . . . don't let us yield to temptation" (NLT). Help me, Father, to always submit to You and Your will—may this always be the desire of my heart. Grant me Your strength to give Jesus Christ the preeminence in every decision I make and in every path I choose. It is only as I submit to You that I can draw near to You with the full assurance I can stand before You and obtain grace in the time of need.

Puriton Quotes:

"*Christian, steep thy soul in the brinish waters of repentance, and God will be appeased. It is an error to think that one act of sin can destroy the habit of grace. Therefore, Christian, if thou hast fallen with Peter, repent with Peter, and God will be ready to seal thy pardon*" *Thomas Watson, 1620-1686.*

"*What an honor to be His [our Father's] children! With the power of our Heavenly Father, of whom should we be afraid? The devil is subject to His power and kingdom. Sin has no power even over the swine, without His providence and permission. Therefore it is well that we should pray, 'Lead us not into temptation'*" *John Bradford, 1510-1555.*

"DELIVER US FROM THE EVIL ONE"

Reading: Matthew 6:5-15
"Deliver us from the evil one" Matthew 6:13

While the King James version says, "Deliver us from evil," most recent translations read, "Deliver us from the evil one." The word might easily be translated as the "evil thing" or "evil one."

Satan is referred to as the "wicked one" (same Greek word as "evil" (see Ephesians 6:16; 1 John 2:13-14; 5:18-19), for he is the source of all evil and wickedness. It was he who introduced mankind to sin, and who has sought to perpetuate it ever since.

Throughout the Old Testament God is seen as the great Deliverer. Psalm 18 is often called "The Psalm of Deliverance":

> *"The LORD is my rock and my fortress and my deliverer; my God, my strength, in whom I will trust . . . He delivered me from my strong enemy, from those who hated me, for they were too strong for me . . . it is God who arms me with strength, and makes my way perfect . . . therefore I will give thanks to You, O LORD, among the Gentiles, and sing praises to Your name. Great deliverance He gives to His king, and shows mercy to His anointed, to David and his descendants forevermore" vss 2, 17, 32, 49-50.*

Two words are linked in this Psalm—deliverance and strength. David acknowledges his enemies are "too strong for me" (the first step in being delivered from the evil one), and that he is delivered by the LORD who is his only Source of strength.

One of the great resources God has made available to His people is His strength: "Be strong in the Lord and in the power of His might" (Ephesians 6:10). God told Joshua: "Be strong and of good courage; do not be afraid, nor be dismayed, for the LORD your God is with you wherever you go" (Joshua 1:9)—words of encouragement to Joshua, and to us today.

Another wonderful encouragement to God's children as we acknowledge our own weakness before the onslaughts of the devil, is that we have a Brother who is greater than he, more powerful than he, and with whom we have been made one—Jesus. Jesus told Peter:

"Simon, Simon! Indeed, Satan has asked for you, that he may sift you as wheat. But I have prayed for you, that your faith should not fail" Luke 22:31-32.

Jesus is our Advocate (1 John 2:1) and sits at our Father's right hand. He is our Representative. Put your name in this scripture instead of "Simon." Make it personal to yourself, for it is as true for you as it was for Simon Peter. Does this not bring comfort to your soul? It should. How often we are strengthened and comforted when we remember the words of Jesus: "I will pray the Father, and He will give you another Comforter, that He may abide with you forever" (John 14:16 KJV). The Greek word translated here as "Comforter," or "Helper" (NKJV), is referring to the Holy Spirit, is the same as that translated "Advocate" in 1 John. Both Jesus and the Holy Spirit minister on our behalf as our prayer, "Deliver us from the evil one" is answered.

This petition is not only meant to be a cry at the moment of crisis, although it is definitely that, but one that should be on our lips constantly. Paul speaks of the "liberty by which Christ has made us free" (Galatians 5:1). Our Father has provided a glorious liberty for His children:

"The creation itself also will be delivered from the bondage of corruption into the glorious liberty of the children of God" Romans 8:21.

This is the status given to every believer in Jesus Christ. The apostle tells us to "Stand fast" in this liberty, and not to become "entangled again with a yoke of bondage." When we pray, "Deliver us from the evil one" we are petitioning God to keep us from the snare of Satan, which we know for sure he has set for us.

The early history of Israel is a type of this liberty:

1) God orchestrated their deliverance from Egypt where they had been held captive for four hundred years
2) God promised them freedom from captivity in Canaan, a land flowing with milk and honey (Exodus 3:8)
3) God led them into their new land, a land prepared by Him for them, where they were to settle and enjoy His provision for them.

God did not destroy the current inhabitants of Canaan, but promised His people victory over them as long as they love Him and live according to His rules. Once they broke the rules they were defeated. So it is with believers today: When we fall into the snare the devil has set for us, we can no longer expect to enjoy the provisions (milk and honey) our Father has promised.

"Heavenly Father . . . keep us from becoming entrapped in the devil's snare." Yes, we can repent of our sins and be restored to that glorious liberty, but how much better to not experience the pains of Satan's traps. God is glorified in our victories, not our defeats.

Puritan Quote:

"'[Father], keep us, that either we may not be assaulted by him [the devil], or we may not be overcome by those assaults': Or from the evil thing, sin, the worst of evils; an evil, an only evil; that evil thing which God hates, and which Satan tempts men to and destroys them by. 'Lord, deliver us from the evil of the world, the corruption that is in the world through lust; from the evil of every condition in the world; from the evil of death; from the sting of death, which is sin: deliver us from ourselves, from our own evil hearts: deliver us from evil men, that they may not be a snare to us, nor we a prey to them'" Matthew Henry, 1662-1714.

"THE KINGDOM, THE POWER, THE GLORY"

Reading: Matthew 6:5-15
"Yours is the kingdom and the power and the glory" Matthew 6:13

What sense is there to pray unless the One to whom we pray is able to answer our petitions? The condemnation against the gods made by the hands of men has always been:

> "But our God is in heaven; He does whatever He pleases. Their idols are silver and gold, the work of men's hands. They have mouths, but they do not speak; eyes they have, but they do not see; they have ears, but they do not hear; noses they have, but they do not smell; they have hands, but they do not handle; feet they have, but they do not walk; nor do they mutter through their throat" Psalm 115:3-7.

As does the Psalmist, Jesus tells His disciples to begin their prayers by acknowledging that our Father is in heaven, and concludes with the expectation that our prayers will be heard and that He has the ability to answer.

Matthew spends a great amount of time speaking of the Kingdom of Heaven beginning with the message of John the Baptist to "Repent, for the kingdom of heaven is at hand" Matthew 3:2.

There are two things that give us confidence when we pray—God is able and willing to grant our requests. This is addressed in the words of our text: "For Yours is the kingdom, the power, and the glory," not for a period of time, but "for ever."

"**Yours is the kingdom.**" God is both Owner and Ruler of His kingdom and governs both His people and property, for He made all things out of nothing. Our Father, who is in heaven, is the Sovereign King of His kingdom, and He bids us come to His throne of grace that we might obtain mercy and find grace to help in the time of need (Hebrews 4:16). He speaks and it is done, and we have this confidence that He hears us when we pray.

Our confidence is also that He has the ability to answer our petitions. Earthly kings may have the authority to grant the requests of his citizens, yet lack the means to make it happen. Not so with our Father, for "Yours is the power."

There is a great difference between authority and power. Abraham knew this, for he was

"fully convinced that what He [God] had promised He was also able to perform" Romans 4:21.

"Yours is the power." God has the power and ability to govern His kingdom, and that includes hearing and answering the prayers of His people.

"Now this is a great encouragement to us, that we go to a God that hath an absolute right, for which he is responsible to none. We go not to a servant or subordinate agent, who may be controlled by a higher power, and whose act may be disannulled; but to an absolute lord, to whom none can say, 'What doest thou?' Job 9:12" Thomas Manton.

We can ask nothing but what God is able to give:

"Now to Him who is able to do exceedingly abundantly above all that we ask or think, according to the power that works in us, to Him be glory in the church by Christ Jesus to all generations, forever and ever. Amen" Ephesians 3:20-21.

"Yours is the glory." Everything God does is for His glory and honor. God will not grant our request unless His name is glorified by it. This was the driving force behind the work and ministry of Jesus: "Now My soul is troubled, and what shall I say? 'Father, save Me from this hour'? But for this purpose I came to this hour. Father, glorify Your name" John 12:27-28, see also 13:31-32.

As God's children, God's glory should be the motive and goal in everything we do. If we pray for that which will enhance our own ego and agenda, we cannot expect God to answer. However, "Let your light so shine before men, that they may see your good works and glorify your Father in heaven" (Matthew 5:16), then that is a different matter:

"O LORD, though our iniquities testify against us, do it for Your name's sake" Jeremiah 14:7.

When we pray with God's glory the intent of our heart, we pray according to His will:

"Thus says the Lord GOD: "I do not do this for your sake, O house of Israel, but for My holy name's sake"' Ezekiel 36:22; "For My name's sake I will defer My anger, and for My praise I will restrain it from you, so that I do not cut you off" Isaiah 48:9.

For every child of God, no matter what we do, our presiding goal and motive should always be the glory of our heavenly Father:

"Therefore, whether you eat or drink, or whatever you do, do all to the glory of God" 1 Corinthians 10:31.

Puritan Quote:
"We cannot empty the ocean with a nut-shell, nor comprehend the infinite God, and raise our thoughts to the vast extent of his power, only we must go to some instances of God's power; that power that made the world out of nothing, and that power which wrought in you where there is such infinite resistance . . . Our wants are not so many but God is able to supply them; our enemies and corruptions not so strong but God is able to subdue them: Surely your heavenly Father will do what is in the power of his hand" Thomas Manton, 1620 – 1677.

David T. Peckham

Other Books by David T. Peckham

Cords of Love –

*Christian Poems -
Thoughts From The Heart.
Written over a forty year
period reflecting the
author's spiritual
struggles and victories.*

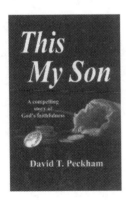

This My Son -

*Testimony and thoughts
from Luke 15.
A forthright and compelling
story of God's Faithfulness*

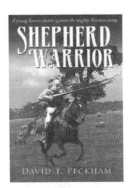

*Shepherd Warrior - Historical Novel
A young Saxon's battle against
the mighty Norman Army
at the Battle of Hastings in 1066*

Warrior Monk -   Historical Novel
A young Saxon torn between
his duty to God and his hatred
for Normans

101 Thoughts From The Word – Volume One
Job through Song of Songs
A book of Devotions

101 Thoughts From The Word – Volume Two
Devotions from the Old Testament
A book of Devotions

101 Thoughts From The Word – Volume Three
Devotions from the New Testament
A book of Devotions